Ways of Reading the Bible

Ways of Reading the Bible

Edited by

MICHAEL WADSWORTH
Fellow and Chaplain, Sidney Sussex College, Cambridge.

THE HARVESTER PRESS . SUSSEX

BARNES & NOBLE BOOKS . NEW JERSEY

First published in Geat Britain in 1981 by
THE HARVESTER PRESS LIMITED
Publisher: John Spiers
16 Ship Street, Brighton, Sussex

and in the USA by
BARNES & NOBLE BOOKS
81 Adams Drive, Totowa, New Jersey 07512

© The Harvester Press, 1981

British Library Cataloguing in Publication Data

Ways of reading the Bible.
1. Bible – Criticism, interpretation, etc.
I. Wadsworth, Michael
220   BS511.2

ISBN 0-85527-537-5

Barnes & Noble Books
ISBN 0-389-20119-7

Photoset in 10/11 pt Andover
and printed in Great Britain by
Photobooks (Bristol) Limited

CONTENTS

PART V

PARABLE AND ALLEGORY

NOTES ON CONTRIBUTORS

KENNETH CRAGG

Formerly Anglican Bishop of Cairo and Reader in Religious Studies at the University of Sussex. Now retired, and acting as Priest-in-charge of a parish near Huddersfield

JOHN DRURY

Formerly Residentiary Canon of Norwich, and now Lecturer in Religious Studies at the University of Sussex. Editor of *Theology*.

DUNCAN FORRESTER

Formerly Chaplain of the University of Sussex, and now Professor of Christian Ethics and Practical Theology at the University of Edinburgh.

BERNARD HARRISON

Lately Visiting Professor at the University of Western Australia. Reader in Philosophy at the University of Sussex.

GABRIEL JOSIPOVICI

Reader in English at the University of Sussex.

STEPHEN MEDCALF

Reader in English at the University of Sussex.

A. D. NUTTALL

Pro Vice-Chancellor, and Professor of English at the University of Sussex.

STEPHEN PRICKETT

Reader in English at the University of Sussex.

ULRICH SIMON

Professor of Christian Literature and Dean of King's College, London.

ANTHONY THORLBY

Professor of Comparative Literature at the University of Sussex.

MICHAEL WADSWORTH (editor)

Formerly Lecturer in Religious Studies at the University of Sussex, and now Fellow and Chaplain of Sidney Sussex College, Cambridge. Shortly to become a Team Vicar in the Liverpool Diocese.

INTRODUCTION

The Bible is a collection of books coming from a variety of historical milieux, and composed of saga and poetry, proverb and parable, visionary pamphlet and gospel. Not surprisingly, therefore, a collection of essays on the Bible is most often devoted to the serious and necessary business of technical biblical scholarship, an intellectual discipline possessed of its own laws and vocabulary, its own methodology and self-authenticating rituals. Problems of language, difficulties of the original tongues in which the biblical record was set down play a large part here, together with the theological appreciation of the material, for the Bible, whatever the faith-presuppositions of the reader, is a set of books which has always called out to the present.

Alternatively, a book or a collection of papers about the Bible may leave out of account historical and linguistic considerations in favour of a concentration upon the literary-critical approach, probing into the narrative style, let us say, of the patriarchal sagas of Genesis, with their powerful, brooding atmosphere, or seeking to analyse the majestic otherness of the words of the Psalms, in whatever language they are read, or endeavouring to thread a way through the gorgeous imagery of Ezekiel or of the Book of Revelation.

Despite an initial reluctance on the part of exponents of these two approaches to benefit from each other, there are signs today that scholars are listening to each other across what has been until recently an impassable gulf. The New Testament critic has learned a little more now about literary analysis, so that he is less likely to treat a gospel as a diagrammatic set of modules or *pericopae* of varying trustworthiness, but more as a continuous narrative work with its own logic and momentum. The literary critic in his turn owes much to the biblical scholar. Indeed he has borrowed from the vocabulary of biblical scholarship terms like 'exegesis' and 'hermeneutic' to apply to the text he is dealing with, whether it be a play of Shakespeare or one of the works of James Joyce. Perhaps it is the essentially paradigmatic nature of the biblical text which has encouraged these borrowings among scholars. If you look on what Walter Benjamin called the *Urtexte*, you cannot but look differently on any other book with which you have to deal, for it is more than the arcane freemasonry of scholarly analysis that has prompted such shifts in approach and appreciation. Suffice it to say that interpreters of modern texts are approaching their quarry these days with an almost 'biblical' reverence. The word, the text, the page, whatever it is, and whatever its provenance, is now no longer

1

what Isaiah denounced as 'precept upon precept . . . line upon line, here a little, there a little' (Isaiah 28. 10).

These considerations have prompted a group of colleagues, most of whom work in the University of Sussex, to plan a volume of essays which underlines the excellencies of both these approaches. Specialists in biblical theology and interpretation are thus to be found among these eleven contributors, side by side with those who work in the field of english literature or in philosophy. To some the Bible is a well-known body of literature, to others not. All of the contributors, however, whether they have come in from the cold to the study of the Bible or not, and whether or not they write from a credal or confessional stand-point, concur in approaching it as a body of literature which is pluriform, and yet regarded by tradition as a unity, which addresses itself to contemporary man, and yet which belongs in its form and thought-structure to an ancient context, which needs the specialist contribution, but which nevertheless calls out for the interpretative skills of those whose work is with texts of a vastly different kind. It is in this spirit that they offer their ways of reading the Bible.

The essays included in this volume fall into five main categories. Part I, entitled Revelation and Tradition, is written against the background of technical, biblical criticism, and asks questions about the nature of the biblical documents as they were originally conceived, in the context of those who gathered and shaped and passed on the literature we inherit. Chapters 1 and 2 thus seek to answer the question, 'What kind of Book?' The next three essays, which make up Part II, Myth and Truth, deal with a problem which perplexes the general reader as much as it irritates a certain kind of biblical critic— What level of truth do these documents possess? The Bible is multi-faceted, the faith it embodies is shifting, developing, changing, from Genesis to Revelation, and yet church and synagogue have regarded it as in different ways embodying 'the lively oracles of God', a proposition which modern critics, from the age of the Enlightenment onwards, have mined away at with a myriad qualifications. A related problem is faced in the course of chapters 6 and 7, in Part III, Translation and Culture Patterns, which survey the attempt made by some modern translators and interpreters to bridge the gap between the biblical world and our own, resulting, in many cases, in a shift from what Barth called 'the language of Canaan', the language of numinous Revelation, to 'the language of Babylon', the language of the secular world, where the voice of God in the desert becomes the sound of stereo in the living room.

The men and women of the biblical world respond to the Revelation of God with urgency. Revelation is indeed a two-fold thing; there is a Revealer, and one to whom the Revelation comes, one who receives it. Thus Part IV, Speech and Action, focuses on the people of the Bible in their dialogue with God and with each other, and their fulfilment of the rôle God has called upon them to play, even if, as in Samson's case, it leads to their destruction.

The parables of the gospels are among the most popular and well-remembered parts of the Bible, constituting, for this reason, that area of biblical study which has attracted critics and scholars from other disciplines. The concluding section of this book, Part V, Parable and Allegory, seeks to determine what underlies the parabolic form in the gospels. Opposite points of view are expressed in chapters 10 and 11, with John Drury (a biblical critic) insisting on the otherness and riddling ambiguity of the form, while Bernard Harrison (a philosopher and literary critic) argues for its immediacy, and for the ease of its contemporary application.

From these foregoing remarks the reader will appreciate that this collection is not in any sense the product of a 'school' or of a single theological approach. Indeed its authors believe that it is high time that those members of the reading public for whom the Bible is a familiar text, as well as scholars working in other, not-so-distant fields, understand the many directions that may be taken by those who approach these documents, and seek to concentrate upon individual aspects of their variety, richness and profundity. It is time too for all to recognize that work on the biblical texts needs to be a co-operative effort on the part of scholars of different disciplinary backgrounds, for, while they will always call out for scholarly, specialist treatment, they are much too important, both in scholarship and in life, to remain the sole preserve of specialists. The whole earth is not yet of one speech and language, nor do we propose, either inside or outside of this volume, to build a tower, whose top will reach heaven. It is our hope, however, that scholars whose primary intellectual concerns lie outside of biblical exegesis and theology will, on reading these essays, feel that they may have something to say about documents they regarded as formerly lying outside their range and capacities, and that, contemplating once more the sorrowful prospect of the tower of Babel, will take heart at finding themselves able to understand one another's speech.
MICHAEL WADSWORTH

PART I:

REVELATION AND TRADITION

There are vast libraries of Biblical scholarship, and they are in the present age expanding at least as far as ever before; but it does not appear that they are much frequented by the general reader. (Frank Kermode in *The New York Review of Books*, 29 June 1978, p. 39)

Recent decades have seen a considerable development in the subtlety of perception brought to the study of the thought of the individual New Testament writers. (J. L. Houlden in *Patterns of Faith*, London 1977, p. 25)

1 MAKING AND INTERPRETING SCRIPTURE

Michael Wadsworth

IN looking at the origins of the Scripture-making process scholars have invested much in the search for original documents or components of tradition. And so, in the case of the Old Testament, there are—so the theory goes—a J writer (the Jahwist), an E writer (the Elohist), a D writer (the Deuteronomist), and a P writer (the Priestly writer), who between them produce the Pentateuch, while in the Gospels of the New Testament the idea of a Q source (allegedly from the German *Quelle* meaning 'source'), which is blended with Mark, and with Matthaean and Lukan material, is still popular in scholarly circles, despite alternative theories which are steadily gaining ground. It is my contention in this essay that we need to adopt a parallel but distinct approach when dealing with the biblical documents, which gives due weight and emphasis to them as literary wholes, rather than as atomistic units of tradition which a later editor has bound together.

Thus the documentary theory of the origins and composition of the Pentateuch may be useful in assessing the historical and theological *Weltanschaung* of each member of a chain of tradition makers, but in many cases, despite excellent intentions to the contrary, it stops short of determining those factors which lead to the attachment of one narrative element to another in the document as we have inherited it. Undoubtedly a methodology which sees breaks and cut-off points in a sequence of narrative events, lying on either side of a documentary divide, will tend to leave out of the reckoning a vein of traditional interpretation, coming from synagogue or church, which reads the same set of events as a richly suggestive continuity. It is not that the search for documents is a wayward approach, but rather that it takes us only so far, or, at any rate, to a point at which it becomes difficult to see precisely what it was that animated a biblical narrative, once the bones and even the flesh and sinews have been laid down.

Midrash and Torah

I have called this essay 'Making and Interpreting Scripture' because I wish to suggest that the process of interpreting Scripture, and even in some cases of rewriting or remaking it—on the part of Jews after the closing of the Old Testament canon—contains an important clue for the understanding of how the books were made, of how their traditions were compiled, in more distant times and over long periods of gestation. For, in a sense, canon or no canon, to the Jew Scripture never stops. 'Behold, we are slaves this day' (Nehemiah 9. 36), says Ezra to the people returned from exile and seeking to build up their nation again. We are slaves like we were in Egypt; the condition of the wandering Aramaean in the formula of thanksgiving prescribed in Deuteronomy 26 is a perpetual one; the child's question at Passover, 'What do you mean by this service?' (Exodus 12. 25), is not merely a perpetual reminder, but a sign that God is passing over, that the Passover is being re-enacted here and now. And so, just as the community tradition has gone into the making of Scripture, community reflection ensures its constant rediscovery, ensures that Moses and the prophets are for ever, in each age, the people's contemporaries. 'What is Torah?' asks one rabbi in a passage from the Babylonian Talmud (Kiddushin 49b) and Torah, remember, stands here, as it often does, as a collective designation for the whole of the Jewish Scriptures, and not merely the Pentateuch. And the answer comes 'It is interpretation of the Torah', *midrash Torah* in the Hebrew. This midrash technique and process, this mode of Jewish interpretation, plays such a vital part in the making of Scripture, that we can understand it against the background of the power at work in the putting together of a biblical text, in the transmission of that text, and in subsequent post-canonical interpretations of that text. It is the germ, the seed of Scripture, and understanding it will help us in our reading of both Old and New Testaments, since with its aid we can see the text with the eyes of the midrashist, who was at one and the same time maker and interpreter, and used his skill to build up his text from traditional material, and—after it had been constructed—to read something new out of the text for each succeeding generation.

For some time now scholars have recognized that exegetical factors at work after the canon's closing owe their being to a parallel phenomenon which operated in the shaping of these same canonical traditions. Thus Geza Vermes writes in *The Cambridge History of the Bible*.[1]

Although intertestamental and rabbinic Judaism may correctly be defined as a 'religion of the Book', religion in which practice and belief derive from the study and interpretation of scripture, it would be false to assume that biblical exegesis is essentially and necessarily a post-biblical phenomenon. No-one familiar with the Old Testament can fail to observe the repeated emphasis laid by some of its authors on the obligation to meditate on, recite, and rethink the Law. It was no doubt a midrashic process such as this which was partly responsible for the formulation of the more recent legal codes, the Deuteronomic and the Priestly, and its influence becomes even more apparent in post-exilic literature (Chronicles and Daniel) and certain of the Apocrypha (Ecclesiasticus). By common though mysterious consent, and using criteria which largely elude us, the Palestine religious authorities decided, probably at about the end of the third century BC, to arrest the growth of sacred writings and establish a canon.

In general, scholars who talk about midrash at work in the Old Testament have used as examples those later parts of Scripture which rework or reinterpret an earlier part, as is the case with the author of this quotation. An awareness of the function and operation of the midrashic process in post-biblical times is thus a useful aid in the task of discovering how the makers of Scripture inherited and reinterpreted earlier fragments of tradition. The present writer would like to suggest that post-biblical midrash can assist the student of the Old Testament, who is interested in the Scripture-making process at a more basic level still.

James Sanders, who has written a useful book about the nature of the Old Testament canon, poses a challenging question at the outset of his enquiry:[2]

What if we actually have only ten per cent of what was available under Temple auspices in the high period of pre-exilic royal theology? King Josiah apparently felt under the judgement of (attributed authority to) the scroll found in the Temple in his day (2 Kings 22), whereas King Jehoiakim destroyed the scroll of Jeremiah in his day. The Old Testament cites literature of ancient Israel which we do not inherit—such as the Book of the Wars of Yahweh and the Book of the Acts of Solomon.

Umberto Cassuto, a distinguished Israeli scholar, comes to a similar conclusion in his magisterial two-volume commentary on Genesis. And so, when he examines the Abraham story, he makes the tentative suggestion that the material which did not find its way into the written Torah may be preserved in later, post-biblical midrash:[3]

The Torah does not reproduce all that the tradition current in Israel used to tell of the first Patriarch of the nation and his milieu. In the Pentateuchal account itself there are still discernible allusions to various topics that are not expressly narrated therein . . . The Torah, however . . . did not elaborate the things that were not essential to its purpose . . . It is possible that in the material cited in the pseudepigrapha and Midrashim some remnants of the ancient tradition have been preserved, but we have no means of determining the matter in detail.

In a detailed study of the exegetical links between the Bible and later post-biblical literature Professor Weingreen goes further than this in the attempt to locate this ancient, extra-biblical material:[4]

. . .talmudic exegesis, in its varied forms, has attracted the serious attention of Old Testament scholars who postulate (a) the existence of a mass of extra-biblical oral material in historic biblical times along with the written sacred texts, and (b) the preservation and further development of these oral traditions in the Talmud.

Finally, a statement in the important mishnaic tractate, *Pirqe Abōth, (The Sayings of the Fathers)* testifies to the fact that a continuous process was going on in the faith communities of Israel from Moses to the men of the Great Synagogue, as the successors of Ezra were called:[5]

Moses received the Torah on Sinai and handed it down to Joshua; Joshua to the elders; the elders to the prophets; and the prophets handed it down to the men of the Great Synagogue.

Weingreen reminds us, in the work cited above, that the term 'Torah' in this passage 'is taken to include extra-biblical authoritative and historical material, as well as the Hebrew Bible itself', and that this axiom 'expresses the nucleus of an historical truth',[6] when it comes to an assessment of the selection process at work in the making and interpreting of Scripture.

In order to understand how later midrash can disclose some of the original interpretative traditions which have dropped from the written Scripture we have inherited, I wish to introduce one document, which is post-biblical (it is early or late first century AD) and exegetical (it is called the *Book of Biblical Antiquities*), which comes from Jewish Palestine, and which uses the midrashic technique in abundance. It was wrongly ascribed to Philo, the Alexandrian Jewish philosopher of the early first century AD, from where it gets its rather ponderous title, the *Liber Antiquitatum Biblicarum* of Pseudo-Philo.[7] As the Latin of the title suggests, the book only survives in a fifth-century Latin translation, but there is no doubt of the book's Jewish provenance or that Hebrew was its original language. The vast scope of this fascinating document has now begun to play a significant part in our scholarly understanding of the midrashic process, its sixty-six chapters continuously retelling Israel's covenant history from the creation to the death of King Saul. It can therefore be seen in the context of a number of post-biblical Jewish writings which extend that process of continuous reflection upon scriptural tradition, which begins within Scripture and which continues after the canon's closure. Examples of works of this *genre* (rewritten Bible if you like) are to be found in the book of *Jubilees*—sometimes known as *Little Genesis* because it reframes familiar episodes from the book of Genesis to suit its own special calendar, based on the 'jubilee' or forty-nine year period; in the document from the Dead Sea Scrolls called the *Genesis Apocryphon* (or *Apocryphal Genesis*) which elaborates in a kind of *novella* the story of how Sarah was taken away by Pharaoh, while posing as Abraham's sister in Genesis 12. 10–20; and in the *Antiquities* of Josephus (which was probably almost contemporary with the making of Pseudo-Philo's book) which, using the techniques of Jewish exegesis, provides Gentile readers with a survey of Israel's history up to the time of the Jewish war with Rome in AD 66–70.

Pseudo-Philo's book will be useful to us, therefore, as a means to understanding something of the growth and making of the parent Old Testament traditions to which it responds. Thus, my method will be to begin with a midrashic interpretation of a scriptural motif or passage in Pseudo-Philo, and then to return to the source of the passage within the Old Testament itself. My aim is to demonstrate that even within the scriptural narratives as they have come down to us there are ghostly traces of ancient story-links which later midrash preserves, utilizes and develops for its own purpose.

Pseudo-Philo and Genesis Chapters 10 to 12

In LAB (as I will call the *Liber Antiquitatum Biblicarum*) Abraham is chosen out of all the families of the Earth to inhabit a land God will show him, because he took a vigorous stand against the building of the tower of Babel, which in the mind of Pseudo-Philo was a monstrously idolatrous enterprise (LAB 6-7). Consider now the account of Abraham's call in Genesis. No reason is there given for it, but it directly follows (Genesis 12) the account of the building of the tower of Babel, with only a list of the descendants of Shem intervening (Genesis 11. 10-32), which, of course, ends with Terah and Abraham. It is almost as if the tower episode in Genesis 11, in which the families of the Earth are visited by God with confusion, is balanced by a story of one particular family among families being called by God out of all the chaos and babel of nationalities in chapter 12.

The documentary theory, however, sees a literary division between Genesis 11. 31-2 (P) and Genesis 12. 1-3 (J), and both this, and the earlier—though still modern—phenomenon of chapter division between 11 and 12 serve to introduce a critical break between tower story and Abraham's call. Thus von Rad in his Genesis commentary observes of the opening of chapter 12[8] that 'The transition from primeval history to sacred history occurs abruptly and surprisingly in vs. 1-3 . . . In v.1, as though after a break, the particularism of election begins, and with it the "scandal".'

The fact that the P writer introduces the journey of Abraham at the end of chapter 11, but like the J writer gives us no reason for it, merely draws forth from von Rad the comment that 'we must free ourselves from the assumption that P had to incorporate into his own work everything that tradition contained.' And yet this is exactly the point that we must bear in mind if we read the sequence of narrative from chapters 10 to 12 as a whole, disregarding for the moment the apparent breaks and cut-off points of J and P. There *are* narrative connections in the story from chapters 10 through to 12 which an inordinate reliance on the J and P writers as self-contained, autonomous chroniclers has tended to obscure; on this occasion, therefore, turning to von Rad's terminology, it makes sense to examine what 'tradition' contains in an effort to discover them.

But first we will discuss the narrative links in the chapters themselves. We notice that the tower of Babel is built 'in the land of Shinar' (11. 2), which is the same part of the world as that out of which Abraham was called, 'Ur of the Chaldeans' (11. 31). I do not wish to dwell here on the view that the J writer (responsible for 11. 28-30 and for 12. 1-3) places Abraham's birth in Haran, while P (the author of 11. 31-32) places it in Ur, since this view, quite apart from its other disadvantages, makes it necessary for the reader to regard 'Ur of the Chaldeans' in the J verse, 15. 7 ('I am the Lord who brought you from

Ur of the Chaldeans'), as an interpolation from P; and I am proposing here that we treat the story sequence as a totality, as a prelude to understanding from ancient Jewish tradition how the sweep of the narrative was understood. Indeed, as Cassuto argues in his commentary, there are implicit links between the pride of the tower builders in the plain of Shinar in chapter 11 and the deeds of Nimrod, the 'mighty hunter before the Lord' of 10. 9 who constructed a series of cities in the land of Shinar and nearby: 'The beginning of his Kingdom was Babel, Erech and Akkad, all of them in the land of Shinar. From that land he went into Assyria and built Nineveh . . . (10. 10–11a)'.

Turn now from Genesis to LAB, and notice how the narrative links between Nimrod, the tower of Babel, and, significantly, the call of Abraham have all been supplied. For Nimrod in LAB is the leader and promoter of the tower enterprise, which Abraham stoutly resists as an act of idolatrous impiety, causing God to rescue and remove him from his birthplace, when the tower building has been frustrated (LAB 6–8). Hints that this midrash is not an entirely fictional reconstruction drawn out of Genesis 10–12 are contained in the suggestive echoing of Nimrod's city building in Shinar in chapter 10 by the hubristic act of tower building, again in Shinar, in the following chapter. There are, however, important clues in other parts of Scripture.

In Joshua 24. 2 we read that the parents of Abraham 'lived of old beyond the Euphrates . . . and they served other gods', independent confirmation, surely, of the idolatrous association of Abraham's homeland. Moreover, if we return to Genesis, to God's words to Abraham at the start of the eerie vision sequence of chapter 15, we can detect, according to Weingreen, an allusion to his rescue from some unspecified danger.[9] The words of Genesis 15. 7 in the English Revised Standard Version, 'I am the Lord who brought you from Ur of the Chaldeans to give you this land to possess', seem unremarkable enough, but Weingreen demonstrates that the Hebrew verb translated by 'brought you out' has 'the active sense of saving, rescuing' in many other places in Scripture—not least in the introduction to the Decalogue in Exodus 20. 2 and Deuteronomy 5. 6, which refers to God's rescue of Israel from Egypt. In short the word 'conveyed the idea of divine deliverance from oppression', and thus God's words to Abraham in Genesis 15. 7 allude to some physical peril from which the patriarch was rescued. For details of the danger Weingreen resorts to the Midrash Rabbah, a Jewish midrashic work of late date, and to the story of Abraham as told in the Qur'ān,[10] but a developed account of the same midrash is found in Pseudo-Philo, where we read that Abraham, for his opposition to Nimrod, is cast into a fiery furnace, reminiscent of Daniel 3, from where he is rescued by God, to the ultimate discomfiture of his enemies.[11] For confirmation of this interpretation of Genesis 15. 7 Weingreen looks to Isaiah 29. 22 'Therefore thus says the Lord, who redeemed Abraham . . .', where the Hebrew word for 'redeem' also bears the connotation of saving or

rescuing elsewhere in the Old Testament. Thus Weingreen concludes:[12]

. . . in ancient Israel, folk stories about the adventures of Abraham, other than those
recorded in Genesis, were in circulation, and . . . indirect references to them are
sometimes implied in biblical texts. This view suggests, furthermore, that the Midrash
has a long tradition, stretching back into biblical times and that there was much Midrashic
material in existence in, what we would call, the Oral Torah. Such extra-biblical folklore
persisted and was ultimately given fixed literary form, with accretions and embellish-
ments, in the Midrash.

As an example of such midrashic embellishment, we find that later
post-biblical tradition, looking for an aetiological explanation of
Nimrod's proud villainy, derived his name from the Hebrew verb *marad*
'to rebel', thus making him that Hemingwayan combination of hunter
and rebel. Fanciful as this exercize in derivative etymology undoubtedly is, the foregoing arguments suggest that the origins of such
an extended and contrived midrashic interpretation stretch back into
the biblical material itself, and to ancient story traditions, now
dropped from the Torah, but still clinging to the edges of the text in a
variety of ways.

One of the primary rules of midrash is that one part of the Torah can
be interpreted by reference to any other part, with a superb disregard
for chronology and historical sequence. And yet from this *a priori* rule,
when applied to biblical chapters in strict sequence, is derived *a fortiori*
the midrashic rule of 'post hoc ergo propter hoc', so that an internal
connection, structurally and thematically, is seen to exist between
Genesis 10 and 11 and between Genesis 11 and 12. Thus post-biblical
interpreters employ more adventurously a rule of literary composition
which is written into the structure of the biblical narratives themselves, and which testifies to the midrashic links seen to exist from the
very start in the making and ordering of these narratives. I am not
making a point here about whether or not these units of tradition are
fictional constructions or indeed about the origins of the Babel
tradition *vis-à-vis* the Abraham tradition. What an analysis of a
midrashic sequence in LAB alongside of its parent biblical tradition
does suggest to me, however, is that the post-biblical interpreter
supplied the narrative links and connections in his exemplar, ciphers of
which are strewn about the biblical narrative like so much living
'bricolage' and in such profusion as to suggest that what later tradition
saw as midrash is, in fact, something very ancient indeed, clinging to
the story line and undergirding it. And here Auerbach's remarks about
the difference between Homer and the Old Testament receive
confirmation and I wish to quote a characteristic observation from the
first chapter of *Mimesis*:[13]

On the one hand [*sc. in Homer*], externalized, uniformly illuminated phenomena, at a
definite time and in a definite place, connected together without lacunae in a perpetual
foreground; thoughts and feeling completely expressed; events taking place in leisurely

fashion and with very little of suspense. On the other hand [*sc. in the Old Testament*], the externalization of only so much of the phenomena as is necessary for the purpose of the narrative, all else left in obscurity; the decisive points of the narrative alone are emphasized, what lies between is non-existent; time and place are undefined and call for interpretation; thoughts and feeling remain unexpressed, are only suggested by the silence and the fragmentary speeches; the whole, permeated with the most unrelieved suspense and directed toward a single goal (and to that extent far more of a unity), remains mysterious and 'fraught with background'.

Of course, Auerbach is making a point for the most part about the psychology of the stories concerned. I would add to his analysis the observation that the absence of foreground facilitates midrashic growth. Nimrod's power in Genesis 10 is widespread, indeed almost unrivalled in its coverage and extent. Homer might choose here to dilate at length on his power in terms reminiscent of the Phaeacian island of Alcinous and end with a brief reflection on the nemesis of the gods that was to overtake the tower building which took place in his realm. Indeed there is in Homeric terms an almost impassable gulf between the Nimrod aretalogy and the tower story, although they speak eloquently enough to each other across it, as the post-biblical commentator noticed. Like a footballer looking for an opening, therefore, the midrashist spots the gap and goes through it, or—to return to the metaphor of yawning gulf—he functions as bridge-builder, even though to him who has eyes to see, to the makers of the *Urtexte*, where the midrashic manner is an ineluctable part of tradition making, no bridges are needed.

Pseudo-Philo and Judges Chapters 17 to 19

We can see how post-biblical midrash makes explicit links in the story sequence which were there from the start in Pseudo-Philo's story of Micah the Ephraimite, the central character of Judges 17 and 18. In LAB 44, Micah becomes an archetypal villain who makes a set of images, which are described in detail, obviously in terms of the current idolatries in the Palestine of his day, where there was a powerful, victorious gentile presence. His mother conspires with him to make the idols and she is Delilah, the woman Samson loved and who betrayed him. Look at the parent tradition in Judges 17, and we can see why these changes were made, for the story of Micah follows the Samson cycle of stories, and the 1,100 pieces of silver of Delilah's blood money (Judges 16. 5) are the same amount as Micah's mother has (Judges 17. 2), which her son steals from her, and restores to her, but which she is said to have cursed. The account in LAB does not record a correspondence in the case of the two sums of money. Indeed Delilah does not receive any money for her pains in the narrative of LAB (43. 6), and the amount used by her son in manufacturing his idols is described in modern first-century currency terms, and does not correspond to the biblical sum. Even so, the writer of LAB has operated in the construction of his account on the principle of 'post hoc ergo propter hoc', using the factor of the identity of the money given to Delilah and owing to Micah's mother to create a sequence out of these two narratives, even though he chooses not to include the detail of monetary correspondence in his account. Now, if we turn back to the biblical version, we discover that what Pseudo-Philo took as clues out of which to string the Samson and Micah sequences together, must in fact have been the reasons why the stories were placed side by side in the first place. The 1,100 pieces of silver introduced in the second verse of Judges 17 is a bridge passage between the Samson and Micah cycles of story. Again, as in the case with my previous example, no explicit bridges are built. The foreground is absent, so that the characters seem to move and go their way in fragmented *tableaux vivants*. But the code is there in the money which Micah's mother, who is unnamed in the biblical account, has cursed. Blood money, stolen money, money for idols, money accursed—the chain is complete, and Pseudo-Philo can now exercize his creative imagination and dive into his own up to date version of Micah's idolatries, so that instead of the comparatively modest graven and molten image of Judges 17. 3, he erects 'three images of boys, and of calves, and a lion and an eagle and a dragon and a dove . . . and his iniquity was of many shapes, and his impiety was full of guile' (LAB 44. 5).

Pseudo-Philo's account makes further links in the chain of biblical narratives. The Israelite tribes are not horrified at Micah's enormities, but they gather for war against Benjamin when members of this tribe rape and murder the concubine of a Levite who is spending the night in their territory. In the eyes of Pseudo-Philo this explains the lack of success the confederacy of tribes has against the renegade Benjaminites at the start of the ensuing civil war. They have not been moved by Micah's apostasy, involving the spiritual downfall of large numbers, which is an outrage committed against the God of the covenant, but they start a war on account of the outrage done to the Levite's concubine, who, so Pseudo-Philo adds, had deserved her fate because of her infidelities.

If we return from LAB to the parent texts we notice the following. Whereas Judges 17 and 18 are devoted to the Micah story, the rest of which is developed in a manner totally unlike Pseudo-Philo's presentation, chapter 19 introduces the unhappy tale of the Levite who travels from his home in Ephraim to take back his concubine, temporarily estranged from him and living in her father's house in Bethlehem. On the return journey the Levite and the girl, now reconciled to him, pass through Benjaminite tribal land where the event takes place as described in LAB. There is no explicit link attested in Scripture between the lack of horror at Micah's apostasies and the confederacy's initial failure in the Benjaminite war. Indeed Micah is no villain at all, as the images he makes are conventional and are allowed to pass the fiercely iconoclastic Deuteronomic censor. The core of the Micah story in Judges 17 and 18 is the introduction of a Levite (not the same one as in Judges 19), who stays as Micah's shrine and serves his images, until he is kidnapped together with them (they must have been portable) by Danites (Samson's tribe) on their way up to new homelands in the North. The tradition of Micah and the Levite in Judges chapter 17 and 18 is therefore concerned with the aetiology of a shrine erected by the Danites in their new city of Dan which they found at the end of their wanderings. The biblical account therefore has the tale of two Levites side by side. One belongs to the Micah story (in Judges 17 and 18) and the other to the tale of the Benjamite war (Judges 19 and 20). And yet just as the 1,100 pieces of silver in Judges 16 is the cue for the introduction of the Micah story after the Samson cycle in Judges 17 and overtones of the Samson story are contained in the fact that the money is accursed, even so the Levite, who travels from Bethlehem in Judah to Mount Ephraim there to lodge with Micah, provides the cue for the story which follows, a story of another Levite who starts out from Mount Ephraim on a journey to Bethlehem, the very opposite direction to that of the first Levite in Judges 17. Again this is a clear case of tradition calling out to tradition, of tradition pressing into service another tradition, which is precisely why Levite 2 in Judges 19 wonderfully retraces the steps of Levite 1 in Judges 17. It is the all-important connection, the midrashic clue acting as the matrix of the two originally independent traditions.

Midrash and modern method

I have concentrated thus far upon individual units of tradition, looking at the biblical text myopically, as it were, so that the midrashic process might be understood as the thread which links those who hear or who respond to tradition on both sides of the canon. And yet midrash can be seen to operate within Scripture upon larger blocks of tradition, as well as within the smaller, story elements.[14] The books of Chronicles are an entire midrashic response to the books of Samuel and of Kings, in which the traditions of David and his successor kings of Judah are thoroughly bowdlerized and revised in the light of new ideals of priestly dedication. There are detailed revisions and lighter revisions, but the midrashist never misses an opportunity. Thus in II Samuel 21. 19 an alternative tradition to the charismatic account of David's slaying of Goliath is mentioned. The real giant-killer here is not David, the stripling with the sling, but Elhanan the son of Ja'areor'egim, the Bethlehemite, 'the shaft of whose spear was like a weaver's beam'. The Chronicler here has his own harmonious midrash, in which he affirms that the man Elhanan slew was Goliath's brother, a man called Lahmi, which is a name he derives from elements of the word Bethlehemite in the passage from II Samuel.

Within Scripture the midrashist could on occasions be a stern moralist as he is in the books of Chronicles or within Hosea's lightening sketch of Jacob, the trickster, the man who took his brother by the heel, and who, through his people, will now be punished for his deeds (Hosea 12. 2–6). Outside Scripture he sees how far the midrashic process can lead him, constructing a *novella* like the book of Tobit, where elements of the Abraham and Jacob traditions feed the imagination, or a Gospel, which is an outgrowth, maybe, but which is still a part of the same exegetical process. Jesus is a Moses or an *Elijah redivivus* actualizing Scripture, a living midrashist, and the reader who holds the Testaments together may pick up the ciphers at every point. The wilderness narratives have fed the accounts of Jesus' Galilean ministry, while angelic visitations both at Jesus' infancy and in the accounts of resurrection appearances have taken entire passages of Daniel into their bloodstream.[15] And here I would urge you to understand that the midrashist in these instances was not indulging in shallow, fictional manipulation of texts, nor investing by way of a literary exercize in the kind of typology that we get, let us say, within Spenser's *Faerie Queene*. Tradition, from the earliest period of Scripture-making, is born out of community reflection upon the text, and for a Jewish Christian, moving in the wake of the Christ experience, the text was never far from his elbow; indeed, it was written upon the tables of his heart. Thus religious experience could not be described in terms other than those used by the midrashist. The Palestinian *tanna* or teacher was a 'repeater' (that is what the Aramaic word means) of Scripture, reading it off for the community against every life experience.

The laws of community composition or of community interpretation were neither arbitrary nor mechanical. There were rules of midrash, tables of exegetical rubrics, from a time shortly before the opening of the first Christian century, but these were applied with a subtle variety and creativity which makes it possible for us to see the Hebrew Scriptures as an organic thing, never halting, always disclosing, never continuing in one stay. The text must be fixed and inviolable. No *lapsus calami* is permitted. The scribe, the *sophēr*, the book man, must never copy a Torah scroll without looking at the words in front of him, for they are God's words, written with the finger of God, and there is tension in the creative symbiosis between such an authoritatively delivered text and such a free spirit of interpretation. And besides, the book could and did kill. If you permit variety in interpretation there will be some casualties. There were in the history of Jewish midrash some Faustian characters who brought calamity upon themselves, by their attention to certain passages considered dangerous, such as Genesis 1, which talked of 'what was before the world was', and Ezekiel 1, which described in the heights of apocalyptic fantasy the divine *Merkabah*, the chariot-throne of God. All that was necessary for the exegete in these cases was to employ caution, and for that you needed to be over thirty, or to be in the company of elders or sages, when you approached these mystical passages.[16]

Nevertheless, a certain young man, we are told (Babylonian Talmud Hagigah 13a), was consumed by fire, when he reached verse 27 of Ezekiel 1 in his reading and meditation. For that verse contained the Hebrew word *hashmal* 'gleaming bronze' to describe the likeness of the human form on God's throne ('And upward from what had the appearance of his loins I saw as it were gleaming bronze'), and such an unutterable, divine breakthrough brought swift heavenly retribution. We rationalists may laugh or murmur that 'the letter killeth', but such events are the result of an intense community reflection, which demands reverence and maturity. Well might St Paul utter in hushed tones that he heard things 'that cannot be told, which man may not utter' (II Corinthians 12. 4) when he reported a similar vision he had had to the church in Corinth.

The Jewish study of Scripture in the time after the canon was compiled was as life-enhancing to many as it was dangerous for some. Freedom must be allied to caution, and above all to reverence. The ordinances and instructions emanating from schools of midrash from the first century BC and after mirror and typify that strange alliance of delicate circumspection and perfervid excitement characteristic of some Christian scholars of bygone generations, as expressed in the anecdote about the great J. B. Lightfoot, the later Bishop of Durham, who responded to a student's over-hasty attempt to grapple with a difficult text with the words 'I have never yet ventured an opinion on that', or in the words with which Edward Clement Hoskyns began one of his sermons:[17] 'Can we rescue a word and discover a universe? Can we study a language and awake to the truth? Can we bury ourselves in a lexicon, and arise in the presence of God?'

It was in this posture that the rabbis in post-canonical times read and interpreted their texts. Scripture reading was a reverent act, since it ushered its exponents into the divine throne-world of God. Ezekiel 1 was thought to lift you to paradise, seen with the eyes of the visionary as a constantly changing terrain, from the garden of Eden, taken from Genesis 2, and embellished with the refinements introduced by Ezekiel, who wades in the water of life in chapter 47 of his book, to the fiery *hekhaloth* or 'chambers' seen by the same Ezekiel in the fluid arabesques of his chariot vision, which he experienced among the exiles by the River Chebar. Small wonder that meditation upon the Torah was held in certain apocalyptic circles to usher in the final stage. The Torah is that by which men shall live both in this age and the next. If Ezekiel could see the heavens opened, then why not that man who, in the words of the book of Jubilees, 'shall begin to study the laws and to seek the commandments, and to return to the path of righteousness' (Jubilees 23. 26). The sectarians of Qumran removed themselves from what they regarded as the corrupt Jerusalem establishment to do exactly this.

Midrash is a living thing because Scripture is a living thing. Scripture is actualized, anchored in life by midrash, because it is life.

But it is one thing to see these things with the eyes of the men of faith who shaped and reshaped and borrowed and monitored these traditions, so that they could live by them, and another thing to ask ourselves what difference it all makes to our reading and understanding of the Scriptures which have generated these enterprises and this commitment. By way of an answer and a conclusion to this enquiry, I put before you the following considerations:

1   We have seen how an acquaintance with post-biblical midrash can lay bare ancient story links within a biblical text, bringing to light in the process decisive structural factors which have bound together elements within a narrative sequence at the early stage of tradition building. Our method, in examining a biblical text, has been to look beyond the documentary divisions of modern biblical criticism at the narrative as a whole. The intention has not been to abdicate the documentary theory, but rather—and I regard this as the most valuable feature of this approach—to emphasize what it is that binds traditions, rather than that which isolates and divides them, to see harmony in a narrative sequence, regarded by tradition as a unity, rather than disjunction.

2   In spite of new initiatives in biblical scholarship, we are still uncomfortably wedded to what the literary critic Robert Alter calls 'excavative theology',[18] to the *Bible and Babel* school, the 'Bible and spade' emphasis. John Sawyer in *From Moses to Patmos* comments on the situation with regard to the biblical story of Abraham as follows:[19] 'It is possibly true to say that many students of the Bible, in schools, universities, and theological colleges, are more familiar with Middle Bronze Age Palestine, Mari, the Hyksos, the Amonites, and the Habiru than with the biblical traditions about Abraham, Isaac and Jacob'.

No-one would deny that it is right to study the cultural background, the *Umwelt* of the patriarchs and of ancient Israel, but, in Sawyer's words this line of study 'has surely assumed an importance far out of proportion to its real contribution to Old Testament study'.[20] Modern biblical critics have on occasions been scornful of biblical tradition, and have not treated it as an historical datum; the text in its givenness, in its ancient, pristine unity, as it was understood by its earliest makers and interpreters, has been abandoned, and the midrashic process has been neglected as a late, derivative and largely fanciful mode of interpretation. The arguments of this essay seek to demonstrate that midrash reaches back into the biblical narratives themselves, and is thus rooted in historical tradition. Yahweh of Hosts is a God who acts in history, so that midrash, far from being the typological 'light fantastick' that some hold it to be, is constantly earthed by the community experience in the *Heilsgeschichte*, the 'Sacred History', which so regulates it and monitors it, that the text actually changes places with life, and becomes, in its turn, a perpetual school of community midrash. This brings me to my third point.

3   Like the adulterous and sinful generation who is constantly asking
for a sign we are obsessed with an old-fashioned historicism, with the
you-are-there school of documentation, with telling it the way it was, or
with the way we think it was. And yet modern critics dealing with
vastly different bodies of material than the biblical documents have
become suspicious of the so-called factual or veridical literary form.
Paul Fussell thus concludes from a study of memoirs of soldiers of the
Great War:[21]

[It is] a sobering thought that memoirs of the kind I have been focussing on here have
been used as fundamental materials for the writing of history. We may be led to the
conclusion that there can be no history; there can be only literary history. Our access to
events, even so significant an event as the Great War, must be through the makers of
plots—that is, poets. As one critic has observed recently, Our evidence [for history] is
itself verbal; a document, a memoir, a charter are semantic acts whose correspondence
with actuality, whose 'truth-function' is no greater than that of other verbal modes.

Fussell refers to the words of the journalist and broadcaster Robert
Kee, an RAF-flyer in the last war in order to underline this point:[22]

From all the quite detailed evidence of these diary entries I can't add up a very coherent
picture of how it really was to be on a bomber squadron in those days. There's nothing
you could really get hold of if you were trying to write a proper historical account of it
all. No wonder the stuff slips away mercury-wise from proper historians. No wonder
they have to erect rather artificial structures of one sort or another in its place. No
wonder it is those artists who re-create life rather than try to recapture it who, in one
way, prove the good historians in the end.

The awareness of the midrash process within Scripture and outside it,
in which saving event and community response become one within the
book and the books about the book, should enable us to avoid a similar
misapplication of criteria, when we are faced with the challenge of the
biblical text.
4   Finally the study of midrash and an awareness of its operations
inside and outside of Scripture enables us to read the Bible as it was
read by the reverent faith-witnesses of the earliest faith-communities,
taking us into the world of the inspired man, the sage, the *hakham*, the
man of the book, and enabling us to understand the Bible as a vital and
perennial source of inspiration. We can see how well medieval
commentators understood midrash long before the advent of documentary theory or excavative criticism if we gaze upon the breathtaking pictured Bible in the Sainte-Chapelle in Paris, where exegetical
clues are picked up and used to suggest pictorial equivalences in the
eleven huge windows full of Old Testament scenes.[23] We can see an
understanding of midrash at work in the *Divine Comedy*, whose author
understood the power of tradition inside and outside the faith
community and read it off against his own life. We can see midrash
supremely illuminating the pages of Yehudah Agnon's short stories,
and in disclosing to us in a reflective, autobiographical essay the
midrashic sources illuminating his fiction, he has left us one of the

most abiding of all apologias for the midrashist, who is never very sure whether he is in the world of the Bible or in some other world, because he stands, like Ezekiel beside the river of his vision, on the threshold between both:[24]

Out of affection for our language and love of the holy, I burn midnight oil over the teachings of the Torah and deny myself food for the words of our sages that I may store them up within me to be ready upon my lips. If the Temple were still standing, I would take my place on the platform with my fellow choristers [*Agnon traces his ancestry to the tribe of Levi*] and would recite each day the song that the Levites used to say in the Holy Temple. But since the Temple is destroyed and we have neither Priests in their service nor Levites in their chorus and song, I devote myself to the Torah, the Prophets, the latter Scriptures, the Mishnah, Halakhah and Agadah, the Tosefta, rabbinical commentaries and textual glosses. When I look at their words and see that of all our precious possessions in ancient times only the memory is left us, I am filled with sorrow. And that sorrow makes my heart tremble. And from that trembling I write stories, like a man banished from his father's palace who builds himself a small shelter and sits there telling the glory of his ancestral home.

Notes

1 Geza Vermes (1970), in P. R. Ackroyd and C. F. Evans (eds.), *The Cambridge History of the Bible Vol. 1*, Cambridge p. 199.
2 J. A. Sanders (1972), *Torah and Canon*, Philadelphia, p. xix.
3 U. Cassuto (1964), *A Commentary on the Book of Genesis*, (trans I. Abrahams), Part 1 Jerusalem, p. 293.
4 J. Weingreen (1976), *From Bible to Mishna, The Continuity of Tradition*, Manchester p. 8.
5 Mishnah Aboth 1.1.
6 J. Weingreen, *op. cit.*, p. x.
7 M. R. James (1971), *The Biblical Antiquities of Philo, Prolegomenon by L. H. Feldman*, New York; D. J. Harrington and J. Cazeaux (1976) *Pseudo-Philon. Les Antiquités Bibliques Tome I*, Paris; C. Perrot and P. M. Boggert (1976), *Philon. Les Antiquités Bibliques, Tome II*, Paris. For questions of the document's date see M. P. Wadsworth (1978), 'A New Pseudo-Philo', *Journal of Jewish Studies*, Vol. XXIX, No. 2, pp. 186–91.
8 G. Von Rad (1956), *Genesis. A Commentary* (trans J. Marks), London p. 150.
9 J. Weingreen (1968), in P. R. Ackroyd and B. Lindars (eds.), *Words and Meanings. Essays presented to David Winton-Thomas*, Cambridge, pp. 209–15.
10 J. Weingreen, *ibid*, pp. 213–14.
11 LAB 6.
12 J. Weingreen, *op. cit.*, p. 215.
13 E. Auerbach (1968), *Mimesis. The Representation of Reality in Western Literature* (trans W. R. Trask), Princeton, pp. 11–2.
14 G. Vermes (1973), *Scripture and Tradition in Judaism. Haggadic Studies*, Leiden, pp. 127–77.
15 M. D. Goulder (1974), *Midrash and Lection in Matthew*, London, pp. 447–9.
16 G. Scholem (1961), *Major Trends in Jewish Mysticism* New York first Schocken ed., pp. 40–79; and G. Scholem (1960), *Jewish Gnosticism, Merkabah Mysticism and Talmudic Tradition*, New York, pp. 9–13.
17 E. C. Hoskyns (1970), *Cambridge Sermons*, London, p. 70.
18 See R. Alter (1975) 'A literary approach to the Bible', *Commentary* December 1975, pp. 70–77.
19 J. F. A. Sawyer (1977), *From Moses to Patmos. New Perspectives in Old Testament Study*, London, p. 15.
20 J. F. Sawyer, *ibid*, p. 17.

21 See A. Fletcher (ed.) (1976), *The Literature of Fact*, New York, p. viii; and P. Fussell (1975) *The Great War and Modern Memory*, Oxford.
22 R. Kee (1971), 'Mercury on a fork', *The Listener*, 18 February 1971, p. 208.
23 See S. Spiegel (1970), in J. Goldin (ed.), *The Jewish Expression*, New York, p. 143.
24 See R. Alter (1969), *After the Tradition. Essays on Modern Jewish Writing*, New York, p. 137.

2 'ACCORDING TO THE SCRIPTURES': LITERACY AND REVELATION

Kenneth Cragg

'LET your Scriptures be my chaste delight. Let me not deceive myself in them nor deceive others about them.' A very proper prayer. But to pray it sincerely is to be involved in serious tasks of mind. For, as the good Augustine goes on: 'This forest [of the Bible] is not without its deer, which repair to it and there refresh themselves, roaming at will and browsing upon its pastures, and lying there to chew the cud.'[1] 'The deer', adds an assiduous footnoter, 'penetrating the forest are to be taken figuratively as those who are gifted to understand the Scriptures'.[2] 'Dears', too, the cynic might observe, 'roaming at will' and making the custody and the understanding of the Scriptures a most puzzling dimension of religious faith.

With a differing metaphor and a sophisticated confidence, W. R. Inge wrote in 1899 that 'We may be thankful that the cobwebs . . . spun over the sacred texts have now been cleared away, so that we can at last read our Bible as its authors intended it to be read.'[3] But 'authors' and 'intention' are themselves question-raising terms. How does authorship relate to that insistent concept: 'The Word of God'? How does intention belong with 'Thus saith the Lord'? How are we to understand inspiration, text, canon, commentary and readership in the status and in the contemporary relevance of sacred writing? What is the nature of holy literacy, the capacity to write and to read in line with revelatory significance? How, indeed, does such significance belong at all? What of its origin, its reception and its transmission?

All these issues are implicit in the phrase 'According to the Scriptures'. How, in the Islamic phrase, are we 'people of the Book'? Scriptures and scriptuaries, text and folk, the holy treasuried and treasured, are clearly mutual. How should they be understood from outside? Are the criteria of their acceptance accessible only to faith? Or also to scrutiny?

It is intended here to discuss the Christian meaning of 'according to the Scriptures' as it may be intelligently argued from the structure of the New Testament. The exposition may be helped by some reference to the sharply contrasted quality of Muslim reception of the Qur'ān. The phrase 'the people of the Book' occurs some thirty times in the Qur'ān to denote the Jews and their holy writings. It could, however, be more fittingly applied to Muslims themselves. There is no faith more essentially documentary than Islam. Its holy Book is celebrated in rivers of calligraphy as the major motif of architectural decoration.

Quranic recitation is the main foundation of all education and theology. The Scripture is the definitive and prime source of all legal and social guidance, while its memorization is the first duty and the fullest reward of faithful piety. That piety's distinctive understanding of its sacred literacy affords a telling angle from which to reckon with the different biblical perspective.

When Paul, in I Corinthians 15. 3 and 4, used the phrase 'according to the Scriptures', he was echoing a conviction which finds notable expression in Luke/Acts and in I Peter, and elsewhere in the New Testament. He means it, as do the other passages, in a retrospective sense. The sufferings, death and resurrection of Jesus are seen as fulfilling their anticipation in the prophets. But Paul's argument has to do with the *traditio* within the first Christian community, the 'tradition' of event and faith within which he claimed firmly to stand and by which alone, despite his rugged independence of spirit, he wished to be tested. Let us defer a study of the retrospective sense of this pivotal phrase—the sense which takes us to what is called the Old Testament, while we explore the other sense of the phrase as it must be applied to the New Testament per se.

It is an obvious fact of the New Testament that its faith-event content is 'according' to its own text. This, which is of course the commonplace—and the crux—of New Testament studies, is nonetheless often strangely overlooked by New Testament readers both inside and outside the community of belief. Jesus left behind no written record of his teaching or his ministry. For these we are utterly dependent upon the memories and the pens of committed hearers and heeders over, and after the lapse of, the years.

The same is true of the taxing relation we must discern between the actualities of Jesus of Nazareth and the primary faith of the Church in the Christ of God. 'The quest of the historical Jesus' is the perennial theme of Christian textual study, and conclusions, or the lack of them, are in long circulation. But the point for the moment is that, confident or sceptical, they must all go to the documents that are generated by the content they debate. Those documents are not debaters but witnesses. The New Testament, Gospels and Epistles alike, is a text which owes itself to what it tells. Its own coming to be as a Scripture happens within its own themes. The writing is *itself* within the significance of what is documented. This fact about it is, or should be, the constant clue to its reading. There is no other 'holy literacy' of just this integral order of history and experience, where event is situated in faith and faith explains itself by event.

Contrast can be readily indicated by reference to the Islamic Qur'ān. Here the text does not in any way participate in the texture of its reception. The subsequent possession of Muḥammad by the soul of his community is tradition (*Hadīth/Sunnah*) in Islam. It does not influence the content of the Qur'ān in any sense. On the contrary, that Scripture is understood to be received *verbatim*, in its Arabic speech, by direct dictation from celestial sources. With a few exceptions, like the *Fātiḥah*, or Opening Surah, which is prayer to God, and occasions where Muḥammad's prayers are set down, it is wholly the Word of God uttered for recitation, first by the Prophet, and then by his hearers. Hence meticulously faithful memorization. Hence, too, devout calligraphy reproducing the very strokes and shapes of the script as the most hallowed expression of the arts.

The text of the Qur'ān, then, does not turn in any sense on the receptive wills of the believing community. Muḥammad, it is held, vocalized the divine speech in faithful reproduction of its syllables and these passed unimpaired into the sacred text and the household of Islam possesses it as the final revelation. Those heaven-sent deliverances of Muḥammad did not linger, like the parables of Jesus, in the retentive memory and custody of disciples to be indited after the lapse of years in such 'forms' or 'sources' as lie behind the final Gospels.

To be sure, the events of the Qur'ān can, and must, be illuminated by relation to the context of their occurrence. Such reference is part of an intelligent exegesis for which commentary relies on the tradition. The sense of the Quranic text is certainly contextual.[4] Not even heavenly speech can be exempt from a time and place of incidence: nor can there be a celestial 'guidance' (*hudā*) which lacks a setting where it guides. But this contextuality of the Qur'ān is one which stays within the twenty-three years of Muḥammad's mission, and God, as an old writer observed, was never heard speaking, *qua* Qur'ān, to any but that single recipient of the exclusive word.

How different is the New Testament picture. The Sermon on the Mount, assuming we have it, is first lost upon the winds of Galilee to be housed within the reverent recollection of that bunch of men and women who were all that Jesus left when, undocumented and undocumenting, he went into his Gethsemane. The recording of a 'love that never faileth', happens in the setting of a small community of discipleship evoking from within its leadership a hymn of Christology in action in I Corinthians 13, years after the historical paradigm in Palestine. The entire significance of the person of Jesus and the realisation of a Messiahship of universal range *via* a suffering redemption emerge, as the New Testament presents them, not in arbitrarily given scripture but in the ad hoc delineation of the experience and the responsibility which believed itself possessed of them.

It is vital, therefore, to receive the New Testament Scriptures in the temper of their own origin. One cannot well infallibilize what does not come that way. If the significance of Christ finds documentation only by risk of such patient apprehension it must not wield authority, or claim acceptance, in other terms. Christian faith is 'according to its Scriptures' in this crucial sense, that its whole content is documented from within experience. So documented, it invites us to read its language in accord with its nature, reckoning perceptively with the event-faith quality from which it plainly speaks.

It is clear, then, that a right literacy with the New Testament will understand it as the steady, literary implementation of a historic Christhood, which could only be acknowledged and stated in these experiential terms. Jesus as the Christ (this being the core of its witness) is so constituted, according to the Gospels and Epistles, as himself to constitute a genesis of faith. This primary fact of the faith brings about two derivative facts, namely those of community and Scripture. These two derivative facts inter-depend. The community needs the writings to explain itself, the Gospels to root it in its believed origins in the Christ-event, the Epistles to educate it in its consequent identity as the people of that Christ-event. Here the spread of place and the movement of time are intimately involved in the will to the pen. The institutional in the Church; moral, social and cultural issues in its life in the world, and the documentary ones in the Scripture; historical, moral and spiritual determinants in the source of Jesus— these belong and evolve together. The New Testament is the evident product of their mutuality.

Time lapsing is an unmistakable factor, in part, no doubt, because of the outliving of the sheer temporal immediacies of eschatological hope and so of the revising of hope's ultimate nature. But not only so. Time took away the owners of direct and immediate memory, while dispersion in the Gentile world carried the faith far from its point and geography of origin. Hence the setting down from oral tradition of *Logia* and stories of Jesus' encounters, acts and teachings.

Universality, too, required the explicitness of things which, earlier, could remain latent or potential. A. D. Nock has the point well:[5]

St. Paul must state why the Gentile converts are to be free from the law and not treated like Jewish proselytes. To do this he must find an explanation of the law's place in God's scheme and he does it in thoroughly Rabbinic fashion. His polemic is fierce and long on this subject because of the menace in the Judaizing view to the universality of the new faith . . . .When all are justified no one had a right to make distinctions . . . . Again he must explain to his pagan converts what is the basis and what are the implications of Christian rites. He must enunciate and render reasonable, moral and other pre-suppositions which to Jews seem self-evident.

It is in this way that the implications of Christian faith, implicit in its origins, become explicit and so 'scriptuarized' in the living context of the fellowship they have created and which proceeds upon them. It is this 'proceeding' which bring Epistles and Gospels to birth. The Christology articulate within them does not arrive, Minerva-like, from heaven by celestial decree.

The range and complexity of that 'proceeding' upon Jesus as the Christ, generating such Scriptures as these, mean that there are nuances and questions for debate. It could not be otherwise in the very nature of the case. But there *is* discernible consensus. Paul, who is at pains to emphasize concurrence with the *traditio*, does not think and write in unilateral autonomy of mind. On the contrary, his experience can be seen to give essential, if also highly dramatic, expression to the sense of the whole. Nor need we stay with that bizarre, if frequently held, notion that he was 'disinterested' in Jesus of Galilee. The Epistles, his and those of others, are not to be assumed to do the Gospels' job. Nor does his point about not regarding the Christ 'from a human point of view' (II Corinthians 5. 16) refer at all (as sometimes obtusely supposed) to disinterest in the earthly Jesus. For he speaks in the same verse of regarding 'no-one from a human point of view', which can hardly mean that he lives in a Crusoe-like seclusion from all society. Plainly he is referring to this-worldly notions of how Messiah might be—notions which are now for ever disallowed in the Messiahship of the crucified.

In this way the New Testament as literature is squarely situated within the significance of Jesus' Christhood. The instinct, implicit in both Gospels and Epistles, is to hold together the self-understanding of the community *and* the history in which it acknowledges its point of departure and of definition. Its very documentation is tied back to origins and interprets them actively as its own *raison d'être*. The faith is in bond to the event and the event is fulfilled in the faith. Were it otherwise, the New Testament would not exist.

This is not to claim some arbitrary legitimacy immune from scrutiny or scholarly question. But it is to say that in and beyond all the minutiae of that scrutiny the New Testament structure, with its Gospels and Epistles, rests firmly on two convictions the mutuality of which is central—the event of Christhood in Jesus and the faith of it as the open fellowship of grace and truth.

It is just here that the duties of scholarship are crucially involved. The New Testament does not make faith itself the event (*pace* Bultmann). Nor does it isolate the event from faith-recognition. The *kerygma* is only history because history yielded the *kerygma*. It is, of course, necessary to enquire whether that sequence of event into writing via community was seriously distorted by factors in the environment. There might be many such—saviour cults, pagan divinization, gnostic instincts, theosophic ideas, and cross cultural traffic of creed and ritual. The conviction on which we proceed here is that a careful assessment of these possible factors does not disqualify the view that the New Testament sequel of faith *is* authentically possessed of the meaning of its history. The alternative is either an impasse of minutiae, or a surrender to despair, neither of which does a more credible justice to the 'happenedness' of the New Testament as literature.

The vital thread in such confidence is a theme which takes us back into the primary and retrospective meaning of the phrase 'according to the Scriptures'.

Before, however, tracing that thread and theme, it is important to note how factors within the life of the Church, as well as those just noted in its environment, impinged on the Gospels. For these involve that quality of 'hindsight writing' which attaches to them all, and most of all to the Fourth. Undoubtedly a context of discourse in the early Church makes for what we may call a stance of interest in the text of the Evangelists. Jesus, interpreting on the road to Emmaus 'in all the Scriptures the things concerning himself', doubtless echoes the interest of the contemporary Church in grounding its retrospect of Messiahship in the exegesis of the prophets. To have sensed that Jesus did so is the echo of its own assurance that this was significantly so of him. The event–faith relationship interacts, in the selectivity, the emphases, the editorial presentations, of the Gospel records. The insights that are, and could only have been, subsequent fuse with the telling of the story that evoked them. New dimensions in retrospect could be seen in parables when their *Sitz im Leben* passed from the Galilean crowds to the households of Corinth or Philippi. The elder brother's rejection of the prodigal, for example, could be read then, not simply as a scorn for the penitent, but as a figure of the Judaizers' disavowal of a Gentile 'repentance unto life'. Likewise the parable of the vineyard, the husbandmen and the son, had an evidently fuller import for the Church of the dispersion than it could feasibly have had prior to that clue-bearing development in history. Yet, either way, it stood central to what we may well call the Messianic perspective of Jesus the preacher.

This is not to say that the latent and prospective meanings of Jesus, thus retrospectively realised, are unwarrantably credited to him in the narratives. Quite the contrary. But it *is* to say that in their very nature these meanings belonged in a fruition to which their significance would lead.

Clearly it is with the Fourth Gospel that this quality of the literature is most salient. Have we not, in this connection, stumbled far too long over a mistaken posture in our reading which has excluded this decisive element of scriptural perspective? We have supposed that we had to judge between *ipsissima verba* of Jesus, falling syllabically from his very lips as if there were a stenographer at hand, and a quite inventive attribution to him by the evangelist of what he never could have said. We have sometimes been urged, within the first option, to suppose that we must choose between a Jesus either true and God, or man and mad, or bad, since otherwise words like 'I came to save the world' would be utterly meaningless, and 'Before Abraham was, I am' quite inconceivable. Should not our categories have been alerted to go deeper by the fact of being left, otherwise, with such stark and crude alternatives? We do not understand Incarnation if we assume a Jesus merely pretending to be man in a masquerade that only fitfully conceals a surreptitious deity.

The clue, surely, is to realise the rich editorial initiatives of the writer, to read the whole as his dramatic presentation of a portrait, firmly rooted in the historical against all gnostic 'airy-thinness', yet sensing and knowing that history in the meaning of its apprehension from a world of retrospect and stating it in terms of its realised significance. 'According to the Scriptures' then has a strong creative, interpretative, dramaturgical quality. The past is contained in its own future and the two together are read and composed as a living present. The present continuous (to borrow a grammatical distinction) becomes the present simple, where events are known from and for their sequel. To sow seed and to sow a harvest are statements of the same event. The harvest is only actual in the sequel by being there at the start. Here the hindsight is assumed from previous experience. One might say: 'The little ships at Dunkirk retrieved an expeditionary force'. One might also say: 'The little ships at Dunkirk retrieved a nation's future'. The *fact* in either statement is simultaneous: the second can only be stated in the sequel. If we turn this kind of situation into direct speech or discourse we reach a right perspective on the Fourth Evangelist. It is not that he is falsifying Jesus' words or imputing what is unwarranted, nor yet that he is quoting as a kind of secretary. Rather, he is presenting the meanings of Jesus as their consequence had made them evident, and doing so with the sort of interpreter's authority by which all literature mediates its vision of the reality by which it comes to be.

Such a sense of things in the Fourth Gospel is liberating, and surely authentic. The future is there in the past, as Thomas Mann insistently explains in his great epic *Joseph and His Brothers*. What happened earlier is discovered later and between the two there is a subtle affinity, for the sake of which we need to enlarge our notion of the 'present' of historical happening to include what Mann calls 'larger entities of sequence', proper to historical recording.[6]

It is not difficult to see this past via its future in the conscious artistry of the Fourth Gospel. We mistake if, reading John 1, we suppose that the two disciples of John the Baptist, there described as following Jesus as 'the lamb of God', did so, there and then, in those realised terms. Had they done so *then*, how could they have been so long and so stubbornly blind to the course of Jesus' Messiahship? Their ultimate discovery of Jesus' identity was, of necessity, post facto. Yet the figure they so followed held for them a sequence of experience which truly had all its future within that first recruitment. The Evangelist narrates as the present of their discipleship what was its essential clue, ultimately realised. They did indeed 'behold the lamb of God.' Hindsight enables the Evangelist to read the future as already present—as in truth it was for them and for the historian—in the opening event.

Or those long eucharistic passages with which John elaborates the story in chaper 6 of the feeding of the multitude. Again the future of the faith is present, and presented, within the portrait of the past. There is this same practice of inspired anachronism in the expression of truth—'He that was' there in 'He that is'.

We may read the great priestly prayer of Jesus in John 17 in this same light. Is it not illuminated, and so read authentically, by these clues to its place in the whole? One does not need to ask how these words were verbally recorded from the lips of Jesus, even as one has no need to enquire how one proves that Hamlet ever uttered the syllables that exclaim 'What a piece of work is man!' Here is a disclosing of the soul in the very throes of wrestling with life and death, with meaning and its measure. What we require of the writer is not an auditor's notebook, but an interpreter's perception. Only as the latter can the truth be found, or wanted.

It is this, we may believe, which John attains in a vivid inner presentation of the consciousness of Jesus: 'I have given them thy word'; 'Thou gavest them to me'; 'I have kept them'; 'For their sakes I consecrate myself'—do we not find here the heartbeat of Jesus' ministry, his partnership with his disciples, his sense of destiny and of divine dependence? The author has mediated meaning with a sure instinct for its measure, because he lives in the continuum of its fellowship and responds to that fellowship's yearning for the literary expression of its inmost secrets.

Examples might be multiplied. But the point, for essay purposes, is sufficiently made. Exacting duties to detail remain in respect of this most lively area of scholarship about the Gospels—the Johannine circle, emphatic history yet gnostic vocabulary, the integrity of Prologue and text, the balance of Judaic/Hellenic elements, and, over all, the master craftsmanship of the anonymous author. Within all these, however, is this arguable key to their reading. It is the central datum of the Christhood of Jesus, read, possessed and written within that other datum of experience to which that Christhood had led, namely 'the seeing of the Father', the 'knowing of the true God and the eternal life'.

We read the New Testament, then, in a double recognition, as a literature made of a faith and a faith making a literature, rooted, alike, in a history, first of the Christ-figure, and then of the Christ-people.

This has brought us back to the promised sequence of the earlier discussion, namely a tracing of the central thread of the story 'according to these Scriptures'. That thread is the Christ in the crucified. Further, since *this* Christ is the shape of the divine obligation to human history, it follows that where we identify the Christ we recognize the divine: 'God was in Christ reconciling the world to himself . . .'; 'He who has seen me has seen the Father'; 'We have the light of the knowledge of the glory of God in the face of Jesus Christ'. The witness is a clear consensus.

What does the faith mean by the Christ-event achieved in the crucified? What, in turn, does it mean by the divine in the Christ-event? Answer takes us back firmly to the ministry of Jesus as, manifestly, do all the Gospels. That ministry moves, in the soul of Jesus, from assurance of 'the kingdom of heaven', which is its central theme. The reality and presence of that kingdom are said to be implicit in the very presence and activity of Jesus—not by arbitrary assertion or pretentious claim, but in the fabric of his teaching, his caring, his healing, in the sheer sincerity of his practice of the kingdom's ways. To usher in that kingdom in a quality of character and deed is to bear a Messianic promise. Hence the Gospels.

But it is precisely the quality of that presence of the norms and claims of the kingdom which evokes the hostility of the world that needs and yet disowns it. The Gospels are clear that the Jesus-story heads towards the tragic. 'The Son of Man must suffer . . .' is the emerging logic. That suffering is in no way artificial in order to fulfil a letter of prophecy. (To this we will return.) It arises directly from the human antipathy to good, from the vested interest of religious prestige and private selfishness, from the perversity of human apathy, enmity and pride. The rejection into which Jesus' ministry moves is seen as symptomatic of evil in the world and kin to all those earlier precedents of suffering prophets who bore in their own persons the hostility of rejectionist society.

It was those precedents, most notably Jeremiah, which generated the vision of 'the suffering servant'. Those same precedents, by the road of those Scriptures, directed the decisions of Jesus as he sensed in his own pathway the shadows of like tragedy of pain and grief. Being Messiah means (if the word is not too soulless) a policy and, only so, an identity. *Who* Messiah is is known in *how* Messiah is. Messianic achievement is the disclosure of Messianic status. Within the consciousness of Jesus, as the Gospels read and write it, these belong together. In a situation entailing directly from his ministry, they see and depict what qualitatively they understand as 'the sin of the world'. In Jesus suffering it, taking it, bearing it, they see and affirm the Messianic fact. That fact, in Jesus crucified and risen, they present, with the Epistles, as the inclusive authentication of 'the power and wisdom of God'. Seeing Jesus they have, in these terms, 'seen the Father' who 'sent' him.

No New Testament writer is in doubt as to the source of that decision. It belongs to Jesus. To attribute it to the Church would be a strange inversion. For it would leave no matrix from which the mind of the Church could emerge to be the shaping, *a posteriori*, of 'the mind of the Christ'. The New Testament is all the other way. The great original is the caring, dying, risen Jesus: the clear derivative is the serving, echoing, depending church.

There are, of course, depreciatory theories of Jesus' readiness to suffer—Schweitzer's, for example, with the suggestion that he meant to precipitate a divine, apocalyptic intervention too sluggish to operate without such desperate provocation.[7] Or there is Brandon's, to the effect that Jesus was a zealot, or a para-zealot, in a bid for power that failed.[8] On such grounds the great *kerygma* was born in its own despite, a redemption plucked from its own travesty. While it is important to explore these possibilities, it is well to accept that the New Testament is the more eloquent against them for allowing them to be conjectured. For in this, as in all else, it is a Scripture so clear in its clues that it has no need to batter the sceptics or starve the ingenuity of the critics.

Its writers steadily relate that suffering Messiahship to two themes—the filiality of Jesus and the tradition of the old Scriptures. His Sonship is an activity of servant-obedience before it is a status of ontology, and only the latter because of the former—witness Philippians 2 and the Epistle to the Hebrews, as well as the sermons in Acts. Christology, in origin, is not about being but doing, not a metaphysic of dignity but a pattern of sacrifice. The resurrection which leads into the former is the climax of the latter. It is not a happy vindication arbitrarily imposed but the undefeated quality of the love that suffers and redeems. Its meaning is that the pattern of the Cross is the disclosure of the divine nature.

That core conviction of the faith-event which is Christianity roots itself in its accordance to the Scriptures. The Gospels and Epistles look back steadily to the precedents by which their confidence in the Christ is kindled, taught and sustained. 'In fulfilment of the prophets' becomes their watchword. The Old Testament, for all its apparent incongruity with the New, is resolutely retained, through all controversy to the contrary, within the Bible of the Church. This Christian will to corroboration from the old certainly derives from the example of Jesus himself. A case can be strongly made for the claim that 'the suffering servant' texts played a significant part in his Messianic awareness.[9] They certainly yielded decisive clues to the interpreting Church.

But they are not slavishly cited. Precedents are not seen to be fulfilled in some purely arbitrary sense. One does not say 'It happened so because the prophets said it should'. For then one would have no sufficient reason, no case showing how the precedent had the right to be one. The matter did not turn on naked prescripts but on living principles, anticipatory only because they were authentic. While it is true that Matthew displays an interest in purely circumstantial parallels, such as: 'He shall be called a Nazarene' (Matthew 2. 23), and even John: 'Not a bone of him shall be broken' (John 19. 36), the over-all retrospect of the New Testament to the Old is integral to relevance and meaning. Whether or not we postulate collections of *Testimonia* as part of the stock-in-trade of Scripture genesis on the part of the Church,[10] the basic concern with the past is its illumination of the mind of Jesus and the congruence of that mind with 'the way God thinks' (see Matthew 16. 23). The Christ-event is the climax of the Christ-hope and both are central to the meaning of history and to the knowledge of God. So the 'new' scriptures ground themselves firmly in the logic of the 'old', breaking out of that tradition in vital obedience to the universality which the 'old' had splendidly glimpsed and stubbornly withheld. It was in Messiahship redemptively achieved that Jewish exclusiveness and Gentile *apartheid* were blessedly transcended. So Paul, in dramatic and passionate advocacy; so the whole New Testament in steady and gathering conviction.

One interesting commentary on that inter-dependence of 'old' and 'new' Scriptures is that the new writings, generated through the identifying of the Christ in Jesus and believing him universal, took their place in life and liturgy alongside the 'old'. Evangelists aiming 'to compile a narrative of the things which have been accomplished', (Luke 1. 1) and apostles educating their disciples in faith by unflagging correspondence out of a pastoral heart, did not consciously see themselves inditing canonical works with a sacred status. But the ultimate standing of their literature as definitive developed out of the very character of its genesis. It came to symbolize as well as to achieve the realisation, in documents, of the meaning of that epitome of the divine-human situation which Jesus had constituted in his living and dying, his dying and living. 'The Word of the Lord', which thereby it became as literature, demands a faith-literacy fitted to its own character. We cannot rightly be absolutist with a Scripture that came hazardously, via the fidelities of a community, about a revelation in life and history, mediated through the minds of a discipleship cast on the raw mercies of a harsh world. We cannot well be infallibilist with a literature which reaches us from a far century, and has within itself a time-span in which its own emergence is at some remove from the events to which it owes itself.

But we can be confident and reverently honest with a Scripture which requires of us a temper of mind appropriate to its own custody of meaning. There are *four* Gospels, not one, not forty-four. In that plurality there are problems, synoptic and other. There are miscellaneous Epistles, with precedents which can be translated into differing times and places and which, for that reason, recruit intelligence and do not abet hard dogmatism. There are occasions in plenty where those who overplay their hand, whether as historians, dogmatists, or ecclesiasts, will find themselves undone. The New Testament, evidently, is the kind of literature, both in its origins and its forms, to refuse all sleeping partnership with its intentions and its meanings. Seen in its own perspectives, it is a Scripture which demands of us resilience of mind, alert to the faith-event it tells—and is.

To be right with the Bible has been the aim and purpose of all the foregoing—a right literacy with the revelation, a true people-of-the-Book quality. But how bewildering have been the attitudes that purport to identify this rightness, how disconcertingly controversial the 'ways of reading the Bible'. There are those adamant advocates of an arbitrary authority, a no-compromise stance about 'revelation' for which any element of individual assessment or rational query implies a slippery slope of relativism where there is no sure footing. These are the all-or-nothing readers for whom any concession to scholarly interrogation invalidates everything. Revelation, on this showing, means an unbending supernaturalism, a disclosure from God to man, faith in which is a divine gift that rests on no other foundation than its arbitrary givenness.

It is possible to make a virtue of this kind of arbitrary notion of revelation as, for example, R. C. Zaehner did in his emotive contrast between the direct, divine, Arabic, syllabic speech of God in the Qur'ān and the indirect, incarnational pattern of the New Testament, which only struggles into revelatory authority laden with a synoptic problem, and much else, to arrive at a canonical status too long debated to be other than finally dubious.[11] Another 'virtue' of this way of esteeming Scripture as absolutist is to see the very abeyance of intelligence it involves as an immolation of reason, and a sacrifice of human pride.

It must be clear from our review of how the faith became literature and literature enshrined faith, in the case of the New Testament, that this posture of mind has no proper place in its readership. Had the case been so, the Scriptures themselves could never have arrived. How then can it be authentic to see them discordantly to their own genesis?

Or there is that wealth of esoteric readership which finds hidden meaning, via allegory and inference, wherewith to fascinate the exuberant and the unwary. It cannot be denied that it has flourished long and far, since the time of the Fathers, and that mysticism everywhere has given it a cherishing. For such reading John the Baptist's disclaimer of worth to unloose the shoe-latchet of Jesus becomes a complete acknowledgement of the mystery of the Incarnation. Or one can explain the clean linen in which Joseph of Arimathea wound the body of Jesus as the same linen sheet in which Peter was offered all manner of living creatures. Thence again we may learn that the Church, represented in such imagery, is indeed buried with Christ. Such ingenuities are legion, fed by the cult of mystery and the sacral aura of a Scripture's status for the individual soul.

While it would be idle to exclude all instinct for the esoteric of this kind, in what might then be a cold and cerebral aloofness, and while some esotericism may be innocent of harm, there is steady need for all such mystifications to be subject to the intelligent discipline of an intelligible whole. It is for this we have cared here. In less than reverent hands the esoteric becomes a menace both to proportion and to truth. No allegory should be sought or asserted against a discernible exoteric sense. Interpretation has a prior obligation to history and to the context—an obligation which 'spirituality' never wisely overrides. Where Scriptures themselves are clearly allegorical one is not in accord with them in being literalist or in finding facts in the figures of poetry. But, for the rest, the very phrase 'according to the Scriptures' argues a criterion of reference, a frame of mind we might almost say, consonant with their own character as history and life.

At the outset it was suggested that some review of the Muslim view of Quranic readership might better underline the different Christian readership of the Christian Scriptures and thus serve inter-communal conversation about the trust of sacred writings. The verbatim Scripture of the Qur'ān is understood in Islam as the direct speech of God. Unlike the New Testament, the Qur'ān is not involved as a document in the experience of its receiving by its people. It does not enshrine, as the Gospels do, the entail of the events which are its text. Indeed, it is itself as text the event par excellence. The divinely ordered phenomenon of *waḥy*, or revelation-inspiration, is the literal miracle of a sublime eloquence on the lips of the unlettered Prophet. Thus its contrast with the Christian book is complete.

That absoluteness of authority, deriving from its nature and its reception, may be taken as a profound religious asset. R. C. Zaehner argued so, in the article earlier noted. He saw the Qur'ān, at least for purposes of his argument, as uncomplicatedly 'the Word of God'. 'For once . . . God spoke plainly in the full light of history: it did not take some four hundred years for the faithful to decide what was holy writ and what was not'.[12] 'A book', he opined, 'is where you would expect to find revelation, rather than in human flesh'. Ignoring the issues in such a magisterial pronouncement, he went on to insist on an entirely arbitrary concept of God's action in revelation qua Qur'ān. There, he claimed, God's inscrutable caprice accepted no humanly related liabilities. The believer appropriately abandons all issues and problems in capitulating to the fact of *Deus dixit*. Whether one should do so, or could be human in doing so, or whether Muslims rightly did so—these were questions which did not arise. By such capitulation mortals were saved the burdens of discursive reason and any theological yearnings of the Spirit.[13]

This view, far as it is from the scholarly acumen Zaehner displayed in other concerns, should not be taken as the *necessary* Quranic account of revelation. Crudely stated it *is* a popular Muslim stance. But it is not one which the Qur'ān itself requires, if we are attentive to the Book's whole significance. It is true that orthodox Islam has understood its Qur'ān as 'a book in which there is nothing doubtful' (Surah 2. 2. et al.) But there is a deeper loyalty that reckons adequately with the considerations, within Muslim premises, which must question the very feasibility of revelation in such rigorous terms.

The first of these would be the phenomenon of prophethood itself. 'We have sent it down upon your heart', say Surahs 2. 97 and 26. 194. The heart is the seat of the emotions and it is with these that awareness of the divine word must engage. The vocabulary of the text is, and must be, *already* current in the culture and the context. Though the sense of *Allah, Ḥaqq, Dhikr, Taufīq*, and other basic terms, is deepened and refined in the Prophet's preaching, this can only be so in that they are already current. 'We have sent it down an Arabic Qur'ān' (Surah 12. 2 et al.), for the explicit reason that Arabic is already there and is the condition of intelligibility. The divine speech quite evidently recruits, indeed needs, the human discourse. It is inconceivable that revelation could issue from and in a total otherness and still 'reveal'.

Harnessing, as it must, ideas, idioms, words, from its potential 'audience', it must also harness and employ the full powers of mind and soul that go with its speaking prophethood. To realise this vital role of the Prophet in his mission is in no way to diminish a sense of its divine givenness. It is to understand it more truly. Muslim piety has no need to fear it may forfeit 'the miracle of the Qur'ān' if it sees its 'matchlessness', literary and revelatory, as standing in a living search and a vital discipleship of spirit on the Prophet's part. Such a sense of things Quranic would generate a truer recognition of Muhammad and would liberate Islamic exegesis from many of its traditional attitudes. The Qur'ān would be more worthily and effectively received.

This is not the place to illustrate where contemporary Muslims are moving towards this livelier possession of their Scripture. The present concern is to see that through all the calligraphic fluency of the Qur'ān runs a comparable theme of revelation recruiting the human and enlisting earthly time and place. There *is* a common element in all the contrasts that divide the verbal and the incarnational—sharp as those contrasts are both in the text and in the tradition of the respective Scriptures.

'Ways of reading', however defined by the nature of what we read, and however obligated to disciplines academic, must finally be responsive to the human world. When the writer in II Timothy 2. 15 speaks of 'rightly handling the word of truth', he uses a Greek word of rare vintage which occurs nowhere else in the Greek Testament or among the classical writers. It could mean 'right dissection' were we dealing with corpses. It visualizes a man picking a sure way across a moor, holding a straight plough in a long field, or cutting stones to suit the pattern of a building—all fitting metaphors of readership. But the 'handling' could also mean serving perceptively the appetites of a hungry family round the table. Bread belongs in the hunger of the world. A literature which, from Galilee to Patmos, is the fruit of crisis and encounter, is best known in facing our own.

Notes

1 R. S. Pine-Coffin (trans) (1961), *Confessions of St. Augustine*, Harmondsworth, p. 254.
2 R. S. Pine-Coffin, *ibid.*, p. 254.
3 W. R. Inge (1899), *Christian Mysticism*, London, p. 272.
4 What Muslim commentators know as *asbab al-nuzūl*, 'the occasions of the sending-down', have always been important in exegesis. The setting of time and place and the incidence of events obviously bear upon the words spoken and how they are to be understood. But these 'occasions' of revelation are not traditionally thought to have affected, or stimulated, in anyway, the content of what was said in them or to them. In his significant study Muhammad Daud Rahbar has painstakingly documented the crucial relevance to exegesis of context and vocabulary and how they inter-relate. See M. D. Rahbar (1960), *God of Justice: Ethical Doctrine of the Qur'an*, Leiden.
5 A. D. Nock (1928), 'Early Gentile Christianity and its Hellenistic background', in A. E.

J. Rawlinson (ed.), *Essays on the Trinity and Incarnation*, reprinted in Zeph Stewart (ed.) (1972), *Arthur Darby Nock*, Vol. 1, Oxford, p. 70.

6 Mann (1978), *Joseph and His Brothers* (trans H. T. Lowe-Porter), Harmondsworth, pp. 551-7 and 667: 'Before the story was first told, it had to tell itself'. See also p.(v): 'Very deep is the well of the past'.

7 A. Schweitzer (1911), *The Quest of the Historical Jesus* (trans), London. His 'logical' or 'consistent' eschatology (as the terms go) for which Jesus' ethical teaching was an *Interimsethik* awaiting the apocalyptic consummation of the kingdom.

8 S. G. F. Brandon (1967) *Jesus and the Zealots*, Manchester. For a strong repudiation of Brandon's thesis and what C. F. D. Moule sees as 'cavalier treatment of the evidence' see M. Hengel (1969), 'Review of *Jesus and the Zealots*', *Journal of Semitic Studies*, Vol. 14, pp. 231 ff.

9 There would seem to be clear echoes of the Servant Songs discernible in the terms with which Jesus, according to the Synoptic Gospels, anticipated his death. 'Ransom' is the most obvious. There is a direct quotation from Isaiah 53.3 in Mark 9.12, in the phrase: 'be treated with contempt'. Or, if not a quotation, an echo. For a case against this view see, for example, M. D. Hooker (1967) *The Son of Man in Mark*, London.

10 See the detailed study of C. H. Dodd (1952), *According to the Scriptures*, London.

11 See R. C. Zaehner (1975), 'Why not Islam?', *Religious Studies*, Vol. 11, pp. 167-79. The same journal also presented an article in reply to Zaehner by the present writer. See A. K. Cragg (1977), 'How not Islam', *Religious Studies*, Vol. 13, pp. 387-94.

12 R. C. Zaehner, *op. cit.*, note 6, p. 177.

13 R. C. Zaehner (1974) *Our Savage God*, London, gives the context in the author's thinking within which his animadversions on Islam in *Religious Studies* were conceived. Though relieved at times by traces of the author's customary scholarship and integrity of argument, both pieces of writing seem rightly to be considered as a gesture of retreat into despair, so emotive and pontifical is the language. The attempt to exclude all theodicy from the doctrine of God and, instead, to assert divine 'thuggery', is to abandon all rational, not to say Christian, criteria. A God 'who tortured his son to death' can in no way be reconciled with the compassion which, in the author's own words elsewhere, is without limit in 'God crucified in Christ'. Sadly *Our Savage God* and the kindred commendation of Islam must be read as a melancholy clue to a despairing state of mind. Islam, the Old Testament and the Cross together deserve a different reckoning.

PART II

MYTH AND TRUTH

For Mircea Eliade who first taught me that there was more to myth than the instant
need to demythologize.
(N. Perrin's dedication of *The Resurrection Narratives: A New Approach*, London, 1977)

The vital problem facing anyone who approaches Christian theology in this way is what
sort of link is there between the myth and the history?
(M. Wiles, in J. Hick (ed.), *The Myth of God Incarnate*, London 1977, p. 158)

3 GOSPEL TRUTH

A. D. Nuttall

THIS essay is the product of both knowledge and ignorance: the sort of knowledge, that is, that may be picked up in the course of a reasonably thorough literary education, together with a truly barbarous ignorance of the Bible (which is of course the matter in hand). Such a state of affairs may well be thought to augur ill.

A man in my position needs a stalking horse and I propose to use George Herbert (who is after all one of the most Biblical of English poets). I hope thus to creep up on the unknown under cover of the known. In the poetry of Herbert I find a peculiar problem. Herbert in his poems adopts a position of prayer; that is, he appears in the poem *in propria persona* as a man praying. He does not, however, confine himself to this *persona*; the poems are partly dramatic in character and frequently offer passages of dialogue, in which the praying Herbert is answered by God. The function of the divine answers is commonly to transcend not just the human failings of the poet but in a way his very virtues too, in so far as they are merely human. The problem is perhaps already apparent. Within the poem the mere humanity of Herbert is externally corrected by God, yet both the human lines of Herbert and the superhuman lines of God were written by Herbert; the ostensibly 'external' correction is in fact supplied by the person undergoing correction and so, perhaps, is not really external at all. God, who all the while was reading over Herbert's shoulder, may well have smiled to see his part so played for him (and, moreover, the action presented as a kind of chastening of Herbert's *pride*).

Of course Herbert is very clever—so clever as to come within an ace of resolving the old paradox of humility, which may be explained thus: is 'I am humble' a self-refuting sentence? If the speaker is unaware that humility is a virtue, it need not be. But Christians are so *instructed*, and in this way the paradox is generated. Herbert engages with this paradox in the third poem called 'Love':

> Love bade me welcome: yet my soul drew back,
>   Guiltie of dust and sinne.
> But quick-ey'd Love, observing me grow slack
>   From my first entrance in,
> Drew nearer to me, sweetly questioning,
>   If I lack'd any thing.
>
> A guest, I answer'd, worthy to be here:
>   Love said, You shall be he.
> I the unkinde, ungratefull? Ah my deare,

41

I cannot look on thee.
Love took my hand, and smiling did reply,
 Who made the eyes but I?

Truth, Lord, but I have marr'd them: let my shame
 Go where it doth deserve.
And know you not, sayes Love, who bore the blame?
 My deare, then I will serve.
You must sit down, sayes Love, and taste my meat:
 So I did sit and eat.

For a while in this poem there is a faint sense of that strange moral *competition* with God which we find in, say, 'Artillerie', 'The Temper', 'The Storm', 'Hope' and 'The Holdfast': the brief endeavour to out-do God himself in self-abnegation, to reject the divine beneficence not from hatred but from sheer altruism and self-contempt. But this of course, as Herbert knows, is itself a kind of pride. And so in 'Love' III the paradox whereby 'I am humble' is self-refuting is gently set aside by God himself. Of course in this particular poem the human speaker has not reached the pitch of congratulating himself on his humility but the danger of such self-congratulation is not wholly absent from the moral penumbra of the poem. Gradually we perceive that the speaker's humility, because it is in a minimal sense self-regarding, is not yet deep enough. To say 'I am not worthy' is presumptuous in so far as it implies that *desert* is in any way relevant to the case. God's answer must be a smiling 'Whatever made you think these things were done according to desert?'. So what is rather needed is the *utter* humility of acknowledging the sheer irrelevance of personal desert. And *this* humility, now defined as the true sort, is by definition non-self-regarding and therefore not liable to the self-consumption we noted earlier. So it might be thought that in the moral structure of his verse Herbert transcends the problem of an asserted humility. The images of God projected by the praying figure are corrected from outside, and humility asserted is engulfed in a humility which makes no claim at all. However, although Herbert is clever he is not quite clever enough; the problem of humility may seem to have been solved, but the problem of the pseudo-divine voice has not, and indeed until he solves the second he cannot really solve the first. Once more, we must say, the lines of the 'external', correcting voice were supplied by none other than George Herbert. Poetical devotion, as Dr Johnson saw, is subject to an irremediable duplicity, which approaches most nearly to mendacity in those writers who profess a puritan plainness of approach. Herbert within the poem may be admirably unaware that he has found real humility, but what of the Herbert who artfully made the whole poem? Such innocence will surely be very hard for him henceforth.

Of course the case I have just put can be blurred and weakened in various ways. For example, it might be said that all our difficulties arise from a confusion of Herbert the 'character' in the poem with Herbert the author, or (which is the same thing) from the error of supposing that the poems are *actually* prayers addressed to God when in fact they are fictions addressed to a reader. To this I give a two-fold answer. First, generations of educated Anglican readers, fully alive to the conventions of poetry, have regarded them as prayers ('poetical devotion', certainly, but devotion for all that). The modern impulse to draw strict lines, to require that everyone declare which language game he is playing, will always seem reductively formalist to such readers. Secondly, even if we grant that such a poem is a fiction, we must forthwith confess that it is the kind of fiction that imitates prayer, and a certain fidelity to the crucial conditions of prayer is surely still required. But here we encounter a curious irony. The one element which can save the praying subject from a hopeless subjectivism is, it would seem, the voice from outside. But that voice, conferring substance on God, is the one element which is not present in real prayer, is the one element of un-realism in the mimesis, is supplied by an act of fiction.

Again, it might be said that when God's answers are drawn from Scripture all my objections lapse. This, however, is not always the case. Herbert's God is somewhat wittier than the God of Scripture (more like Herbert?). Nevertheless it might be said that in any live religious tradition believers are not confined to the repetition of revealed formulae. The believer has to be able to say, not just what God said, but what he would say in endlessly changing situations. Indeed, saying what God would say is part of the ordinary job of the parish priest. But the curious thing about the world of Herbert's poetry is that God *actually* replies, and this does not usually occur in life; it is not so much the *content* as the *fact* of the reply that is crucial (though it remains important that the content is illicitly elaborated). God never answers Donne, and in this respect at least his poetry is the cleaner for the difference.

Again, it might be said that in any personal lyric there is a necessary distinction between the 'I' of the poem and the poem's author. For example the lover in the poem may cry that he is in every way exhausted, while the author may betray in the vigour of his writing a state of abounding imaginative health. I answer, of course, that this will serve well enough for those poets who acknowledge clearly that their work is fiction. But Herbert is not thus. My argument is *ad hominem*, addressed to the author of the Jordan poems.

Again, wherever the words given to God are transcribed by Herbert from a mystical vision, he escapes my charge. I leave it to the reader to judge in particular cases how probable this is.

Lastly, it might be said that the voice of God in Herbert's poetry may well be supplied (or deemed to be supplied) by conscience, and this disposes of our difficulty. This objection has some force, but I nevertheless submit that if we substitute (for example) 'sayes Con-

science' for 'sayes Love' the effect of a subjective universe shattered
from without is virtually lost.

The suggestion that there is an ontological problem in George
Herbert therefore survives. It does not survive unscathed, but it
survives. Note that throughout the argument the unimpeachably
divine character of Scripture was never questioned. This was natural,
because our concern was with Herbert's good faith, and as long as
Herbert believed Scripture to be the Word of God he was guilty of no
deliberate breach of truth in employing the words of Scripture to
transcend the merely human utterance of his praying subject. As we
saw, the trouble was rather that he did *not* at those moments in his
poem confine himself to scriptural words, and that he ascribed a saving
force to an audible reply from God which seldom if ever occurs in real
prayer.

But Herbert lived in the seventeenth century, when belief in
Scripture came more easily than it does today. What happens when a
modern innocent turns his attention to St John's Gospel, thinking it
(for he knows no better) a book written by a man or by men about a
person supposed divine? It is no longer *given* that the entire text is
divine. Rather we have a situation in which a work purporting to
provide theological, moral and historical truth includes dialogue with
the supposedly divine person. Does this mean that within the Bible
itself (that is, in the body of writing which stood as a kind of rock in the
discussion of Herbert), the Herbert paradox is in fact repeated?—that
Herbert in all good faith was leaning on men who had problems very
like his own?

John says at the beginning of his Gospel that the Word which *was*
God became flesh and dwelt among us. He makes it plain that this
incarnate God is to be identified with Jesus, that Jesus made the world,
entered it and was rejected by it, that Jesus 'the true light that
enlightens every man was coming into the world' (1. 9). This Jesus,
then, was more than man. But within a page this divine man is
speaking, and we need urgently to know: are the words Jesus's own or
are they John's (for John was only a man)? If we choose the first
interpretation, or indeed a modified version of it whereby the words
of Jesus could have been believed by John to have been Jesus's own, our
course is easy. But if we choose the second, and suppose that John is in
any degree constructing the dialogue of Jesus, then at once the
Herbert problem confronts us. It might be thought that we do not
have that special irony we find in Herbert, whereby a kind of moral
solipsism in the praying subject is presented in such terms as to make it
clear that only a voice from outside can resolve it; a voice from outside
is then seemingly produced, but turns out after all to be a fiction of the
benighted subject. In John the problem assumes a different and more
universal form. It is the world, not the author on his knees, that is the
benighted subject, and that night is presented in such a way as to make
clear that only the intervention of superhuman power can dispel it.

Not even an exceptional man like John the Baptist can give true light (John 1. 8–9); only the supernatural can irradiate the natural. But, we are told, this indeed happened and the Evangelist can tell us the superhuman words of the superhuman man. But, if John, natural man, to any considerable extent concocted those words *for* Christ, both his argument and his good faith are in ruins. Only the superhuman will serve, and the superhuman is the one thing which natural man, however pious and willing, cannot undertake to provide.

But now we begin to see that the contrast between Herbert as contending with moral solipsism and John as contending with naturalism is partly unsatisfactory. The similarity, in fact, is stronger than the difference. The praying Herbert within the poems fails, not because he is cut off from moral contact with his fellow creatures, but simply *qua* creature: he fails because he is not God, and this is equally true of every other human being. Thus, Herbert's predicament within the poem is implicitly universal, and moreover the universal situation turns out to be identical with that proposed by John. And so the distance between them shrinks. What we took for a distant analogy is something a good deal closer than that. At the same time, however, the word 'solipsism' retains a certain paradoxical appropriateness. The solipsist trembles lest all outside himself should prove an illusion, leaving him, as Hume said, 'environed with darkness'. The Christian trembles lest all outside humanity and nature should prove an illusion, leaving his entire species benighted. The phrase 'collective solipsism' or 'solipsism of the species' may seem contradictory, but the religious mind instantly endows it with a perfectly coherent meaning. Even the etymological element represented by *sol* in *solipsism*, the element of alone-ness, persists in the collective version, since now the fear is that, if the human race is in no sort of relation with the transcendent, then the entire race is horribly alone. The kind of moral solipsism which Herbert wrestles with in his poems is really—for all his interest in the Individual praying by himself—collective solipsism.

Solipsism, once it is permitted to pose itself as a problem, can only be cured from outside. Self-comforting fictions produced by the suffering subject will not serve, precisely because they are produced by the subject. This reasoning applies indifferently to individual and to collective solipsism. 'External' cure in the case of the individual solipsist means cure from a person or thing other than himself. 'External' cure for the collective religious solipsist consists in cure from a being who does not belong to the human race or the natural order. Christianity differs from most if not all religions in recognizing this necessity and supplying, through the Incarnation, the required external cure.

But now I must draw a distinction. I said earlier that even when Herbert draws his divine replies from a live tradition, he remains at fault in so far as his dramatic resolution depends on an *actual* reply from God; what is most dramatically effective in the poems is the fact that the man praying actually *hears* (however faintly) the voice of one saying 'Child', so that external cure appears in exactly the way most urgently required—but then this turns out to be fiction. By parity of reasoning we must seemingly allow that the Evangelist is in better case. For even if the *content* of Jesus's speeches were feigned by him, we need not suppose (need we?) that he doubted the *fact* of Jesus's appearance on Earth. *That* he spoke is as important as *what* he spoke.

Here my argument begins to see-saw uncomfortably: lose Herbert, save John, lose John, save Herbert. Thus, to save Herbert we might say: 'The *fact* of an audible reply to prayer is not the only external cure recognized by the Christian. Indeed the antithesis between fact and content is in one respect highly misleading. The very nature of Jesus's moral and spiritual teaching proclaims it Other than the world, and this *fact* about *content* supplies an adequate corrective to the merely human'. This would mean that the fiction whereby Herbert has God speak at the end of the poem becomes a venial fiction, since it is no longer on the *fact* of a reply that the very existence of an external correction depends. But if we apply this reasoning to the Gospel and suppose that the Evangelist supplied part of the *doctrine* of the Gospel, since it is now *doctrine* which most crucially supplies the necessary correction of the merely human, then the good faith of the Evangelist is in serious jeopardy. Conversely, as we have seen, if the mere fact that God has appeared and spoken is crucial, then Herbert is in trouble and the Evangelist is safe.

It is by now obvious that I have run up against questions of fact and probability. The question 'Is the Jesus of John's Gospel a construction of the Evangelist, a construction of tradition or Jesus himself?' is of course a question for scholars. Such faint echoes of controversy as reach my ears suggest that the most extreme view, namely that the Evangelist has largely constructed Jesus for us, is by no means out of court. But I make no pronouncement. I confine myself to deductions from theoretical possibilities.

But first I propose a *Gedankenexperiment*. Let us read a passage of dialogue in John on the assumption that it is a piece of fiction, a work of literary art. Let us take Jesus's conversation with Pilate in John 18. 33–38:

> Pilate entered the praetorium again and called Jesus, and said to him, 'Are you the King of the Jews?' Jesus answered, 'Do you say this of your own accord, or did others say it to you about me?' Pilate answered, 'Am I a Jew? Your own nation and the chief priests have handed you over to me; what have you done?' Jesus answered, 'My kingship is not of this world; if my kingship were of this world, my servants would fight, that I might not be handed over to the Jews; but my kingship is not from the world.' Pilate said to him, 'So you are a king?' Jesus answered, 'You say that I am a king. For this I was born, and for this I have come into the world, to bear witness to the truth. Every one who is of the truth hears my voice.' Pilate said to him, 'What is truth?'

This is a remarkably early specimen of what literary critics call discontinuous dialogue. When Jesus is asked if he is King of the Jews, he answers neither yes or no, but instead asks a question of his own. When he is asked what he has done, he answers not that question but the earlier one with the mysterious 'My kingship is not of this world'. Even so, he skips one logical stage; to make the logic fully explicit he would presumably have had to say something like 'I am a king, yes, but not of the Jews nor of anything earthly'. This logical ellipse seems to trouble Pilate and he asks, seeking confirmation, 'So you are a king?' and hears in answer the words 'You say that I am a king'.

Now the usual story told by scholars of drama is that the discontinuous dialogue in favour with the *epigoni* of Harold Pinter really began with Chekhov. Chekhovian dialogue sounds like this:[1]

LIUBOV ANDREYEEVNA: How you've aged, Feers!

FEERS: What can I get you, Madam?

LOPAHIN: They say, you've aged a lot.

FEERS: I've been alive a long time. They were going to marry me off before your Dad was born. [LAUGHS] And when Freedom was granted to the people, I'd already been made the chief valet. I wouldn't take my Freedom then, I stayed with the master and mistress . . . . [PAUSE] I remember everyone was glad at the time, but what they were glad about, no one knew.

LOPAHIN: Oh, yes, it was a good life all right. At least, people got flogged!

FEERS [*Not having heard him*]: Rather! The peasants belonged to the gentry, and the gentry belonged to the peasants; but now everything's separate, and you can't understand anything.

Again, notice the systematic absence of 'logical fit'. Of course the literary critics allow that although Chekhov is for practical purposes the *fons et origo* of this manner, it is always on the cards that Shakespeare, who could do anything, did this. And indeed he did. Here is a passage from 2 *Henry IV* III ii. 199–210:

SHALLOW: By the mass, I could anger her to th' heart. She was then a *bona roba*. Doth she hold her own well?

FALSTAFF Old, old, Master Shallow.

SHALLOW: Nay, she must be old, she cannot choose but be old, certain she's old and had Robin Nightwork by old Nightwork before I came to Clement's Inn.

SILENCE: That's fifty-five years ago.

SHALLOW: Ha, cousin Silence, that thou hadst seen that that this knight and I have seen? Ha, Sir John, said I well?

FALSTAFF: We have heard the chimes at midnight, Master Shallow.

Thus far back and no further. By and large, it takes a modernist to relish discontinuity, to rejoice more in silence than in palpable structure, and Shakespeare is merely (as so often) the exception that proves the rule. Elsewhere as far as the eye can see lie tracts of *connected* writing.

So what are we to make of the Gospel? Is it a freakish anticipation of modernism? A very little thought suggests that it is not. The principle of discontinuity which holds in both Shakespeare and Chekhov is quite different from that which holds in the Gospel. The world of Shakespeare's Gloucestershire scenes in *Henry IV* and Chekhov's

Cherry Orchard is in a manner one place: a world of ill-disciplined servants, ill-managed material circumstances and asthenic yet poignant emotions. Here dialogue is above all desultory; discontinuities occur not only between speeches but in the middle of speeches, showing that the characters are not only failing to communicate but as individuals lack coherent, autonomous drive. Madam Liubov's orchard, Justice Shallow's orchard; both are symbols of a sort of sweet-smelling death. But in the oblique answers of Jesus we sense rather an awful life.

The dialogue with Pilate may be discontinuous, then, but it is anything but desultory. We are not made to watch people drifting away from each other and themselves into a kind of reminiscent vacuum, but rather disputants locked in combat. The discontinuities of Jesus (and of Pilate—for he begins to learn the game) are evidently deliberate. They are at the very lowest a way of holding the initiative at all times. Answer a man directly and you are playing his game, dancing to his tune. A constitutional inability to answer a straight question seems to have marked out Jesus from the first. The people looked for him and at last found him in Capernaum (John 6.25) and asked him when he had arrived there, which is a simple enough question. Jesus does not say 'Yesterday' or anything resembling that. He says, 'You seek me, not because you saw signs, but because you ate your fill of the loaves'. That is, he immediately assumes the initiative and overrides them. When later the Jews ask (John 8.19) 'Where is your Father?' he answers (*answers?*) 'You know neither me nor my Father; if you knew me, you would know my Father also'. Here we begin to see more clearly that together with a seizing of the initiative there is further a technique of deliberate transcendence. Jesus's (non-) answer implies that their assumptions in asking the question were all wrong, that they were thinking on the wrong plane. Yet, note, he could have told them this and yet preserved the form of a direct answer; that is, he could have said, 'In Heaven'. But of course such an answer would not have quickened the minds of his listeners anything like as effectively as the answer he chose. Which perhaps is as much as to say, that he chose to express his transcending answer in a form obfuscated for rhetorical purposes. Later in the same chapter (John 8. 25) he is asked, 'Who are you?' and answers, 'Even what I have told you from the beginning'. This could of course be a perfectly normal exasperated response, except for the fact that Jesus has not as far as we know been telling anyone in any straightforward sense who he is from the beginning. Nor need we postulate a *lacuna* in the text, for we are told that the Jews themselves found his answer unintelligible. So we must place this answer in the same category as the others. It too is a transcending non-answer. Later in the same dialogue Jesus says to the Jews (John 8. 56) 'Your father Abraham rejoiced that he was to see my day!' and they not unnaturally react: 'You are not yet fifty years old, and have you seen Abraham?' Jesus answers (and here 'lack of logical fit' seems too weak a description) 'Before Abraham was, I am!' (John 8. 57–58).

Nor is it only with outsiders that Jesus speaks thus. Simon Peter said to him (John 13. 6) 'Lord, do you wash my feet?' and Jesus said, 'What I am doing you do not know now, but afterward you will understand' (John 13. 7). Obviously in this last example it would be absurd in any sort of discourse to give the formally apposite answer, 'Yes, I am washing your feet'. Clearly Simon Peter is not querying the fact, but the propriety of the fact. He means, 'You're surely not going to wash my feet, are you?'. But, equally obviously, Jesus might have begun his answer by saying, 'Yes, I am indeed going to do this'. But he prefers a baffling ellipsis and a statement which transcends the merely social morality of Simon Peter's question.

Looked at coldly this technique of arrogant obliqueness, once analysed, can appear singularly infuriating. The basic mechanism is surprisingly simple, and it is easy to turn out such dialogue by the yard. For example:

WHITE: Are you going to the Conference on Friday?
BLACK: Am I? Persuade me.
WHITE: Gombrich will be there.
BLACK: If you like Gombrich, that is the sort of thing you like.
WHITE: Why, don't you like Gombrich?
BLACK: Let's say that I don't.

To write such dialogue is a curious experience (now I testify) partly because one senses a powerful latent evil in the smiling, quizzical answers of Black. One thinks wildly for a moment that the whole story of Christ is latent in his mere style; people who talk in this way, one feels, are liable to be crucified (or made to drink hemlock). But while the gaps in modernist dialogue imply a kind of anti-nature, the gaps in Jesus's dialogue imply a transcending complement, a supernature.

I have suggested that there is no analogue earlier than the Gloucestershire scenes of Shakespeare's *Henry IV* for the discontinuous dialogue of the Gospels and that even that example was in truth scarcely analogous. Certainly the dialogue of even the most mysterious Greek tragedies—*Oedipus Coloneus* for example, or *The Bacchae*—seems pellucidly consecutive beside the dialogue of John's Gospel. The non-answers given by the Delphic Oracle are perhaps to some extent comparable. These responses, however, do not in practice intimate substantial transcendent verities, but prudently ambiguous practical predictions. The hieratic ambiguity has an evident function. Morton Smith has described a tradition of Delphic secrecy in sectarian Jewish religion at the time of Jesus and seems at one point to assign a similarly prudent motive to the Jewish practice.[2] The followers of Christ may have been in some respects libertine and it was merely wise to keep such goings-on hidden. But this explanation scarcely covers the words of Jesus as we have them. Jesus seems less concerned with concealment than with some shocking revelation. There seems to be a Northern tradition of responses at once dour and equivocal, at least as old as the Sagas and at least as young as R. L. Stevenson, which makes some faint approach, but it is faint indeed. But half a page ago I mentioned hemlock; does the example of Socrates shed any light? The Platonic dialogues, considered as a dramatic form, are at first sight far too consecutive. Paradoxically, it is rather in the *Apology*—a mono-logue—that we find a kind of parallel to the utterance of Jesus. After all, the whole of the *Apology* is a kind of answer and a non-answer to a series of questions. Did Socrates corrupt the young? He answers, 'Would a man wish to make his fellows better or worse?' (transposing the discussion to the *a priori*). What punishment did he deserve? He answers, 'Maintenance free of charge in the Prytaneum' (rejecting the very notion of punishment).[3] And all the while, amid the wreckage of his conventional legal defence, we sense an enormous mystery.

The excuse of Socrates for his appalling incivility was that he had seen something incommensurate with the world he inhabited. The way Plato put it was that he had apprehended the Ideas which exist beyond the sensible world, but this is probably already too definite. The excuse of Herbert was essentially the same; he had heard a voice from beyond humanity, or, if he had not, he blasphemed his own law. The Evangelist's situation we have seen to be essentially similar and we must grant that the same conditions apply to Jesus himself, but here there is an extra twist. For Jesus did not claim to have heard the divine voice. He claimed to be the divine voice. This is the highest point in an escalating series of difficulties, and here we find no resolution, but rather a knot drawn tight.

So our contrast between the 'feigned-audible' answer of God in Herbert and the less contentious physical availability of Jesus begins to lose its urgency as it is replaced by a more importunate doubt. Everything now depends on the nature of the Jesus who was thus available. Was he man or was he God? We are driven to concentrate no longer upon the physical availability of a certain body, but rather upon the veracity of a certain claim.

I have deliberately delayed discussion of the most tantalizing of all Jesus's answers to Pilate: 'You say that I am a King' (John 18. 37). We may distinguish three kinds of equivocal answer. The first is merely evasive, the second obliquely adumbrates a universe of discourse which transcends the assumptions of the original question, and the third directs attention to a realm which is *radically* transcendent, so utterly Other as to resist any kind of specific illustration in human terms. Jesus is a king but has nothing specific in common with other kings. In what way, then, is he a king? One is driven back on a kind of tautology; he shares with other kings the property of sovereignty or rule. So Pilate repeats the question, 'So you are a king?'. And Jesus uses in reply an idiom which at one level implies simple assent, but at another more formal level merely bounces the question back: 'You say that I am a king'. Even if it were shown that in Aramaic the idiom 'you say', like the American 'You've said it', was regularly used as an affirmative, so that Jesus is committing himself to rather more than 'King is your word for it', in a situation as tense as this one would suspect that the speaker might nevertheless be taking refuge in the literal meaning of the words. Imagine a man being interrogated during the McCarthy investigations:

'Are you or have you at any time ever been a Communist?'
'You've said it'.

In such circumstances such a reply would immediately sound uneasily equivocal and I have little doubt that the Senator from Wisconsin would press for a less ambiguous answer. Thus, even if Jesus may be said to have assented to Pilate's question (and even that is doubtful), he does so in an idiom which at another level merely retorts the question back upon Pilate; moreover his choice of this idiom is probably not accidental. He answers, but in another way he merely echoes, and the mystery lies somewhere between the assent and the echo, no longer to be specifically hinted. George Herbert wrote a poem in which Heaven answered him in an echo only, but an echo which was at the same time miraculously informative:

O who will show me those delights on high?
ECHO: I.
Thou, Echo, thou art mortall, all men know.
ECHO: No.

This will serve as an emblem of what happens in Jesus's dialogue with Pilate, but it is an emblem only, and not a strict parallel. In the poem the blankness of the echo is almost too easily defeated by the little miracle of literary ingenuity; each repetition is made into a perfectly meaningful and intelligible answer. But in Jesus's answer to Pilate the element of blank intransigence is less easily dispelled.

I have argued that the discontinuous answers of Jesus are virtually unique and that this uniqueness requires a special explanation. My own response has been that the hiatus between question and answer arises from the extraordinary, other-wordly character of the answers. Behind 'You say that I am a king' stands nothing less than 'I am God'. Under such pressures the ordinary fabric of discourse gives way. At the same time, however, Jesus's words have a stylistic context, which I take to be one of immemorial Jewish irony. This irony is hard to describe but, once noticed, easily recognized. Oddly enough, there is a touch of it in Pilate's 'Am I a Jew?' (John 18. 35) (was the Roman governor going native?). The Talmud might be described as in part a book of entirely pious jokes about God. Here, if you like, is a real analogue to what Jesus is doing. But the effect of this discovery is not to remove the uniqueness of Jesus's language but to emphasize it.

True, in both cases the irony often arises from the baffling gap between human and divine, but in the Talmud the human speakers, merchants, rabbis, all are merely human and God is other than they. Jesus alters the very grammar of Talmudic humour, applies it in the first person singular and assumes a position in the joke which no one had presumed to occupy before (unless it was Lucifer).

But now further differences between Herbert and John begin to press upon us. My argument against Herbert is largely *ad hominem*. That is, when I am asked by what absurd ideal of literalness in language and unquestioning humility in man I censure Herbert, I answer, the ideals are Herbert's own. The England of Elizabeth had been predominantly Calvinist, and the England of Herbert's time was still powerfully puritan in its theology. It was not I but the author of 'Jordan' i and ii who affirmed that only the plainest truth would do for devotion. It was not I but a theology still potent in Herbert's time which affirmed that the very effort to deserve the love of God was itself a kind of pride. But how much of this applies to John? I have suggested that nothing less than the *ipsissima verba* of the divine man will do, but John may not have had even the concept of accurate verbatim quotation. At least, it is a pretty safe rule that no Ancient ever quotes another accurately. Plato's quotations from Homer are always perfectly metrical, perfectly Homeric but rarely if ever impeccable. More importantly, it seems that Plato thought it consistent with his piety to his dead teacher to attribute to him philosophical views he never held.

Perhaps, then, John never asked himself point-blank whether Jesus really said *x* or *y* but contented himself with writing down only what seemed 'right', or harmonious with memory and tradition. Does this mean that the *ad hominem* charge of mendacity cannot be put? I answer, the problem has assumed an altogether starker form and will not go away. If John is in bad faith it will not be because he has like Herbert personally supplied the words which God might have said but rather because he has pretended *simpliciter* that Jesus was God; likewise, if John was honest, his honesty does not consist in the accurate transmission of words duly vouchsafed to him, but rather in the truthful recounting of the most extraordinary of all *facts*. You do not need a puritan theology or a scholarly training to know the difference between explaining how Jesus was God, and pretending that Jesus was God. In any case, if my argument is not *ad hominem*, it is *ad deum ipsum*. It scarcely matters that puritanism with its emphasis on plain truth has not yet emerged, since what is now in question is not the accurate tradition of a transcendent truth or the propriety of such discourse under God, but the original self-declaration of God, if God it was. Let us take it step by step.

First, let us suppose that John, for political or missionary reasons, produced the claim to be divine on Jesus's behalf. That is hideous bad faith. In a Greek or Roman of the period it might have merited a milder description. After all, the classical world at that time abounded in *theioi andres*—so much so that the word *divine* meant little more than 'charismatic', and I deliberately choose a debased English word. But John was a Jew, and Jews, however well informed about Greek philosophy, had an altogether heavier conception of deity. The Word, the Logos, is taken from the Greeks but in no docile spirit, for it is instantly *made flesh*, a most un-Greek conception. In a famous passage in the *Confessions* Augustine says how he read in the Platonists of the divine Word, 'but that the Word was made flesh and dwelt among us I did not read there' (Confessions 7. 9). John was no crypto-Hellene. He knew that to describe a Jew as calling himself God was not in the least like referring to the self-deification of an Emperor. Here, if you like is the equivalent moment to my appeal to puritanism in connection with Herbert. At the very least, the Jewish conception of deity is puritan, while the Graeco-Roman conception is Cavalier (in the pejorative sense of the word).

Secondly, let us suppose instead that John was repeating, in good faith, a tradition about Jesus which he believed to be true. In this case we can bring no charge against John. Instead we must interrogate (theoretically of course since it is in practice impossible) the earlier transmitters of the story. And, at every stage, either the teller is inventing the claim to be divine (and that is hideous bad faith) or else he is repeating what he believes to be true—until we come at last to the historical Jesus. One might suppose the story to have grown by insensible degrees, but the supposition is not easy. Even if we assume that at an earlier stage Jesus claimed divine parentage and no more, and this was inflated through mis-hearing and the unconscious distortions of memory, the original claim is, in a Jewish context, sufficiently stark. It is an assertion of the intersection of the transcendent with the natural. Somewhere, some such claim must have been introduced. And always it must have been clear that it was either an awful lie or a more awful truth.

Lying behind a great deal of what I have said is the old, fierce alternative *aut deus aut malus homo*, 'either God or a wicked man'. But in truth there is one other possibility, and that is that Jesus was mad. After long hesitation I find that this explanation, initially so repulsive, is the one I think most likely to be true. After all, I write, not as an Evangelical Christian, but as one brought up by unbelieving parents in an unbelieving culture, true to that nurture and that culture by mature conviction, and yet, with all this, exasperated by the enervate professions of believers. It is as if one's very scepticism is somehow dishonoured when it finds itself confronted by such half-belief. When I say that Jesus may have been mad, I am working on the assumption that the possibilities of natural explanation should be exhausted before supernatural explanation is invoked. The natural explanation turns out to be a less simple affair than it seemed. The supposition that Jesus was wicked is of course in immediate difficulties. To many people the supposition of madness will be equally difficult. But this reaction rises in part, I suspect, from two false presumptions: first, that madness is the opposite of intelligence and second that madness is incompatible with goodness. In fact, most dull-witted people are sane and many mad people are luminously intelligent. Some mad people, likewise, have more than the common allowance of charity. There have been many mad men who thought they were God. The special irony with Jesus is that, so far from being a case of megalomania compensating for utter incapacity, his real claim upon our reverence is immense. The emperor Caligula thought he ruled the universe and really ruled the known world. Jesus thought he was God and was really the best of men.

This essay is essentially a plea to people to see what a knife-edge thing the Gospel of John is. People seem to have acquired a way of talking about Scripture which somehow absolves them from the need to notice the one extraordinary thing that Scripture says, as if they do not, in these sophisticated times, need to make any sort of decision on the point. Perhaps they have all gently agreed (clerics and laymen, all) that Jesus was somewhat deranged and told lies. This, as I have confessed, is my own provisional position. It still dismays me that they take up this position with such complaisant equanimity, with no more, so to speak, than a nod and a wink across the boardroom table—as if this were the least of the questions that confronted them. It is, at the lowest, bad literary criticism (like discussing *Romeo and Juliet* without once acknowledging that the play is about love). This barbarous reader took no belief to his reading of the Gospel. But the first thing he encountered was a frontal challenge to that unbelief.

Notes

1 A. Chekhov (1959), *The Cherry Orchard*, Act II, in E. Fen (trans) *Plays*, Harmondsworth pp. 361-2.
2 M. Smith (1973), *The Secret Gospel: the Discovery and Interpretation of the Secret Gospel according to Mark*, New York.
3 See H. Tredennick (trans) (1969) *The Last Days of Socrates: Four Dialogues*, Harmondsworth, pp. 55-6, 70.

4 THE COINCIDENCE OF MYTH AND FACT

Stephen Medcalf

THREE scholars of English literature—C. S. Lewis, Hugo Dyson and J. R. R. Tolkien—conversed on myth nearly fifty years ago on a warm night—19 September 1931—under the trees and in the New Buildings of Magdalen College, Oxford. What they said can be reconstructed from three letters of C. S. Lewis's and from a poem of Tolkien's, variously entitled *Mythopoeia* (Mythmaking), *Misomythos* (the Hater of Myth) and *Philomyth to Misomyth* (the Lover of Myth to the Hater of Myth).[1] The lover of myth, not surprisingly, was Tolkien. Perhaps it is surprising that the hater of myth was Lewis, though less so when one knows that this conversation removed in him—who had 'admitted that God was God'[2] more than two years previously—an inhibition against becoming a Christian.

But he did not exactly hate myth. Four years earlier, he had defined a myth as 'a description or story introducing supernatural personages or things, determined not . . . by motives arising from events within the story, but by the supposedly immutable relations of the personages or things . . . and not . . . connected with any given place or time'.[3] Confusedly he hated such stories because he loved them, believed them false in fact, and could not make up his mind whether, had they been true, he would still have loved them. In 1928 he had declared that only if they were fictions could myth and symbol do their proper work of expressing absolute Spirit: for if mythical beings actually existed they would have 'empirical' value as objects of fear, desire or other passions. Therefore 'the symbol is never *given* as a fact, but *taken* by free spiritual activity': if all mythology were proved true, 'the poets would throw it away and invent a new one, warranted untrue'.[4]

Religion in general, Christianity and the Gospels in particular, he had condemned as inimical to the spiritual life, because of their idolatrous involvement with fact. But his views were changing under the influence of another literary scholar, Owen Barfield. In June of 1931 Lewis was planning a book affirming that imagination is 'a truth-bearing faculty'.[5] His views on Christianity and the Gospels were about to change: and it is this change I wish particularly to consider, as a standard to measure what it means to read the Gospels as myth.

On the evening of 19 September 1931, then, Lewis said that 'myths were lies and therefore worthless, even though "breathed through silver"[6]'. There was a rush of wind which shook the leaves from the trees. You look at trees, answered Tolkien, and label them simply 'trees': positivistically, you think that God created simple and separate entities characterized by clear and distinct qualities, and named accordingly:

> . . . the petreous rocks, the arboreal trees,
> Tellurian earth, and stellar stars, and these
> Homuncular men. . . .

You liken the perception of those qualities to the processes, which register marks on the gramophone record and the photograph. But 'trees are not "trees" until so named and seen'. Both naming and perceiving are responses of consciousness essentially like that to which they respond, 'panning the vein of spirit out of sense'. The first and perpetually necessary movement of perception creates myths, and from it all concepts are abstracted:

> . . . There is no firmament
> Only a void, unless a jewelled tent
> Myth-woven and elf-patterned: and no earth
> Unless the mother's womb where all have birth.

These primal perceptions are valid because, although man is fallen, he was made in the image of his Creator, and therefore 'We make still by the law in which we're made'. Through man the light which comes from God is refracted, 'splintered from a single White to many hues'. The doctrine is Coleridgean: the secondary or poet's imagination is an echo of the primary imagination or consciousness, which in its turn is a 'repetition in the finite mind of the eternal act of creation in the infinite I AM.[7]

Lewis, in whom positivism jarred and blended with idealism, seems to have been persuaded. Only a fortnight earlier, indeed, 'overwhelmed' by seeing *The Winter's Tale*, he had decided that the point of the play is its image of resurrection, and written that the value of plays and novels was becoming for him 'dependent on the moments when . . . they succeed in expressing the great *myths*'[8]. He was willing to believe in the symbolic truth of the myths of, at any rate, poets and pagans.

They went indoors and continued on something he was not ready to believe—Christianity—but soon returned to myth: yet to points so differently emphasized that maybe the principal speaker was not Tolkien, who records no further, but the third man, Hugo Dyson.

What was then holding Lewis back from Christianity was not 'so much a difficulty in believing as a difficulty in knowing what the doctrine meant. My puzzle was the whole doctrine of Redemption!'[9] The world, or an individual, might be in such degradation as to be beyond rescue 'unless something quite beyond mere natural help or effort stepped in': but in what sense could this be effected by 'the life and death of Someone Else . . . 2000 years ago?'. Christ's example helps us, no doubt: but the Gospels and St. Paul have beyond this, at their centre 'expressions which I could only interpret in senses that seemed to me either silly or shocking'—'propitiation'—'sacrifice'—'the blood of the Lamb'.

Dyson and Tolkien showed him that:

if I met the idea of sacrifice in a pagan story I didn't mind it at all: again, that if I met the idea of a god sacrificing himself to himself [Odin] I liked it very much and was mysteriously moved by it: again, that the idea of the dying and reviving god [Balder, Adonis, Bacchus] similarly moved me provided I met it anywhere *except* in the Gospels. The reason was that in Pagan stories I was prepared to feel the myth as profound and suggestive of meanings beyond my grasp even though I could not say in cold prose 'what it meant'.

With certain differences of stress, what Tolkien had said under the trees about myth could now be applied to the Gospels. He had spoken of 'God expressing Himself through the minds of poets using such images as He found there', so that our imagination and its myths are valid as an echo of God's creating fiat. But if the story of the life and death of Christ is recognized as 'God's myth, where the others are men's myths'[10], then the analogy can be reversed. We can understand by the way in which we respond to poetry how we may apprehend God's acts. We accept the story as '*true*, not in the sense of being a "description" of God (that no finite mind would take in) but in the sense of being the way in which God chooses to (or can) appear to our faculties'.

Tolkien had argued that our understanding always derives its substance from the primal myth. Thirteen years later, Lewis gave his own version of this point. 'Human intellect is incurably abstract. . . . Yet the only realities we experience are concrete'[11] While we love this man, bear this pain, enjoy this pleasure:

we are not intellectually apprehending Pleasure, Pain or Personality. When we begin to do so, on the other hand, the concrete realities sink to the level of mere instances or examples. . . . As thinkers we are cut off from what we think about; as tasting, touching, willing, loving, hating, we do not clearly understand. . . .

'Of this tragic dilemma myth is the partial solution. In the enjoyment of a great myth we come nearest to experiencing as a concrete what can otherwise be understood only as an abstraction.'[12] If you look for an abstract meaning in, say, the story of Orpheus and Eurydice, 'the myth would be for you no true myth, but a mere allegory': nevertheless when you encounter it, although you do not *know*, you *taste* great abstract truths about music, poetry, dream, imagination, vision, memory, grief, love, death and resurrection. 'What flows into you from the myth is not truth but reality (truth is always *about* something, but reality is that *about which* truth is) and therefore, every myth becomes the father of innumerable truths on the abstract level'.

We may draw out the paradox that in order to understand a myth, one is impelled to find an abstract truth in it: but when one has done so, the myth still seems to illuminate the truth, and not the truth it. And, as with the story of Orpheus and Eurydice, so with God's myth, the story of Christ—much more indeed, in proportion as what is expressed is further beyond our understanding. In reading the Gospels, we may taste redemption: legitimately we may allow them to father theologies of redemption: but 'the doctrines we get *out of* the true myth are of course less true: they are translations into our *concepts* and *ideas* of that which God has already expressed in a language more adequate, namely the actual incarnation, crucifixion and resurrection.'[13]

Lewis's doctrine may usefully be contrasted with Lévi-Strauss's explanation of the undoubted fact of the polysemous quality in myths: that they have no meaning of their own, but serve to structure and hence to confer meaning on other contexts of fact. Lévi-Strauss's theory is valid in some cases, but Lewis is thinking of a fertility of inherent meanings: what he understands by myth is something like the romantic symbol or the idealist concrete universal. Myth, that is, is a little, but not properly, like a perfect case of a universal pattern, as it were a perfectly drawn triangle: a little more like, but still not properly, a perfect instance of a moral, social or aesthetic ideal, like Sir Philip Sidney giving his cup of water to the dying soldier. It is still more like the figures in Sidney's own *Arcadia* or Spenser's *Faerie Queene*, or what both Sidney and Spenser thought the lover recognizes in the beloved. For these contain in themselves the whole power of the ideals they shadow, while Sidney himself was a man following an ideal. But a myth is still more concrete, more effective in changing those who encounter it, more complex and more polysemous: perhaps inevitably, if it is going to be all these, Lewis's definition demands that it be transcendent or supernatural. Shakespeare created a myth in the play which was in Lewis's mind in September 1931, *The Winter's Tale*: or perhaps, since the figures of the play are not supernatural, nor very polysemous, he only, as Lewis put it, 'expresses' the myth of resurrection. But *The Winter's Tale* suggests what was coming into Lewis's mind about the Gospels, insofar as what he was thinking of was the unity of myth and ideal truth.

However, the idea that 'the story of Christ is simply a true myth' found a further response in Lewis' mind from something that had been lying there for five and a half years. 'Early in 1926 the hardest boiled of all the atheists I ever knew sat in my room on the other side of the fire'[14]—there is little doubt that this was a conversation of 27 April 1926, with the political philosopher T. D. Weldon,[15] of whom Lewis wrote that he 'holds that Hobbes alone saw the truth, tells me I am an incurable romantic'[16]—and remarked that 'the evidence for the historicity of the Gospels was really surprisingly good. "Rum thing" he went on. "All that stuff of Frazer's about the Dying God. Rum thing. It almost looks as if it had really happened once".'[17]

Weldon's remark had peculiar force in the 1920s and early 1930s, during the high tide of the influence of Frazer's *The Golden Bough*, when one finds typically and poignantly in the last section of *The Waste Land* the recognition that the story of Christ's death and resurrection is one among many myths of dying and rising gods, and as little powerful or helpful as they. But this sense that the existence of parallel myths invalidates the myth of Christ is reversed, if that myth 'really happened': the others then become not only reflections but confirmations of that one in which God expresses Himself not through the minds of poets but 'through what we call "real things"'. This myth, and this uniquely, is identical not only with truth but with fact.

From this second modification of Tolkien's remarks, there follows a third. Our response to the total unity of myth, truth and fact, must correspond to its given-ness. There is nothing in the myth's meaning for us to supply, nor anything in its circumstances except what historical ignorance allows: it is all created, all given by God. If there is to be a response of creative energy in us, it must be practical, not aesthetic: not in retelling the myth, not in conferring our sense upon its matter, not in artistic creation—although even in this the myth of Christ has doubtless by its mere overflow and side effect given a larger impulse than any other, even the Buddha's—but as it is when we read the greatest writers, in ourselves. 'If God chooses to be mythopoeic—and is not the sky itself a myth?—shall we refuse to be *mythopathic*?'[18] I take the notion here to be that which Hopkins expresses in his own language of inscape and instress, when he says that he kisses his:

> . . . hand to the dappled-with-damson west:
> Since, tho' he is under the world's splendour and wonder
> His mystery must be instressed, stressed.[19]

But the pathos, the embrace, the wonder and delight, the instress is to be as much greater, as God is more manifest in Christ than in the sky. In something that makes this unlimited demand, Lewis' original objection, that a symbol given as fact would attract to itself passions which would limit its expression of spirit, is simply swallowed up.

The ideas brought up in this conversation are not essentially new: they go back past Coleridge and the idealists to the Neo-Platonists. Something like them formed the intellectuals' exegesis of paganism during its last centuries. Lewis will almost certainly have known its exposition in a sort of pagan catechism *On the Gods and the World* probably written in AD 362–3 by Saturninus Salustius Secundus.[20] Salustius was a close friend of the emperor Julian, Julian the Apostate, and the passage on myth in his essay is clearly connected with Julian's *Hymn to the Mother of the Gods*: it is therefore part of Julian's restoration of the old religion in a Platonic and mystical form, and written in deliberate contradistinction to Christianity. Salustius says that we talk about the gods in myths partly because the mythic form imitates the way the gods work in creating the world: 'For one can call the Universe a myth, since in it bodies and things are apparent, spirits and understandings hidden'.[21] He cites as an example of interpretation the myth of Attis, how he was castrated because he deserted the Mother of the Gods for a nymph: it represents, says Salustius, the point at which the Creator ceases to generate things that are born and die, lest He produce something worse than the worst. 'These things,' he adds, 'never happened, but always are: the understanding sees everything simultaneously, where the discursive reason recounts things, some before, some after'[22]—echoing an earlier phrase of his, that the substances of the gods 'do not come into being . . . but always are'.[23] And he concludes:

Thus, because the myth has a natural relation to the world-order, we imitate that world-order—how could we order ourselves better?—in keeping a festival of the myth, which appropriately happens at the spring equinox, when generation ceases, and the days become longer than the nights, symbolising the return of the Creator to the spiritual world.[24]

The high regard for myth, the belief that it expresses eternal truth in sacramental form, the feeling that all creation is made on this pattern, and the injunction to copy the myth, all remind one of Lewis: and one could add something that Lewis does not specify, the appropriateness of the spring season not only to the myth of Attis, but also to Christ's resurrection and its festival. Salustius' approach—one might say Lewis's—is in part a refinement of the old nature worshippers' explanations of their annual rituals, such as the myth of creation recited at Babylon (of Marduk killing Tiamat, the chaos monster) at the annual spring festival.

But Salustius insists that these things never happened: Christians in his time and ours insist on the fact. Salustius indeed regards the world of particulars in which they could happen as worse than the eternal world, and creation as somehow regrettable, while the Christian insists that creation is the work of God's love. For the Christian the 'true myth', the Incarnation, is the most direct part of the act of creation: for Salustius the myths are only means to a spiritual truth which can be better stated, a means useful to provoke the understandings of the wise to activity and to rebuff the invincibly ignorant (by whom he principally means the Christians) but inferior to the more abstract as well as more spiritual idea.

Naturally, therefore, Salustius' allegorical interpretation of myth separates idea from symbol. Lewis in 1931 was becoming aware of the possibility of an identity of idea and fact. The very happening must be the meaning. He was following, I think, not only the romantic quest for symbol, but the instinct which has led Christendom to the doctrines of the hypostatic union of God and man in Christ and of the real presence in the bread and wine, and to the recognition that the eucharist is not only the means of communion or adoration, but an action to be done. The hidden divinity is one with the factual, the actual, the going on of events.

If myth became fact, it became something not only concrete but detailed. So far we have applied the doctrine of the 'true myth' to a still abstract form of the story of Christ, little more than one could glean from the Apostles' Creed together with a general sense of His character. Lewis's scattered comments on the Gospels do something to remedy this:

1   Christ, in that He 'holds bread, that is, corn, in His hand and says "This is my body"'[25]: in that He dies and rises again is like the Corn King of pagan myth, but found at a point in time and history. But 'the connection between this and the annual drama of the crops'[26] was foreign to the whole Jewish world in which he moved; it is not made in the New Testament except, with a force having nothing to do with nature religions, once in the gospel of John—'unless a grain of wheat falls into the ground and dies'[27]—and once in Paul's first Epistle to the Corinthians—'What you sow does not come to life unless it dies. . .'.[28] It seems that the story of Christ does not follow the old myth; the old myth, and all the processes of nature which underlie it, seem more like a foreshadowing of Christ.

2   The literary appeal of the Bible, Old and New Testaments alike, is only felt by romantics. 'David weeping over Absalom, Moses at the burning bush, Elijah on Carmel, the Horror of Great Darkness, the Maniac among the Tombs—what have these passages to say to an unbeliever unless he is a Romantic, or to a Counter-Romantic unless he is a believer?'[29] But in the Old Testament 'the truth first appears in *mythical* form and then by a long process of condensing or focusing finally becomes incarnate as history'. However, the truth, when it is condensed from myth to fact, 'undergoes a certain humiliation. Hence the New Testament is, and ought to be, more prosaic, in some ways less *splendid* than the Old.'[30] 'What is everywhere and always, imageless and ineffable, only to be glimpsed in dream and symbol and the acted poetry of ritual, becomes small, solid,—no bigger than a man . . .'.[31] Yet the New Testament, keeping the power of myth to awaken an imaginative response, may even be thought a deeper poetry than the Old.

3   The Gospels are full of details which suggest either invention, to give an imaginary scene verisimilitude, as in the modern novel, or reportage; pictures like Jesus 'doodling with his finger in the dust', conversations such as that which follows the healing of the man born blind, and the 'unforgettable''And it was night' when Judas goes out to betray Christ.[32]

4   Lewis wrote that:

There are characters whom we know to be historical but of whom we do not feel that we have any personal knowledge . . .: such are Alexander, Attila, or William of Orange.

There are others who make no claim to historical reality but whom, none the less, we know as we know real people: Falstaff, Uncle Toby, Mr. Pickwick. But there are only three characters who, claiming the first sort of reality, also actually have the second. And surely everyone knows who they are: Plato's Socrates, the Jesus of the Gospels, and Boswell's Johnson.[33]

Jesus is recognizable even in his contrasts, 'peasant shrewdness, intolerable severity, and irresistible tenderness': we accept Him at His own valuation, even when He says 'I am gentle and lowly in heart'.[34]
5   His personality is also numinous 'lit by a light from beyond the world'.[35]
6   He does not give us His teaching in the 'fool proof, systematic fashion we might have expected, or desired'.[36] To a literalist He is 'the most elusive of teachers'. But that elusiveness demands a 'response from the whole man . . . steeping ourselves in a Personality . . . suffering Him in His own way, to rebuild in us the defaced image of Himself'.[37]
7   He talked in His native poetic tradition—in the parallelisms of Semitic verse. Thereby He made what He had to say hard to forget. But it seems almost inevitable too that 'that great imagination' which formed the world for delight should, when it used human speech, speak sometimes in poetry.[38]

There is in this series, which I think broadly represents Lewis' developing ideas, something like what Kant called a 'Copernican shift' from outer to inner.[39] At one time, Lewis laid stress on Jesus' ignorance, 'humanly speaking',[40] of the myth of the Dying God: later, on His imagination. These are both comments—equally daring—on Jesus' subjectivity: but the former directs attention at an impersonal and objective pattern. Lewis identified the mythic pattern of the Corn King straightforwardly as something derived through a pattern in nature from the 'Death and Re-birth pattern' which was first in God: and argued that Christ's apparent unconcern with the Corn King story is evidence of this derivation. There is something missing, a short cut taken, which makes this account less convincing than it might be. Do we, could we, have access to and recognize a pattern in the mind of God anterior to both creation and incarnation? And, since great poets at least have strange access to their own unconscious and to the general experience of mankind, to what may Jesus not have had access? What in any case is the relation between our creating and perceiving of pattern? Lewis was reluctant in the 1930s to investigate these borders of consciousness. He believed strongly that one cannot describe the process of consciousness, cannot look out of the corner of one's eye to catch seeing in the act without distorting or annihilating what one is conscious of. This doctrine, true in itself, has a polar opposite equally so: that, unless one explores one's self-consciousness, one is at the mercy of one's native projections and patternings of the world. Perhaps Lewis's opinion is also connected with a reluctance to grant what Tolkien stressed—that we are united with the world in our partial creation of it.

Yet on the other hand, it seems that to begin with the Gospels or Christ in them, were too concrete, imminent, compulsive, for Lewis to make any comment on the experience of reading them. Perhaps he would have thought such further explorations too merely aesthetic, a delay and distraction from the acceptance of Jesus as the Son of God which he made nine days after the conversation with Dyson and Tolkien.

His early remarks seem haunted both by his regard for the givenness of Christ's impact, and by a longing for fixities, such as Tolkien had rebuked in him, and for patterns. A consequence of the latter instinct is that when he tried to imagine the Atonement, in the passage from *The Lion, the Witch and the Wardrobe*, he lapsed into the thing that had kept him back from Christianity, an abstract doctrine of the Atonement clothed in allegory.

Another early assertion of his, that the Bible only appeals as literature to romantics, seems both wrong and inconsistent with his praise of its realism. It was the dialectic of idealist-romantic and historical-empirical that was so telling in the September conversation. Yet he continued to overstress ideal and myth.

There remained, after he had accepted that 'the Word was made flesh', something of the Neo-Platonist in Lewis. It seems no coincidence that the main defect in his theology and ethics of the next twenty years is, as Austin Farrer points out, a taint of the idealist instinct to maintain the independence of the mental subject from the bodily world, so that he tended to 'overlook the full involvement of the rational soul in a random and perishable system'.[41]

This is beautifully, and in a way deliberately, apparent in his novel, *Perelandra*. Its hero Ransom, trying to solve a moral problem on the planet Venus, realises that:

the triple distinction of truth from myth and of both from fact was purely terrestrial— was part and parcel of that unhappy distinction between soul and body which resulted from the Fall. Even on earth the sacraments existed as a permanent reminder that the division was neither wholesome nor final. The Incarnation had been the beginning of its disappearance.[42]

Here Lewis chooses as his third term *truth*, something from the ideal world, in place of the existential 'mythopathic' response. The effect is seen in the way he constructed *Perelandra*, and throws a strong contrasting light on the very different qualities of the Gospels. The *story* of *Perelandra* is that of Eve: but the inspiration of the book was a symbol: Lewis had a 'mental picture' of floating islands, and then built up 'a world in which floating islands could exist'.[43] Already (in *Out of the Silent Planet*) he had played with the idea that other planets might be unfallen worlds, and that in them our myths might be facts. So that the world of floating islands became a world where nothing is fixed, where the condition of living is to adopt what each minute brings you, perpetual self-abandonment to the will of God, and the root of evil is the wish for 'a defence against chance, a security for being able to have things over again'.[44] In Perelandra as in Eden, there is one moral command that seems arbitrary—not to dwell, not to sleep and wake on the fixed land. Once the nature of Perelandra is grasped from outside, the reason for the command is plain—to desire the Fixed is to desire 'to put in our own power what times should roll toward us'.[45] But Perelandra can only be grasped from outside by yielding to, or else consciously rejecting the temptation to break that limiting command. Until that happens, the act to be resisted remains opaque fact: then and only then is it seen as sharing the translucent symbolism of its world.

At the climax of the book, the moment when Ransom realises that on Perelandra myth and fact are not divided, he realises too that in such a world the fight to destroy the Tempter may have to be a physical combat. I would note two points about this climax. First, Ransom is persuaded that the interior voice, which forces him to realise this, is not his own thought, when it says 'It is not for nothing that you are called Ransom. My name also is Ransom'.[46] He is a trained philologist: he knows that *Ransom* is derived from *Ranolf's Son*: he could never have invented that: and it causes him to accept 'that the whole distinction between fact and myth, was purely terrestrial'. He is in a world, where, not obscurely and brokenly as in ours, but plainly, substance is meaning and figure fulfilment. Called Ransom by tellurian accident, he is to be the ransom of Perelandra. He is then to act out one aspect of the Atonement—the willingness to be killed to save a world: the Atonement conceived not (as in *The Lion, The Witch and The Wardrobe*) as a limited comprehensible thing, but as an incomprehensible mystery standing behind what we do.

The point about the name only developed as Lewis wrote. In *Out of the Silent Planet*, *Perelandra*'s predecessor, it is explicitly said that the man's real name is not Ransom: at one stage in the writing of *Perelandra* the 'real' and other name was given.[47] Ransom's realisation that an apparent accident was part of a design and a mere fact a symbol, reflected what happened in Lewis's mind.

In the actual, physical and symbolic fight with the tempter comes the second point to which I would draw attention. Ransom is given fresh strength by the realisation that he is fighting what is scarcely a corrupt being, but the one thing for which 'perfectly unmixed hatred'[48] is proper: corruption itself. He is filled 'not with horror but with a kind of joy . . . from finding at last what hatred was made for'.[49] In Perelandra the partial meanings we recognize are made explicit, emotion fits act. Something about the actual writing is again reflected here: Lewis was well aware (and comments on it in the case of George MacDonald) of the moral and aesthetic danger for writers of fantasy, that they may create objects to indulge immoral feelings. It is also possible that, as with *Ransom*, there is a figural naming: the tempter is called the Unman, which (Lewis may have known, may have expected to be recognized, may have brought up from unconscious memory) is a translation of Thomas Mann's way of referring to Hitler: *Unmensch*. In this world, as Lewis points out elsewhere, it is not lawful wholly to hate even Hitler, even in the year in which *Perelandra* was written— 1941. In a world where figures are fulfilled, it might be different.

If *Perelandra* works, as I think it does, it works because there is a whole fictional world created in which myth, truth, fact and the response to all three are not dissociated: a world not unlike Sidney's or Virgil's Arcadia, Spenser's Faerie, or Bohemia in *The Winter's Tale*: a world in which the 'And it was night' admired by Lewis in St John's Gospel—the union of physical darkness, of the power of spiritual darkness and of the alienation of Judas from Christ, drawn attention to at the moment when all three were coincident—is consistently applied at all times and through all qualities.

But how is myth become fact in the world that we experience to be expressed—in the fallen or at least finite world of the going on of events, where wholeness of moral meaning or of beauty flash out only momentarily? Even Shakespeare can only bring the return of Hermione in *The Winter's Tale* off on the stage momentarily and at the cost of some strain. One should not expect, one does not find, that in the Gospels the world takes steady symbolic shape even round the light of the Word made flesh—at least one does not find it so in the awareness of the onlookers and recorders.

John continues his light effects with the 'lanterns and torches' at the arrest of Jesus,[50] the 'charcoal' of the fire at which Peter warmed himself,[51] and the morning 'while it was still dark' when Mary Magdalene came to the tomb.[52] Throughout his gospel, we find such other effects as Jesus saying 'As long as I am in the world, I am the light of the world' before he heals the man born blind,[53] and at the prologue the movement from the light shining in darkness, as of night, to the lightening, as of dawn, of every man coming into the world. But one does not find that John is describing a steadily translucent symbolic world like Perelandra: rather each effect leaps into life as it comes, reminiscent though it then is of earlier effects.

To study the delicate union of myth and fact in the Gospels, and the relation of the mystery of 'God's myth' to the fulfilling of men's myths, requires a functional definition which will not pre-judge whether myth is history or whether its origins transcend our imaginations. Late in life, I think—in his critique of the experience of reading, *An Experiment in Criticism*—Lewis gave the definition we need. He distinguishes myth (whether the ancient myth of Orpheus or Kafka's *Castle*) from legend, romance, epic and novel, as a story as powerful in brief summary as in development. This suggests or implies further characteristics. The story does not move us by suspense or any other narrative art; it is felt to be inevitable, 'more like a thing than a narration'.[54] We do not project ourselves imaginatively into the characters or their lives, though we feel 'that the pattern of their movements has a profound relevance to our own life'. The experience is grave: 'it is as if something of great moment had been communicated to us'. Trying to grasp this communication, we create a series of explanations, yet when all explanations have been tried, 'the myth itself continues to feel more important than they'. The subject matter is preternatural and the experience of hearing it numinous.

Compared with the definition quoted at the beginning of this essay, this is the definition of a man who is at ease with myth because he has lived with it. Lewis has abandoned determination of the story by 'the supposedly immutable relations' of personages who transcend its events—a criterion which was perhaps associated with his hankering after transcendental pattern: he no longer thinks of myth as detached from time and place—doubtless the September conversation helped here: and he attends to the power of the story in a way which promises more light on the 'mythopathic' response.

We can identify at least three 'myths' in this sense in St Mark's Gospel:

1 That of the dying and rising God, immemorial.
2 That told by Peter, according to Acts, at Pentecost:

Jesus of Nazareth, a man attested to you by God with mighty works and wonders and signs which God did through him in your midst, as you yourselves know—this Jesus, delivered up according to the definite plan and foreknowledge of God, you crucified and killed by the hands of lawless men. But God raised him up, having loosed the pangs of death, because it was not possible for him to be held by it.[55]

3 That told by Plato in the *Republic* some four and a quarter centuries before Pentecost, as part of the argument whether it is better to seem or to be good. He imagines the ideally good man, a man of justice, integrity and nobility

who wants, to quote Aeschylus, not to seem but to be righteous. So we must not let him seem righteous, because if he did, honours and rewards would flow in on him for what he seemed: then it would be impossible to know whether he is righteous for righteousness' sake, or for rewards and honours. So we must strip him of everything but righteousness: . . . never doing anything wrong, let him have the reputation of utter evil, so that he may have been put to the test for righteousness, in that he is unaffected by bad reputation and its consequences. But let him go on unmoved to death, all his life thought of as unrighteous, being righteous. . . . Being the kind of man he is he will be whipped, his body will be stretched and bound, his eyes burnt out, and finally after all other sufferings he will be crucified [or impaled—the Greek words are interchangeable].[56]

Clement of Alexandria seems to have been the first Christian to observe that Plato 'all but prophesied the scheme of salvation'.[57] Plato may have had Socrates' fate in mind, though indeed the story is more like Christ's. That the awe which clings about it is not due solely to association with the life of Christ is suggested by Plato's description later in the *Republic* of the philosopher creating a perfect state as like a painter 'looking at the ideal form of what is just and good and temperate . . . and taking as his guide that which Homer himself called the divine image and likeness born among men'.[58] Plato would not have been surprised if his story had an air of something heavenly.

Mark could have known all three stories, but is not likely to have been influenced by the two Gentile ones. The likeness, however, to the pattern of his gospel of the story attributed to Peter, of the man in life and death rejected by men and vindicated by God, is commonly thought to support the tradition that it was from Peter that Mark received his information about Christ.

But this likeness, together with the inevitability with which a terrible myth shakes itself free as we progress through Mark, may also be used to support the form-critical theory that the original facts about Jesus have been shaped by preaching and commentary—have been preserved and incorporated according as they fitted the need of the community in which they were recounted. This theory would push the gospel in the direction of *Perelandra*: somebody's sense of truth is held to predominate, and one would expect the detachment from the world of fact, the symbolization of event, the clearness of interpretation, the identity of value and fact, the polarization of value, the exact correlation of emotion and object, the supremacy of necessity over chance, in short the figurally fulfilled world of *Perelandra*. Mark and the other gospels may be the fantasy of individuals or of a Church projected on to the facts. If the Church, one may interpret the result positivistically—Mark simply reflects the situation of the early Christians—or theologically—Mark represents the interpretation given by the Holy Spirit through the Church. In the latter case we have returned exactly to our starting-point—to a poetic myth 'panning the vein of spirit out of sense': we play down the condensation of God's myth as fact.

But I confess I do not believe the theory. Chronology alone calls it in question. In its original form, when some generations were held to have passed between Jesus' life and the final form of Mark, the theory of a smoothing and shaping of oral tradition made sense. (Significantly, its proponents still use the word 'tradition' in an odd and perhaps unconsciously ambiguous sense). But it can only have a limited application if the gospel was written circa AD 65 or earlier—not much more than thirty-five years at most after the events it describes. The distortion at that distance of time will be like that noted in a letter to *The Times* of January 1978, at the same distance from the Nuremberg Trials—'It may be that we still stand too close to this formidable trial for anyone of our generation to make a valid assessment of its place in the history of human affairs in all their plenitude'.

Moreover, even at points where the brief, intense Petrine story is most fully in control of its material, the text exhibits features which suggest that myth was condensed into fact from the very event. The story of Peter's denial, for example, is structurally and emotionally part of the myth. Mark interweaves it with the moment when Jesus is obliged by the high priest to admit Himself 'the Christ, the Son of the Blessed',[59] the moment when divinity 'seated at the right hand of Power, and coming with the clouds of heaven'[60] brightens out at the impulse of its degradation. The to and fro of Peter's heart corresponds: he follows Christ to the trial, but at about this same moment denies Him. The cock crows, a detail which catches all imaginations: I suppose because a cock crow is triumph, the victory of the new day—not Peter's triumph, and therefore, with its jeering note, a suggestion that this day may be the triumph of evil. Yet Jesus had foretold it: in some sense He still accepts, is not defeated.

But fit as it may into the myth, there is nothing that one thinks of more as having *happened* in the Gospel. It is the subject of the essay in which Auerbach demonstrates the unity through the Gospels of two aspects of reality kept apart by the aesthetics of classical antiquity— high tragedy and ordinary people in their ordinary lives, in this case a fisherman at a police action. He suggests that one sees a reforming of the static classical ethics in the 'tremendous "pendulation"'[61] of Peter's heart: and points out the randomness of the narration (we are not told how Peter got away)—the randomness of the characters, the maid and bystanders, brought into the story—'the use of direct discourse in living dialogue'[62] unparalleled in classical historians—and the involvement of the narrative in its circumstances, with 'neither survey nor artistic purpose'[63] in its setting and background.

The form critic would have it that the story was preserved because it comforted backsliding Christians. There is no specific evidence for this, but it may be true. I suppose most readers however prefer the explanation for which there is external evidence to corroborate the facticity, the internality and the pain with which it is told—that it was preserved because Peter would have it preserved.

Immediately again after a moment of epiphany in the narrative of Jesus' arrest, as Jesus says 'But let the scriptures be fulfilled'[64] there follows 'And they all forsook him and fled. And a young man followed him, with nothing but a linen cloth about his body; and they seized him, but he left the linen cloth and ran away naked'.[65]

Those who argue that everything in the narrative relates to some plain teaching, or else to a fulfilment of the Scriptures, are reduced to explaining this incident from such Old Testament texts as 'he who is stout of heart among the mighty shall flee away naked in that day'[66] and '[Joseph] left his garment in her hand, and fled and got out of the house'[67]: which in their inadequacy cast doubt on the theory capable of proposing them. Yet the darkness, confusion, stripping, flight of the incident make it fit the story well enough. Or at least it would fit, one would not be disconcerted by it, if it were told centrally, less in the manner of a footnote, and in the first person, as the narrator's subjective reception of the total event.

The traditional explanation that the young man is indeed the narrator (which, supported as it is by the suggestion in Acts that Mark's mother owned the house of the last supper, I think I accept) still does not account for the tone. Mark may be claiming a tiny position as an eyewitness, but he does not put his point of view at the centre. The narrative does not turn subjective: its centre is always Jesus.

There is a further point, valid whether the young man is the narrator or not. The inclusion of details like 'linen cloth cast about his nakedness' (the RSV smooths the text by leaving out *cast* and *nakedness* which, conspicuous and vivid in the Greek, slightly support the idea of a man remembering his actions and the feel of them) suggests things accumulated, not integrated, in the heap. It suggests a wish to include all known incidents, because in the overwhelming crisis described, meaning may be latent anywhere. Mark dare not leave anything out because, like Ransom in Perelandra, he may be moving, if not in a whole world, at least in circumstances where there is no chance: among symbols like the name Ransom in Lewis's fiction—or (since we are not in a fiction, but a history) like the name Ransom in Lewis's experience of writing—a chance thing may become relevant: as indeed for some readers the linen cloth becomes relevant at the appearance of the young man with a long white robe cast about him, who announces the resurrection. But the verbal echo is not close. If Mark himself recognized the likeness, could he too have wondered about and doubted it? Certainly this sense of discovery—of an urgent, never quite fathomed meaning opening beyond the text is central to the reader's experience of Mark.

That Mark was moved by the idea of a relevance possible rather than discerned is suggested by his preservation of Aramaic phrases among the Greek, when they were puzzling, because one wanted the exact words. The healing words—*talitha cumi*,[68] *ephphatha*[69]—may have power in them, the affectionate diminutive *Abba*[70] addressed to God is strange—a child's word—and precious. Much stranger, agonizingly strange is *Eloi, eloi lama sabachthani*.[71] Those who explain the linen cloth out of Amos and Genesis argue that early Christians saw an obvious explanation in that Jesus was quoting Psalm 22. He may well have been: that it was not an obvious explanation to early Christians is suggested by the fact that Luke and John omit it.

Perhaps this wish, not to lose the possibly relevant, accounts for the cornerstone of form criticism, the abrupt successive anecdotes. That Mark is a narrative unity, governed by the approaching death and the 'myths' surrounding it as they loom through the earlier incidents, no one who heard Alec McCowen's dramatic recitation of the entire gospel in 1978 will doubt. It has the unity one expects in reminiscences covering three years—if the instance is not too trivial, a university novel: detailed time-reference at beginning and end, association of likeness between. But within that unity there are pebbles of exact, economical description, as hard as possible.

This hardness is particularly apparent in the implicitness of Mark's meanings when compared, particularly, with Matthew. Mark presumably was aware that there is an appropriate text for Christ's entry into Jerusalem on a colt: but he (and Luke) omit any explanation where Matthew (and John) give it. As in Jesus' explanations of His parables, only those to whom understanding is appropriate will receive it.

This last notion was an ancient commonplace: Salustius repeats it, and it is implicit in the whole concept of Gnosticism. What is extraordinary about Mark is the degree to which he insists that those to whom understanding is not appropriate normally include everyone except Jesus. Jesus explains the parables to His disciples: but that is far outweighed by the stress on their uncomprehendingness. The principle of uncomprehended relevance is built into the story in the reactions of the participants. Over and over again one has 'And they were exceedingly astonished' and 'You do not know what you are asking'. Alec McCowen evoked a burst of laughter from his audience at a notable exemplification of this—when, after the feeding of the five thousand and of the four thousand, what seems a calculatedly arranged sequence comes to a climax as Jesus asks his disciples, who had forgotten to bring bread, 'Why do you discuss the fact that you have no bread?'[72]

This double structure—a partial bafflement of narrator and reader overgone by a total bewilderment of the participants in the story— reaches a crescendo if Mark really did end his gospel with the women's reaction to the Resurrection 'they said nothing to anyone, for they were afraid'.[73] The doom-laden narrative is reversed; the prophecies of victory improbably fulfilled: the reader finds all that is gone before reinterpreted—but the participants are left with 'blank misgivings of a creature, moving about in worlds not realised'.[74] Granted that such an ending is stylistically and syntactically unlikely, whatever followed could only increase the heightening sense that God's act overthrows our expectations while our responses lag behind.

Luke comparably embodies a perpetual newness in his narrative of the Resurrection when two men ask 'Why do you seek the living among the dead?'[75] and recalls it when at the Ascension again two men ask 'Why do you stand looking into heaven?'[76] John ends with the assurance that Jesus transcends what we have heard, for if everything he did were written 'the world itself could not contain the books'.[77] Matthew, on the other hand, in his narrative of the Resurrection and in his ending stresses naturalness and confirmation, just as he stresses fulfilment and interpretation in his narrative. He comes nearest to satisfying the conditions of form criticism—the *Perelandra* pattern.

But essentially Matthew too gives the sense of the other Gospels, which their being four enhances: that the reader is thrown into a sequence of events he cannot master. The effect of the *Perelandra* pattern, in which the formula 'myth become fact' is distorted by identifying myth with transcendent pattern, is a certain diminishing, because a world embodying such a formula is a world that can be grasped. And this of course fails to do justice to Lewis's original intuition that 'God's myth' cannot be grasped, only allowed to remake us. Lewis pointed out that human myth and fact share the capacity to father innumerable abstract truths. We can perhaps add that the Gospels, like natural fact, have the capacity to father innumerable myths—Corn King, righteous man, God's chosen and more—and still to 'feel more important than they'.

The Gospels never come near putting us into the false state where we seem to understand from a centre which is possible only for God. St John, who might be thought to diminish the strangeness of Jesus by his theological introduction, states our condition. We are in that darkness to which Judas went, the darkness which cannot comprehend the Word, but only be enlightened by Him.

If myth had become fact in the events before the gospel-makers recounted them, a probable explanation is that this is the way Jesus' own imagination arranged His life. His entry into Jerusalem on a colt looks as if He had arranged it to proclaim Himself the King who comes humble to Zion. His actions at the last supper seem deliberately to confer sacrificial meaning on His death. And if He was aware of acting the part of sacrifice in even the strictly Jewish context, C. S. Lewis's objection that He does not seem to have been aware of acting the Corn King scarcely holds: like a poet's, His imagination might draw on depths greater than He knew in the words and myths He employed.

Are we then saying, if Christ deliberately made myth of fact, that He is in effect a romantic hero, a 'man of destiny'? In the greatest of romantic heroes, Napoleon, there was undoubtedly a union of myth and fact. The ingenious J-B. Pérès very conclusively showed that the history of Napoleon is the myth of Apollo. Their names are identical, probably derived from the Greek *apollumi*, 'destroy'. Napoleon merely has the Greek intensive *ne* attached, so that the name suggests 'true destroyer', 'true Apollo'. Bonaparte, 'good part', suggests day as opposed to night. Both were born on an island in the Mediterranean: Corsica replaces Delos because it bears the same relation to France, where Napoleon was to reign, as Delos to Greece. Pausanias also calls Apollo the Egyptian god, not however because he was born there, but because there he was honoured as a god: as Napoleon was. Napoleon's mother was called Letitia, 'joy', no doubt suggesting the dawn, and echoing Apollo's mother Leto. Napoleon had three sisters, no doubt Apollo's sisters the Graces, and four brothers, the seasons. For Napoleon sustained three of his brothers as kings while he was in power, as Apollo does Spring, Summer, Autumn: to the fourth in his decline he gave the mere principality of Canino, the 'hoary', a picture of Winter's reign, at a time when the people of the North—the winds—invaded France and replaced its flag of many colours with one of white. Plutarch tells us that Apollo's wife was the Moon, the Egyptians thought of her as the Earth, Isis, mother of Osiris' (the sun's) only son Horus, the god of agriculture. Napoleon was given two wives and one son, born at the spring equinox, time of agriculture. Napoleon defeated the revolution, a version of that coiled (*revolutus*) serpent the Python, killed by Apollo. Napoleon had twelve marshals who moved, the zodiac, four stationary, the cardinal points. The sun in the spring attempts to move North: after three months is turned back, as with Napoleon at Moscow. Finally as the sun seems to emerge from the seas of the East, only after a reign of twelve hours to plunge into the Western ocean, so Napoleon comes from Egypt to reign, and after a reign of twelve years vanishes into the Atlantic'.[78]

This was written as polemic, but it is striking enough to require some explanation, and I think it possible to give one. No doubt there is a myth here in our functional sense, a story of rise and fall, movement between East and West, South and North, from mystery into mystery. Napoleon did act out the rise and fall story for which innate human consciousness and cultural tradition reinforcing one another have found an image in the sun's course. He was, in fact, affected by this image: 'If I had to have a religion', he said, 'I should worship the sun— the source of all life—the real God of the earth'.[79] He was a self-dramatizing romantic at the height of the romantic period: quite possibly this pattern affected him in breaking away from an obscure provincial island, quelling disorder, consciously emulating Alexander the Great (who himself made much of a relation to the sun-god), over-reaching himself geographically and otherwise, and bringing about his own fall. No doubt people loved to see some such pattern in him: his name may well have helped him against competitors—had he not had a well-omened name, he would doubtless have chosen one, as Stalin, Hitler, Ataturk did. No doubt too something in the minds of those who settled on exile for him in a lonely island on the other side of the equator responded to the same pattern. The rest is coincidence, aided by the ability of the human mind to discover factors which will group, as in the growth of a crystal in impregnated water, round any symbol.

It has probably been true of almost any great man, as Anthony Storr says of Churchill in 1940, that at some moment:

his inner world of make-believe coincided with the facts of external reality. . . . It is an experience not unlike that of passionate love, when, for a time, the object of a man's desire seems to coincide exactly with the image of woman he carries within him. . . . England . . . needed a prophet . . . who could dream dreams of victory when all seemed lost. Winston Churchill was such a man; and his inspirational quality owed its dynamic force to the romantic world of phantasy in which he had his true being.[80]

Is there a difference about Christ?

De la Taille said that at the last supper Christ 'placed Himself in the order of signs'. David Jones, who loved that phrase and built his *The Anathemata* round it, opposed to signs the *utile*. And it is clear that Jesus built His death, the terrible inexhaustible crucifixion of the King out of the *utile*. On the one hand, the myths of willing sacrifice and of 'reigning from the tree' express something perfectly real about his approach to death: on the other there is the basest utility, the political decision 'It is expedient for you that one man should die for the people'[81]—although that too can be made, as St John saw, symbolic—and a death in which the sufferer is peculiarly the passive object. He made the one from the other.

But unlike the romantics, Jesus seems not to use symbols for self-expression, but to communicate comfort: showing Himself as the peaceful Messiah by a donkey, or as the self-offered sacrifice by wine, where Napoleon crowns himself to manifest his imperial nature. There is a throw-away quality about His life: Napoleon would have done otherwise, and thought that 'Jesus should have performed His miracles, not in remote parts of Syria in front of a few whose good faith can be called in question, but in a city like . . . Rome, in front of the whole population'.[82] This was Jesus' temptation in the wilderness, to create a Perelandra of figural fulfilment, perfectly translucent, out of the world and its kingdoms. His anger at the evil that seeks for a sign, and his calling Peter 'Satan' when he tried to make Him avoid the cross suggests the same thing. He made His symbols by submission to the *utile*, not by subduing it. His Messiahship is so wrought out in bitter fact, in the *utile*, that the last events of His life can be seen precisely as the purging of our instinct to fantasize unwelcome events.[83]

So far the difference between Christ and a romantic hero is moral. There is a further difference which I can best express by comparing His story to Plato's about seeming and being good, in which the *utile* and the ideal good triumph both in their opposite modes. It catches something of the inevitability of Christ's life. For Plato, even to embody an ideal in this contingent and perishing world is to diminish and corrupt it. What happens to the good man, therefore, is an echo of the fact that his story is told at all. It is equally inevitable that in this world of appearance the true reality can only be manifested for Plato in its own destruction: and that in this manifestation it will still make its claim on those capable of receiving it.

The contrast with Plato is naturally like that with the neo-Platonist Salustius. Neither Judaism nor Christianity holds that the world of happening is only appearance or necessarily corrupting. Nevertheless the inevitability that Plato expresses has its analogue both in detail and in outline in the story of Christ. In His swift uncompromisingness, His call to the Kingdom of Heaven, His insistence on love and on sacrifice, Christ is at odds with the world, and His death seems inevitable. Plato's story is about the Best: Peter's story is about the man perfectly related to God: end concepts with nothing adequate for comparison. Both stories are about the interaction of the Best with the *utile*, the contingent and the bad. Both Plato's myth and Jesus' life concern an intention which shows itself in the actual and despises any seeming which is not perfectly part of intention. Jowett observed that St John mastered the problem which defeated Hegel, of describing *alētheia praktikē*, 'truth idealized and yet in action'.[84] But one feels that it was not John but Jesus.

For His sayings display the appropriate inevitability in little. They make claims which are so extreme in their assertion of a personal domination over time, death, all, and their combination of this with a moral demand, that one wonders how they could come into the human head unless they represent something about the consciousness of whoever said them.

Some of them seem to embody fragments of myth. It is difficult to match the quality of these. One can compare the visions of the Rabbis: 'Forthwith, Rabbi Eleazar ben 'Arak began his exposition of the "Work of the Chariot", and fire came down from heaven and encompassed all the trees in the field'.[85]

But so far as I can find out, none of these makes the personal claim that Jesus makes in, for example, 'I saw Satan fall like lightning from heaven'[86] or 'All things have been delivered to me by my Father'.[87] In these sayings, and above all in the account of His trial the gospel writers portray what Eliot only pointed out in the achieved martyr and saint of *Murder in the Cathedral*, but described in *Burnt Norton*:[88]

> The release from action and suffering, release from the inner
> And the outer compulsion . . .
> . . . both a new world
> And the old made explicit, understood. . . .

When Jesus is using something already symbolic, His use usually transforms the original. Riding the donkey does not do this: here he fits the archetype, meaning by it 'this is what my life means'. But often we say 'This is what the archetype meant' as if He fills a gap in it. This is most conspicuously true of the last supper: of which, and of the images of sacrifice which may have been in His mind, Isaac's and the suffering servant's, Aquinas' words are true:[89]

> Types and shadows have their ending
> For the newer rite is here.

His words over the bread, and cup, the most certainly authentic words ascribed to him, attested in three Gospels, by St Paul and in the liturgy, have the same characteristics as many others of His sayings: a claim for Himself involving gigantic symbolism, personal reaching out to His hearers, and a terrible poignancy. All the myths we have outlined concentrate on them. They may indeed be called the nodal point of the Bible, bringing together exodus, Israel, covenant, passover, blessing, sacrifice, Messianic feast, as well as themes from outside the Bible, spring, meal, dying God. In contrast with Salustius' myths, what they express unquestionably happened. They contain a command which the Christian obeys, willing as it were to be included in the text of the Bible and in the imagination of Jesus, working out the union of myth and fact in this as part of the mythopathic process.

Probably the last thing on which the New Testament critic of the last fifty years and the common reader will agree is whether one can discern the character of Jesus. The common reader can only assert, with the same vigour as C. S. Lewis does, that in the four Gospels we experience a recognizable character, a particular mind and imagination described in detail such as could scarcely have been invented except by someone curiously resembling Jesus. Only—one continually returns to Plato's metaphor for the good—to look into Jesus' imagination is like looking into the sun. It is difficult to see what is at work there, virtually impossible to think of questioning it, but its power is overwhelming. If His words are taken, as they demand to be taken, for given, they light the world, in flashes or continuously, sometimes to our hurt, sometimes to our comfort.

In the fulfilment of previously existing myths, there is no reason to think—though the argument is purely negative—that anything but Jesus' own imagination was at work, operating at times at the levels at which the imagination of poets and inspired men work. In the myth-like quality of his life (discounting a little, in Matthew specially, for midrashic narration)—in the wedding of active symbolizing and submission to the *utile*, as if He drew their nature out of things, in the inevitability and moral demand—His imagination seems to merge, through His understanding of fate as the Father's will, with what happens to and around Him. There is no gap in the story. The division that C. S. Lewis postulated about the Corn King myth, implying that 'humanly speaking' Jesus played a pre-existing pattern in creation which He did not know of, a pattern laid down by the eternal Word, does not seem to represent the Gospels. Austin Farrer suggests that the myth quality is the product of Jesus' imagination working on the images of the Old Testament, validated by the Resurrection:[90] but that discontinuity too does not do justice to the consistency of the Petrine story reflected in Mark, of vindication and rejection in life and death. We simply do not know the balance between Jesus' imagination and the other factors involved. But we can, I think, say that Lewis describes the Gospels best when he comes nearest to Tolkien's Coleridgean language, and speaks as if one feels in Christ's imagination something like the imagination that made the worlds.

Imagination has two advantages over *myth* to describe the patterning of the gospels: first it suggests creative action rather than a self-contained attraction, and secondly it comes closer to St John's image, the Word.

The true formulation, no doubt, is only 'myth became fact' for the literary critic: for the ordinary believer and the theologian the truth is 'the Word became flesh'. The New Testament never uses the word 'myth' except for the delusive stories of paganism. And Clement of Alexandria, seeing in Christ a fulfilment of paganism as well as of Judaism, still thought of the myths as dreams, half-lying stories of which Christ is the truth, is the real Orpheus, the new song.[91]

But perhaps the literary critic's formulation can help the theologian's at a time when people talk as if 'the Word became flesh' is itself a myth. Then it is worth stressing that there is a sense of 'myth' which does not concern something that we project or comprehend, but something that reaches beyond our minds.

Even with this sense of myth, it is probably better to say that 'the Word became flesh' is the key to myth, than that it *is* a myth. That is another subject, but it is worth noting in conclusion another book which helped to suggest the idea of myth become fact to C. S. Lewis, G. K. Chesterton's *The Everlasting Man*. Chesterton gives Clement's doctrine in many memorable phrases. Of the story of Bethlehem he says 'it is the broken speech and the lost word that are made positive and suspended unbroken.'[92] I think that this lies behind the finest meditation of our time on the relation of human myths to God's myths, or rather of human words to the Word of God, the section of Eliot's *Ash Wednesday* that begins:[93]

> If the lost word is lost, if the spent word is spent
> If the unheard, unspoken
> Word is unspoken, unheard:
> Still is the unspoken word, the Word unheard
> The Word without a word, the Word within
> The world and for the world;
> And the light shone in darkness and
> Against the Word the unstilled world still whirled
> About the centre of the silent Word
>
> O my people, what have I done unto you

Notes

1 I am indebted for permission to quote from Tolkien's poem, Copyright © The Estate of J. R. R. Tolkien, communicated by the kindness of Mr Christopher Tolkien. My two other principal sources for the conversation are R. L. Green and W. Hooper (1974), *C. S. Lewis: A Biography*, London pp. 116–8 and H. Carpenter (1977), *J. R. R. Tolkien, A Biography* London, pp. 146–8.
2 C. S. Lewis (1955), *Surprised by Joy*, London.
3 Letter from C. S. Lewis to Owen Barfield, cited in L. Adey (1978), *C. S. Lewis's 'Great War' with Owen Barfield*, Victoria, p. 34.
4 C. S. Lewis, *The Summa*, cited in L. Adey, ibid., p. 90.
5 Letter from C. S. Lewis to T. S. Eliot, cited in R. L. Green and W. Hooper, *op. cit.*, p. 126.
6 J. R. R. Tolkien, *Mythopoeia*.
7 S. T. Coleridge, *Biographia Literaria* chapter xiii.
8 Letter from C. S. Lewis to Arthur Greeves, cited in R. L. Green and W. Hooper, *op. cit.*, p. 115.
9 R. L. Green and W. Hooper, *ibid.*, p. 117.
10 R. L. Green and W. Hooper, *ibid.*, p. 118.
11 C. S. Lewis, in W. Hooper (ed.), (1971) *Undeceptions*, London, p. 41.
12 C.S. Lewis, in W. Hooper (ed.) *ibid.*, p. 42. I have altered the truths ascribed to the myth of Orpheus.
13 R. L. Green and W. Hooper, *op. cit.*, p. 118.

14 C. S. Lewis (1955), *op. cit.*, p. 211.
15 C. S. Lewis's diary. I owe this discovery to the labour and kindness of Dr Clyde Kilby.
16 C. S. Lewis's diary, cited in H. Carpenter, *op. cit.*, p. 18.
17 C. S. Lewis, (1955), *op. cit.*
18 C. S. Lewis in W. Hooper, (ed.)., *op. cit.*, p. 43: see also H. Carpenter, *op. cit.*, p. 45, who puts the remark into Tolkien's mouth.
19 G. M. Hopkins, *The Wreck of the Deutschland*, verse 5.
20 G. Rochefort (ed.) (1960), *Saloustios Des Dieux et du Monde*, Paris, trans in G. Murray (1912), *Four Stages of Greek Religion*, Columbia and (1925), *Five Stages of Greek Religion*, Oxford.
21 *Ibid.*, III 3.
22 *Ibid.*, IV 9.
23 *Ibid.*, II 1.
24 *Ibid.*, IV 10.
25 C. S. Lewis (1947), *Miracles*, London, p. 137.
26 C. S. Lewis, *ibid.*, p. 138.
27 John 12. 24.
28 1 Corinthians 15. 36.
29 C. S. Lewis (1962), *They Asked for a Paper*, London, p. 47.
30 C. S. Lewis (1947), *op. cit.*, p. 161. I owe my later criticism of this point to Miss Nicole Mezey.
31 C. S. Lewis (1962), *op. cit.*, p. 159.
32 C. S. Lewis, in W. Hooper (ed.) (1975), *Fern Seed and Elephants*, Glasgow, p. 108.
33 C. S. Lewis, in W. Hooper (ed.) *ibid.*, p. 110.
34 C. S. Lewis, in W. Hooper (ed.) *ibid.*, pp. 110–11.
35 C. S. Lewis (1955), *op. cit.*, p. 222.
36 C. S. Lewis (1958), *Reflections on the Psalms*, London, p. 112.
37 C. S. Lewis, *ibid.*, pp. 113–4.
38 C. S. Lewis, *ibid.*, p. 5.
39 E. Kant (1787), *Critique of Pure Reason*, Preface to second edition.
40 C. S. Lewis (1947), *op. cit.*, p. 138.
41 Owen Barfield et al. in J. Gibb (ed.), (1965). *Light on C. S. Lewis*, London, p. 41.
42 C. S. Lewis (1943), *Perelandra*, London, p. 165.
43 C. S. Lewis, in W. Hooper (ed.), (1966) *Of Other Worlds*, London, p. 87.
44 C. S. Lewis (1943), *op. cit.*, p. 53.
45 C. S. Lewis (1943), *ibid.*, p. 239.
46 C. S. Lewis (1943), *ibid.*, p. 168.
47 Information from Mr Owen Barfield.
48 C. S. Lewis (1943), *op. cit.*, p. 177.
49 C. S. Lewis (1943), *ibid.*, p. 178.
50 John 18. 3.
51 John 18. 18.
52 John 20. 1.
53 John 9. 5.
54 C. S. Lewis (1961), *An Experiment in Criticism*, Cambridge, pp. 43–4.
55 Acts 2. 22–24.
56 Plato, *Republic* II 361b–362a.
57 Clement of Alexandria, *Stromata*, V: Migne 256.
58 Plato, *Republic* VI 501b.
59 Mark 14. 61.
60 Mark 14. 62.
61 E. Auerbach, (1968), *Mimesis* (trans W. Trask), Princeton, p. 42.
62 E. Auerbach (1968), *ibid.*, p. 46.
63 E. Auerbach (1968), *ibid.*, p. 41.
64 Mark 14. 49.
65 Mark 14. 50–52.
66 Amos 2. 16; see D. E. Nineham (1963), *The Gospel of Mark*, Harmondsworth, p. 397.

67 Genesis, 39. 12; see D. E. Nineham (1963), *ibid.*
68 Mark 5. 41.
69 Mark 7. 34.
70 Mark 14. 36.
71 Mark 15. 34.
72 Mark 8. 17–21.
73 Mark 16. 8.
74 W. Wordsworth, *Ode: Intimations of Immortality*, ix.
75 Luke 24. 5.
76 Acts 1. 11.
77 John 21. 25.
78 J. B. Pérès (1827), in G. Davois (ed.) (1909), *Comme quoi Napoleon n'a jamais existé*, Paris. I owe my knowledge of this edition to M. G. Hutt.
79 Vincent Cronin (1973), *Napoleon*, Harmondsworth, p. 534.
80 A. Storr, in A. J. P. Taylor et al. (1973), *Churchill: Four Faces and the Man*, Harmondsworth, p. 245. I owe this quotation to the Bishop of Tonbridge.
81 John 11. 50.
82 V. Cronin (1973), *op. cit.*, p. 533.
83 See C. Booker (1969), *The Neophiliacs*, Glasgow, especially *ad fin.*
84 G. Faber (1957), *Jowett*, London, p. 181.
85 Babylonian Talmud, Hagigah 14b.
86 Luke 10. 18.
87 Matthew 11. 27: Luke 10. 22.
88 T. S. Eliot, *Burnt Norton* II.
89 St Thomas Aquinas, *Hymn for the office of Corpus Christi* (trans J. M. Neale).
90 Austin Farrer, in C. Conti (ed.), (1976), *Interpretation and Belief*, London, pp. 174–5.
91 Clement of Alexandria, *Exhortation to the Greeks*, chapter 1.
92 G. K. Chesterton (1925), *The Everlasting Man*, p. 210.
93 T. S. Eliot, *Ash Wednesday V*. See S. Medcalf (forthcoming) *An Anatomy of Consciousness: A Study of the Works of T. S. Eliot as a Single Poem*, Brighton.

5 CRITICISM AND TRUTH

Anthony Thorlby

Part I

AT a time when the study of literature is turning from criticism towards a kind of phenomenology, that is to say, away from questions of purely artistic value or textual meaning and towards questions of what an imaginative book is in relation both to the world and to its readers, then the Bible presents a phenomenon of the greatest interest. In particular, the Bible throws into high relief the value—or lack of it—which we are prepared to attach to two things: the inventiveness of the imagination and the aesthetic quality of words. These things are hard to separate though it is a fundamental principle not only of literary understanding but of aesthetics generally that it is possible to distinguish between them. They are commonly referred to as content and form, and their relationship is made still harder to comprehend by the further aesthetic principle that beauty in art, including literature, consists in a perfect blending or harmony of the two.

Study of the Bible, as may be seen from the way the Bible has been studied and interpreted during the past three centuries, presents a fascinating temptation to try to lever form and content apart. It has attempted to do this by re-examining from increasingly radical and modern points of view both what the Bible says and the ways in which it says it. In both its content and in its form imaginative elements have thus been discovered, as might be no more than natural in a work of literature. But the Bible is supposed to be true, and truth has itself come to be seen as standing between the two poles of the scientific Enlightenment: on the one hand, the certainties of reason expressing themselves in the language of logic and of mathematics, and on the other, the empirical certainties of sense experience. The character of 'ordinary' language, which has to establish true connections between the two, still remains something of a puzzle, noticeable especially with regard to its origins, which are manifestly not of a rational kind; but the possibility of giving an entirely true account of the world—namely one that would be both rationally and empirically correct—has long been an article of faith that variously dominated, derived from, supported or clashed with men's religious beliefs.

The fate of the Bible is especially instructive in this context; for once it was placed in this new field of intellectual force its unity began to disintegrate. The first major transformation it underwent was in the

79

direction of Deism: reason might accept as a necessary truth that the orderly behaviour of the universe must be due to an all-wise First Cause and Creator, or that the orderly behaviour of men demanded a moral law and even an institutionalized church. But the ways in which the Bible established these truths were evidently fanciful, while the pretensions of the Church far exceeded this rational and moral mandate. Even the fact of clothing these truths in the colours of the imagination seemed to bring them into disrepute, apart from the social evils of bigotry and fanaticism to which their misrepresentation almost inevitably gave rise.

The Bible has been placed in this vulnerable position, of course, as a result also of the Reformation. In saying this, it is important not to perpetuate misinformed polemic. When Calvin (for instance) argued that 'Scripture has its authority from God, not from the Church' he explicitly wrote that 'the Scriptures obtain full authority among believers only when men regard them as having sprung from heaven, as if there the living words of God were heard.'[1] The critics of the Bible in later centuries clearly do not begin by regarding it in this light; the 'inner Testimony' they cultivated sprang from the practice less of lifelong repentance such as Calvin preached, than of secular philosophy and some rudimentary science. Nevertheless, for all those opposed to the authority of the Roman Church, there was no other authority than Scripture, joined with a new-found freedom of personal conscience, 'that certain mean between God and man, which does not allow man to suppress within himself what he knows';[2] joined, but all too easily disjoined, so that there soon began a two-fold movement within Protestantism: what Barth has called a 'fatal slide' into the doctrine of inner inspiration, and at the same time a public proclamation, a holding high for general inspection, of the veracity of the biblical accounts.

Protestants found themselves, so to speak, alone with a book; and in the solitude of their study, under no constraint to read it only as part of a larger act of worship—to read sacramentally and symbolically, as of old—they were not slow to find that this book was full of inconsistencies. Worse, it was, by the rational standards of the other books they were beginning to study, full of implausibilities (to put it mildly), miraculous interferences with the necessary laws of nature that were an insult to their own intelligence as well as to the kindred Spirit they revered as the author of all truth. No one, as far as I am aware, then thought to compare the Bible with the standards he might have applied to literature; and obviously he could not apply to it conceptions we might nowadays consider. The first person to do so sympathetically was Herder, as we shall see; for the rest, comparisons of the Old Testament with other primitive legends and fairy stories became commonplace amongst the French *philosophes*—Boulanger,[3] for example, or Dupuis[4]—who discovered thereby nothing more interesting than superstitious ignorance.

The first centuries of the 'new learning' and then of the Enlightenment were, in fact, remarkably slow in developing an adequate
conception of the imagination, imaginative literature, and even of art.
Consequently, to have treated the Bible in a literary manner would
doubtless have sounded like a very oldfashioned, even medieval
procedure, a return to habits of thinking in allegories and discovering
significances in tropes and types and figures of speech. Even before the
'new learning' began, the development of Aristotelian science and
logic could no longer rest upon the intellectual foundation of the *artes*,
amongst which grammar had once held pride of place, that 'science of
correct speech and interpretation of the poets,' as Quintilian called it,
and which for Augustine was equally indispensable for studying the
authors of the Bible. 'Up to the twelfth century, the *artes* were the basic
schema of the world of thought,'[5] but the *Institutiones* of Cassiodorus
had long since been forgotten when those of Calvin appeared, to found
theology on logic. Yet a comparison of the Bible to literature, or still
more generally to the arts, might have served better the cause of
religion, which Deists no less than orthodox believers (why, eventually
even Voltaire!) wished to defend. The fundamental assumption would
then have had to be made that, to the extent to which biblical narrative
and expression are 'artistic', that is to say, imbued with imagination
both in their content and form, to that extent also they demand
imaginative not scientific comprehension; their representations are
symbolic not literal.

Why should words, of all things, provide a form of representation
that is so much nearer to truth than drawing, or painting, or carving,
or acting—to say nothing, of course, of the central and sacred 'acts'
which represented, made present again, the mysterious experiences
from which the Church itself was created? What is represented in the
mosaics, the bas-reliefs, the manuscript illuminations, and ikons
which survive from the early periods of Christianity is quite easily
grasped (except where the iconography has become unfamiliar), even
though the *style* of representation does not give a superficially
'accurate' account of reality. Moreover, the details vary, even though
the themes do not; yet who would take offence at such inconsistencies,
changes, infidelities to the 'original' as critics of the Bible were to take
offence at its verbal unreliability? Well, various Puritans did, of
course, and some of them damaged the material fabric of the Church
as a result. Their objection was not (needless to say) to finer points of
artistic irregularity, but to the entire notion of making any idolatrous
fabrication of spiritual truth (though the word 'idol' means originally
'image', from a common root that also gives 'idea'). At that epoch, the
possibility that all words might in their own way be 'idols', images,
signs, or symbols was not considered. The failure to do so exposed the
Bible in the end to charges of inaccuracy and superstition more
devastating than the fury of the iconoclasts. The biblical scholars who
were contemporaneous with, if not sympathetic towards, them came

near to breaking the sacred texts of Scripture as irreparably as those Puritans broke the Church's other idols, which happened to be made of wood and stone, instead of from words.

The change that came about between Calvin's attitude and intentions with regard to the Bible and its fate at the hands of later generations of Protestants may be illustrated by two quotations. Calvin writes, after rehearsing the argument from design, and concluding that the 'mirror of the Deity in his works' is inadequate to inspire belief:

Unless this certainty [i.e. of faith], higher and stronger than any human judgement, be present, it will be vain to fortify the authority of Scripture by arguments, to establish it by common agreement of the church, or to confirm it with other helps. . . . Conversely, once we have embraced it devoutly as its dignity deserves, and have recognized it to be above the common rule of things, those arguments—not strong enough before to engraft and fix the certainty of Scripture—become very useful aids.[6]

A century-and-a-half later, when Locke had his famous meeting with 'five or six friends' whose discussions led him to write *An Essay Concerning Human Understanding*, we know from a note made by one of those present (James Tyrell) that what had been discussed was: 'the principles of morality and revealed religion'. Locke says that he came to realise 'that we took the wrong course, and that before we set ourselves upon enquiries of that nature, it was necessary to examine our own abilities, and see what objects our understandings were or were not fitted to deal with'.[7] First make up your mind about what you consider 'the origins, certainty, and extent of human knowledge', and then take a critical, unbiassed look at Christianity and Scripture. It was a decision which not only set the direction of British philosophy for centuries but, by its more-or-less direct consequencies, ensured that no significant theology or even metaphysics would ever prosper here.

Locke may also have ensured for English society a relative immunity thenceforth from the dangers of fanaticism; his concern for rational criteria of Christian belief was prompted by his awareness of what was likely to happen when men were unable to 'distinguish between the delusions of Satan and the inspirations of the Holy Ghost'.[8] But he certainly put the Bible into an impossibly exposed position in his other two writings on religious subjects, *The Reasonableness of Christianity* and *A Discourse of Miracles*. He was a religious man and knew well enough that much of what is revealed in the Bible as true constitutes a kind of truth that is 'above reason' and in no way to be either deduced or inferred by reason from what may ordinarily be known. Why, then, should a man believe any part of it? Locke hits upon the disastrous solution of proposing two supernatural criteria which can evidently be put to simple, empirical test: first, that of prophecy (the Old Testament prophets had always said that a Messiah like this would come, and here was just the man); and secondly, that of miracles. The latter he assessed on the basis of what he calls 'power', which might just possibly be understood as an embryonic theory of intuition,[9] but is much more likely to be seen as the experimental readiness of an essentially detached and unprejudiced mind to be impressed. Come on, impress me, and I'll accept the truth of what shows most power. If that was what he wanted, Locke should have read the legends of Isis and Osiris (say), or simply remembered a few of the classical ones he had already read. But precisely and very curiously, he seems to forget that he is dealing with written evidences of power. His own faith is such that he writes as though he were looking actually at the miraculous events of Biblical history, rather than at written accounts of them. The power of a miracle, however, cannot be thought of so empirically, as though it were a controlled experiment to observe how much distortion of natural forces takes place. A much closer analogy might be to a poem or play, which transforms our normal modes of perception (for the time that we listen and watch), and thereby exhibits an extraordinary power over our imagination.

The rest of the theological story is well known as far as England is concerned. The English Deists wanted to rescue the truth of religion— they continued to refer to it even as the Christian religion—from the uncertain ground of the Bible. For John Toland (*Christianity not Mysterious*) supernatural signs could not be allowed to lend revelation any authority it did not intrinsically possess; and it possessed only such as is consistent with our common notions. If the Bible were really God's word, nothing contradictory, difficult to comprehend, or other than useful and necessary could be contained in it. The fact that it is full of material which does not conform with these exacting rational standards would have to be explained by the early Church's having misrepresented the simple message of Jesus. Toland concludes that he is dealing with a book that may not be trustworthy and imagines for himself a real Jesus who shared his own rational view of God, and of the universe, and was not responsible for the superstitions that had been fabricated around him. It was the germ of a theological idea which was to persist and inspire increasing popular assent, though little impressive writing in English, in subsequent centuries. It was soon supported, a generation later, by a more scholarly step in the same direction which Anthony Collins took in his *Discourse on the Grounds and Reasons of the Christian Religion* (1724). Collins saw that the proof from prophecy rested upon allegorical interpretation and could not be regarded as literal fulfilment. He took historical interest in the Bible further than Toland, stressing that the atmosphere of Messianic expectation amongst the Jews of Jesus' day encouraged the apostles to interpret Scripture allegorically in Jesus's favour, for they wanted to believe He would be their real, temporal deliverer, rather than a mysteriously spiritual one.

It is tempting to regard David Hume as having given the *coup de grâce* to this tendency in English theology, so intelligent, humane, and charmingly ironical a philosopher is he; but doubtless accidental and historical circumstances operated as effectively as good intellectual reasons. At all events, his *Dialogues Concerning Natural Religion* and especially his essay *On Miracles* appear to leave any case for religion, either historical or philosophical, in ruins. His *Natural History of Religion* already begins the destructive work on largely empirical grounds, by contrasting the theoretical capacity of reason to infer from nature 'so sublime a principle as its Supreme Creator' with the 'narrow spirit', 'bloody principles' and 'grotesque intolerance' of actual religions. Far from supporting morality, religious zeal makes man insensitive, he argued, to values of justice and humanity. Hume's profound understanding of the matter is shown best, however, in his evident realisation and consistent care that he should not propose philosophy itself as a final solution, let alone a superior theological solution, to the problems raised. He is sensitive to the existence of thoughts, feelings and questions about God as a reality in the lives of men, and his adoption of the dialogue form for his final discussion of religion is more than a formal device. This is not a matter in which philosophy totally proves, but one in which men must decide whether and what to approve. It is very striking, for instance, that the 'chairman' of the *Dialogues* approves at the end the position of the man (Cleanthes) who would appear intellectually not to have won.

The humanity of Hume shows itself basically in his readiness always to assume a difference between the character of the world and the capacities of human intelligence. At best, he believes, there may be some faint analogy between them. The question of analogy, of what we initially assume to be the right expression for our experience, is crucial. For one man, the world is like a machine; for another it is alive, like an animal. Reason can explore the differences and consequences of these assumptions, but it can do no more. It cannot prove either of them to be certain, and any attempt to establish the nature and existence of God upon this uncertain foundation will be exposed to contradiction and lead to scepticism. The case with regard to miracles is even more precarious. For here the foundation is not the merely imaginative one of analogy but the even more uncertain ground of human testimony. Hume uses Locke's criterion of the 'force' exerted on the mind by a miracle, but he subverts it by thinking always of the all-too-human agents through whom this force is now supposed to reach us. He never forgets that he is dealing with a book, written probably long after the event, and prior to that with human impressions and intentions. The bedrock of religions based on miracle—and for Hume there can be no other kind, nor in point of historical fact have there been—turns out to be the dreadful quicksands of men's 'knavery and folly'.

The effect of Hume's writing on religion looks very largely negative, and it is hard not to suspect him of irony when he says 'we may conclude that the Christian religion not only was at first attended with miracles, but even at this day cannot be believed by any reasonable person without one. Mere reason is insufficient to convince us of its veracity'. Certainly in its time and place Hume's approach struck damagingly at the efforts of theologians to accommodate Christianity, or religious belief of some kind, to the rationality of the scientific Enlightenment. There has always been, of course, another thread in the cord of Christian belief, the dark one of confessed ignorance and impossibility which runs from Tertullian to Pascal to modern existentialists. I do not wish to suggest that Hume has much personal inclination to follow it, or even to hold it simply like a ruled margin down the edge of his page, as it seems to me St Thomas does; but he should also not encourage us to discard it as worthless. It bears some similarity after all with the thread of scepticism which he intertwines into his own reflections on natural law and 'the authority of experience'. That authority is not absolute either, and though 'the proof against miracle, from the very nature of the fact, is as entire as any argument from experience can possibly be imagined', Hume knows well enough that no amount of improbability, any more than any amount of probability, since it is based solely on fact, can ever pass over into complete certainty. No, he does not like miracles and would gladly be rid of them, with the help of that 'sufficient number of men of such unquestioned good sense, education and learning, as to secure us against all delusion'. But who are these men and how many would ever be 'sufficient', if the behaviour of the world in its most important events resembles that not merely of an animal, but of a human animal, if (in a word) fact is a matter of history, that is to say, of testimony not measurement? And what degree of 'good sense, education, and learning' is enough to render us 'secure against all delusion' there? Hume recognizes that he is dealing with both a primitive and a basic trait of the human imagination, something more than a tendency to lie; he calls it a 'propensity for the marvellous' and a 'love of wonder', and sees that eloquence thrives on it; it gives rise to that remarkable mixture of history and fiction which is typical of all early literature, 'and it can never be thoroughly extirpated from human nature'. There is surely a double irony, which is to say perhaps none at all, in Hume's conclusion to the essay *On Miracles*: 'Whoever is moved by Faith . . . is conscious of a continued miracle in his own person, which subverts all the principles of his understanding'.

Hume places religion in such a non-negotiable position for any man of good sense, education and learning, that it might seem unwise to try to say any more. Plenty more was to be said, however, not all of it marked by such evidences of a closed mind as Paley's, and much of it was said in German. The attempt to find, after all, some basis of higher accommodation between Christianity and 'the principles of (enlightened) understanding' distinguishes the main drive of German theological and biblical scholarship during the century following Hume—exactly as though he had never written. The movement begins indeed with Hermann Reimarus, a scholar born a little too early to have been able to know Hume's work, and it was continued by philosophers and theologians protected from the influence of Hume's scepticism—and alas also of his style—by Kant. Reimarus seems to go back rather to the ideals of Locke, whose writings were well known in northern Europe, being echoed in Germany by Christian Wolff, and he makes quite explicit mention of the English Deists. This is in his now famous *Apology*, which Reimarus kept secret in his lifetime and of which only anonymously printed fragments appeared for a long while after his death. The book marks the beginning of the 'quest for the historical Jesus',[10] a form of enquiry which was to become a major preoccupation in Christian thought from Reimarus's day to our own. It certainly represents the most sustained effort there has been to produce a specifically modern reading of the Bible, through the medium of arriving at (from the scriptural texts and any other historical and archaeological evidence available) a clear non-miraculous account of what actually happened in Israel at the beginning of the Christian era. In a word, the fiction was to be separated from the fact, and the Bible as literature to be distinguished from the Bible as history.

No enterprise has ever thrown more light on Scripture, or on what precisely may be said 'in a word'. Even where the result is to convince a reader of the basic assumption that no miracles happened then because miracles never do, it must also convince him that what has happened in the minds of anyone who ever believed in the truth of the unified text—in all its factuality *and* its miraculousness—can have been little short (in Hume's words) of 'a continued miracle in his own person'. This must have been the case especially as regards the minds of Paul and of the Evangelists, who produced the original documents in what we might call the miraculous mode. If we ignore Hume and assume that no miracle occurred there either, then we are faced with the puzzle of how and why these men can have written and actively propagated what they presumably knew to be untrue. It is necessary, of course, to say 'presumably', because everything now does turn upon what is presumed really to have taken place both in fact and in the minds of the first witnesses to the facts. Reimarus and any author who follows his example, for instance, Renan, about a century later or Goguel more recently still, is obliged to write an account that is more believable than the New Testament as it stands. And to the extent to which he may be successful, to that extent also he will change the nature of the belief which Christianity demands. Whatever he succeeds in explaining in a more 'likely' fashion no longer needs to be 'believed'; it moves the imagination not to religious meditation or action, but to the calm, disinterested contemplation of history.

We will not therefore be at all unfair to these writers if we suggest that, though none of them had any intention of discrediting the reputation of Jesus of Nazareth—let alone of God—it is inconceivable that their books could have inspired two thousand years of devotion. Their alternative, and generally much fuller, explanations of what happened must either make us attribute some peculiar magic to the verbal formulation of the Bible—which in the case of the New Testament it does not seem to have—or else make us suspect that no book of any kind would by itself be capable of doing this, not even the Gospels. Christianity, we see, would scarcely have established itself by being merely an important, well documented bit of history, nor by being a particularly beautiful bit of literature, if those are the terms in which its status as a book obliges us to think. It was evidently established by the activity of a community of people, and by the life and person of one of them in particular, as it was experienced by his first apostles, who tried to live up to this experience and at the same time relate its essential features in a way that would enable other people to see what it had been like. The Gospels simply give a rather plain account of what had to be done and related to this end, while quite obviously not giving anything like an adequate historical explanation, nor much in the way of literary embellishment.

What, then, did Reimarus suppose that the Christians, including Christ himself, had really been doing and relating, if it was something other than the Bible so plainly says? In the so-called *Fragments* of his *Apology*, Reimarus finds grounds for suspicion in the very fact that the apostles and Evangelists were relating their story for a doctrinal purpose. Everything turns for him on their need to re-interpret Jesus's original teaching that the kingdom was at hand so that it still made sense after he had been put to death. In itself this thought is neither new nor unorthodox, but it rendered both the new doctrine and the entire history suspect in Reimarus's eyes, when he tried to bring the actual events into a naturalistic focus in his mind. He was placing himself, of course, in a very odd position with regard to his textual sources, which he appears ready to believe 'were simply fabricated and false', while accepting that there must be some historical foundation for every incident, which consequently needs to be analysed and explained. Moreover, unless he is going to accept that the apostles were truly converted to a spiritual conception of their master's mission—and what could possibly have done that except something as miraculous as what they related?—they have to remain, in fact, as much motivated by worldly ambition after the Crucifixion as before it. On this point Reimarus is consistent and clear: these men expected 'power, honour, and glory' in a plain political sense, together with the free food, money and good living which they had learnt to enjoy when accompanying Jesus. And they were so determined to get these things, that they were 'inspired'—if that is the right word—to lie, to alter entirely their master's original message and image, steal his body and declare he was risen, fabricate stories of miracles and posthumous appearances, allow the gibberish they talked together in an advanced state of intoxication at Pentecost to be mistaken for 'the gift of tongues', and to commit murders in order to safeguard party-political funds (Acts 5).

It is a breathtaking book of historical reconstruction and one which, at a remove of two centuries, may safely be regarded as a great aid to faith. If this is what you have to believe in order to avoid accepting miracles in the way the Gospels relate, then there is surely less credulity involved in believing the Bible. Though Reimarus did not know it, at about the same time that he was writing, Hume enunciated a principle which might have given him pause, namely: 'That no testimony is sufficient to establish a miracle, unless the testimony be of such a kind, that its falsehood would be more miraculous than the fact which it endeavours to establish'. Reimarus deserves more credit, however, than Hume for having explored in detail what an alternative, non-miraculous history of Christ and Christianity would look like. It turns out to be a piece of highly implausible fiction on which surely no one would ever have staked his life, least of all its authors. But then, of course, these men staked (and lost) their lives on their own version, not Reimarus's, or rather they staked them on something which no written record could itself adequately describe or communicate, let alone prove and validate; their writings were, as we know, very much an afterthought. There is a sense, therefore, in which Reimarus still agrees with the Church (though not with the would-be sure-established churches of his day): there is 'no sure proof of the truth' of Christianity, and miracles do not provide one. As Hume reminds us, for a thing to be miraculous, it must contradict all normal experience; the word in effect means 'no sure proof'. Reimarus only just misses a quite modern and more profound conception of belief when he argues that, had God wished to convince men of the resurrection, He could have made sure that everyone saw it and took unambiguous note of it as a historical fact. Where he betrays the misplaced philosophical confidence of his age, however, is in concluding that, since God manifestly did not do this, the entire salvation story of the Bible must be mere imposture, a fatal combination of mankind's desire to deceive and be deceived.

The Enlightenment has a great deal more Biblical criticism of this kind to show. Underlying all of it is the arrogant assumption of European progress and superiority over all former times and other peoples; and the lighthearted manner in which stupid and wicked behaviour was imputed to even the most venerable names as well as to mankind generally, is to be explained by the confidence with which these new Europeans believed corrective knowledge could now be dispensed. One of the most witty examples is provided by Voltaire in his attacks especially on the Old Testament (*La Bible enfin expliquée* is the best known of many similar writings), and his purpose is as usual to undermine orthodox historical authority for the churches' long-standing abuses of religious power. He employs the usual techniques to discredit Scripture, relativize it and destroy its theological content: first, there are the contradictions in the text itself, then there are similarities to the myths of other peoples, and finally there is the absurdity of associating the Highest Principle of Truth and Morality with stories like these. The meaning that these criticisms have for Voltaire, which is revealed as much by the style in which he delivers them as by either his scholarship or his conclusions, illustrates the primary, determining role of a factor he cannot see: namely, his fundamental, unquestioned and—in its own way—religious view of the world. He simply does not believe that God would either be or do anything which he, Voltaire, did not find sensible and polite, and which all men might not be persuaded to find so. In large measure, however, the contradictions in the Old Testament, together with God's still sometimes harsh and un-Christian behaviour there, even indeed the comparison of biblical style, imagery, and myth with pagan instances had in fact been commonplaces of Christian thought since the earliest times. Commentators both Jewish and Christian had developed ways of explaining them in terms of allegory, textual redaction and authenticity, and by 'looking up' all other knowledge of the world in the Bible—as in 'an encyclopaedia which contained all knowledge useful to man'[11]—in order to discover its true meaning. Voltaire, armed with considerably more knowledge and with his own Encyclopaedia, simply reverses the process; he is, as it were, facing the other way spiritually. And the result is not an expansion of faith but a sharpening of polemic, often with no higher regard for consistency or fairness, despite Voltaire's principles. Thus, for example, when Isaiah's prophecies prove wrong Voltaire mocks him, and when they prove right he argues that the text must be a later addition. The distortions of polemic can be appreciated, doubtless, also for their own sake, as an art in itself, no less than the arguments of scholasticism; as for instance in Voltaire's observation:

On voit avec un peu de surprise [que Dieu] ait condamné Adam à la mort, et toute sa posterité à l'enfer pour une pomme.[12]

Part II

In retrospect, the attacks on the Bible which flourished under the complacent assumptions of Deism look for the most part like a rather lower form of criticism by contrast with the altogether higher variety made possible by the revival of metaphysics in Germany during the eighteenth century. This was a complex revival, to which many factors contributed of a literary and historical kind, turning it into something that two of its most influential initiators, Spinoza and Kant, could have scarcely foreseen or intended. They were men of a rational and enlightened stamp for whom it was indeed necessary to know *Dei aeterna sapientia* (Spinoza) and the 'categorical imperative' of moral conscience (Kant), but quite unnecessary—in fact impossible—to learn these truths from the implausible and circumstantial evidence of the Bible. They believed such truths to be inherent in the categories of human understanding, and it is their prior presence there which enables us to understand what Christ meant to teach by word and example, just as they also enable us to understand the rational order of the world. Their view was still a form of Deism, then, but Deism with a difference; for the effect, if not the only interpretation, of Spinoza's philosophy and of Kant's was radically to redefine the relationship between the categories of thought: objectivity and subjectivity, materiality and spirituality, finiteness and infiniteness, and so on.

It was here that Hume, finding no good grounds for establishing metaphysical connections, had concluded that at best there might exist some 'faint analogy'. Kant specifically wished to resist Hume's scepticism; and seeing that the Englishman had considered the relationship directly of things to knowledge, as though the world of things were quite distinct from that of thought, Kant argued that thought is constitutive of the world we know. To argue this proved decisive, though it probably did not lead Spinoza, and certainly not Kant, as far as it did their Romantic successors towards identifying all being, including that of God, with the spirit as it is present in man. The once-popular Romantic reading of Spinoza as a pantheist, for instance, depends on an essentially aesthetic and imaginative intuition of the unity of 'life' in all its attributes that is hard to find in the austere text of Spinoza's metaphysics. There is an unmistakably aesthetic quality in the feeling for wholeness which permeates so much of the speculative thought, literature, and even metaphysical philosophy of the generation in German culture extending from Herder to Hegel and beyond, and it derives from their enthusiasm for art, for the creative capacities of the mind, and for the organic life—as distinct from systematic order—of nature.

The change of perspective achieved by this generation may be gauged by the way in which David Strauss, who acknowledges both Herder and Hegel particularly, has learned to read the Bible. Within fifty years of the publication of Reimarus's *Fragments,* he writes: 'We do not hesitate to regard as delusion the disciples' idea that Jesus rose and appeared to them, or their expectation that he would soon return in the clouds of heaven; it was nonetheless a delusion that contained a great deal of truth'.[13] Now, in making this apparently self-contradictory remark that the New Testament is both true and false at the same time, Strauss is not arguing for a self-sufficing, rational truth independent of the Bible and exemplified there only in allegory and parable. He intends to re-establish at a higher level the truth of precisely those things in the Gospels—'the supernatural birth of Christ, his miracles, his resurrection and ascension'[14]—which at another level he has destroyed 'critically', as he puts it: that is, by his 'criticism of the history of Jesus'. He is engaged, in fact, in the 'higher criticism'.

The word 'criticism' had acquired a rather complex meaning in German by Strauss's time. With Kant it meant analysis of the mental

forms which shape the world we are conscious of; and for him it also
meant recognizing, beyond the limits of consciousness though not of
belief or moral intuition, a world of things-in-themselves, or (more
precisely) a 'thing-in-itself', of which by definition we cannot say what
kind of thing it is. Reason at best points towards it, by discovering
irresolvable contradictions (antinomies) in thinking about the world:
for instance, that the world both must and yet cannot have a
beginning; or that, as regards its physical and temporal extent, it is
both finite and infinite. Kant might have seen in the Bible some sort of
symbolic fusion of these contraries, but his intellectual temper
prompted him rather to guard against 'confusing' impossible acts of
knowledge. The more so since his philosophy seemed to offer the
possibility instead of the mind's gaining complete knowledge of itself;
knowledge of limitation and contradiction was on the verge of passing
over to a higher level of understanding. In what sense it does so pass
over for Kant is a matter of debate, but he certainly leads criticism
within sight of a promised land of higher, critical certainties.

Strauss was evidently confident of having arrived there, thanks
largely to Hegel, who claimed to have resolved Kant's antinomies.
Contradiction, Hegel taught, was not a limitation of human thought,
but its dialectical life, not a reason for halting but for going on; the
mind's self-realisation was a process, and negation a necessary phase
in it. What the 'thing-in-itself' is becomes known, or rather (since
'known' implies a knower distinct still from what he knows), the thing
becomes knowledge. And since the thing itself, which is there from the
beginning, is in the first instance Life or Being—though at that primal
stage it is undifferentiated and therefore unnameable—this is the
same as saying that Being becomes knowledge or that Life is revealed
as identical with mind. A marvellous Romantic message, and one
helped on its way by the coincidence in German of the meanings 'mind'
and 'spirit' in the one word *Geist*! There is in Hegel's philosophy a
profound imaginative appeal sustaining all its speculative logic and
systems, and its roots are both aesthetic and religious. He was
convinced of the essential spirituality of life, since his student days
when he shared common enthusiasms with Hölderlin and Schelling,
who were to become respectively one of the greatest poets and one of
the most Romantic philosophers of their generation. Hegel's writing
grew by contrast notoriously rationalistic and abstract, but he was
trying to formulate in new conceptual and logical terms the same basic
vision as theirs of an ideal wholeness of spirit and world. No matter
that this absolute character of the thing had been declared beyond the
reach of reason by Kant; it is inevitable that the mind begins by
distancing itself from the immediacy of lived existence, and by
individualizing itself within the whole, which thus disintegrates into
the myriad parts of particular knowledge. This is the mind's necessarily
negative phase; but in understanding how and why it must be passed
through, mind transcends its own limitation and is reunited, at a

higher level of coexistence and comprehension, with its elusive, mistaken old antagonist, the world.

The principle of mediation on which Hegel's celebrated dialectical form of thinking is founded cannot be analysed in any detail here. Two observations may suffice to indicate its peculiar spiritual character. First, he discovered this strange logic of the spirit in his earliest writings, which were essays on *The Positivity of the Christian Religion* and on *The Spirit of Christianity*. Each essay tackles the paradox that the religion of the Church should have become something altogether unlike its founder, and *thereby* have propagated itself. The first assumes Jesus to have 'recommended a religion of virtue . . . formed for the needs of our spirit'—to have been a sort of Kantian moral teacher, in fact—who was, however, forced by circumstances to 'bring himself, the teacher of religion, into play'[15] in order to lend it authority; which authority has been much abused, etc. The second essay is more subtle (and obscure) in explaining how the original experience of love amongst the disciples whilst Jesus was alive, became transformed after he died. That first community 'lived without actively struggling against the world',[16] Hegel asserts. While Jesus lived, 'his individuality united for them in a living being the indeterminate (or infinite) and the determinate (or finite) elements in one harmony. With his death, they were thrown back on the separation of visible and invisible, reality and spirit'. Finally, after the resurrection, 'the opposition between the living and the dead Jesus vanished and the two are united in God . . . The need for religion finds its satisfaction in the risen Jesus, in love thus given shape'.[17]

Hegel's manner of dealing with the question of whether the resurrection actually occurred, permits a second, closer observation of the logic which was to dominate his future philosophy:

To consider the resurrection of Jesus as an event is to adopt the outlook of the historian, and this has nothing to do with religion. Belief or disbelief in the resurrection as a mere fact deprived of its religious interest is a matter for the intellect whose occupation—the fixation of objectivity—is precisely the death of religion.[18]

His constant aim will be to overcome this phase of 'European intellectualism', as he calls it here, a phase which 'extracts all spirit from the contents of consciousness and crystallizes the latter into absolute objectivities, into realities downright opposed to spirit'.[19] As he developed later his 'higher criticism' of mankind's spiritual evolution, this kind of spiritually negative phase became an inevitable part of the process whereby mind (spirit) passes from the immediacy of experience to final, absolute, reintegrated knowledge. By regarding truth as a spiritual process, rather than in fixed propositional form, he came to discover the same process, and thus the same truth, revealing itself in logic and metaphysics (themselves no longer separate fields), in the New Testament story and in the subsequent history of theology. Everywhere pure Being must suffer negation and be buried in its own contrary (which his *Science of Logic* defines as pure Nothing), in order to realise the potential contained within itself. Unless the seed fall into the ground and die, it will not live; that is the logic of life's continuance, both in nature and in the soul.

The life of the spirit is not one that shuns death or avoids destruction. It endures its death and in death maintains its being. It only wins to its truth when it finds itself in utter desolation. It is this mighty power, not by being a positive which turns away from the negative, as when we say of something that it is nothing or it is false, and then, being done with it, pass onto something else; on the contrary, spirit is this power only by looking the negative in the face and dwelling with it. This dwelling beside it is the magic power that converts the negative into being.[20]

Hegel might be writing here still about the spirit of Christianity, but is, in fact, introducing a much larger account of Europe's spiritual and historical evolution. A single logic embraces for him man's external history and the process of knowledge, making the history of metaphysics logically identical with the metaphysics of history. It is sentences such as these which explain how the Bible could be assessed both positively and negatively at the same time by a Hegelian theologian like Strauss, for whom they saved a great deal more than Christianity alone from eighteenth-century scepticism. Strauss speaks for his generation—from George Eliot to Matthew Arnold, to mention two names nearer home—when he writes, for instance: 'the critic is intrinsically a believer . . . he is filled with veneration for every religion, and especially the substance of the sublimest of all religions, the Christian, which he perceives to be identical with the deepest philosophical truth'.[21] Note that it is the very 'substance' of Christianity which Strauss venerates, by which he means its central, miraculous events, even though, as his *Life* shows, 'the attestations to their historical validity are peculiarly weak'. Note also that 'the deepest philosophical truth' is said to be 'identical' with this religious substance, and is not to be thought of as some other, more general idea of morality or divinity; for 'if the idea have no corresponding reality, it is an empty obligation or ideal'.[12]

We are debarred, almost by definition, from asking what this 'deepest philosophical truth' is which is identical with the substance of Christianity. Criticism is forever arriving at it dialectically, leaving a trail of havoc behind as regards the 'positive' truth of the textual material it has examined, but confident still in the redeeming 'spirit' of its own form of enquiry—which, however, tends to vanish again into pure Nothing, just when it seems at last to reach its goal. Perhaps fearing this, Strauss expanded his critical enquiry to almost four times the length of the four Gospels put together, revised his book four times, and then at the end declared he must begin again on the history of dogma, for it is there that the crucial 'substance' of Christianity now takes refuge:

Hitherto the object of criticism was the Christian content as it lies before us in the Gospel reports as the history of Jesus. Now this content, called into question by doubt, reflects upon itself and seeks refuge in the interiority of the believer, where however it exists not as mere history, but as self-reflected history, i.e. as confession and dogma. Against this dogma appearing in its immediacy, as against any form of immediacy, criticism must indeed awaken in the form of negativity and a striving for mediation.[23]

Strauss borrows the term 'mediation' directly from Hegel, of course, to signify the process whereby thought passes beyond what is immediately given in experience, converting it into the opposite state of reflection, and then moving beyond that to annul the negativities inherent in reflection. It is this process that constitutes the 'philosophical truth' of the higher criticism, and Strauss sums it up as follows in his book on Reimarus:

In the view of the Church, Jesus was miraculously revived; according to the deistic view, his corpse was stolen by the disciples; in the rationalistic view he only appeared to be dead and revived; according to our view, the imagination of his followers, aroused in their deepest spirit, presented their master revived, for they could not possibly think of him dead. What for a long time was valid as an external fact, first miraculous, then deceptive, finally simply natural, is hereby reduced completely to a state of mind and into an inner event.[24]

The crucial moment in this train of ideas lies in the recognition that an event cannot be considered wholly in itself as objective, but that it is mediated through the minds of those first present at it, and continues to be mediated through the meditations of all who hear of it. Moreover, while the first attempts at mediation result in a false separation being made between what are mistakenly accepted as objective facts on the one hand, and on the other, a variety of subjective views of them as miracles or delusions, object and subject come finally to be reunited by a further act of mediation. The inner event of the apostles, who did not know or represent it as such (but objectively), becomes the inner event of Strauss, who does. Then the inner event of critical comprehension rejoins the original inner event of creative representation; and the negative element, to which the immediate life of the spirit always gives rise in the mind that tries to grasp its own life in the physical-historical accidents apparent to it, is itself negated in turn by critical examination of this antithesis. *Duplex negatio affirmat* QED. Thus runs the writ of Hegel's logic. It sustains the laborious enterprise of Strauss's mythological reading of the New Testament—for it is by means of his concept of myth that Strauss synthesizes the contradictions which analysis reveals—and it was to displace the focus of religious interest for over a century away from the immediate meaning and problem of belief onto the higher historical understanding of the phenomenon of Christianity.

Most of the instances from the Old Testament which Strauss adduces have been well known since the earliest times of typological, prophetic, allegorical and similar readings of Scripture, as indeed they have to be if they are to support his case for seeing in them the moulding influences upon the imaginations of the first Christians who could not but represent their experience of Jesus by their light. There is consequently nothing very original in his analysis of the Gospels except his (borrowed) method. The importance of this should not be underestimated, however; it had already enabled Hegel (in his *Lectures on Religion*) to explain the 'higher' meaning of all earlier manifestations of religious belief, culminating in Christianity, and then at last in his own philosophical understanding of Christianity. And it was to help generations of intellectually disturbed Christians to pass between the Scylla of untrustworthy history and the Charybdis of irrational revelation, and yet to feel still that they and mankind were pursuing a spiritual course. But the safe passage was effected at the price of making the life of Jesus interesting primarily from an aesthetic and critical point of view, and then of justifying the interest of aesthetics and criticism in a quite absolute and also abstract way. The reader is encouraged to respond to the spiritual meaning of the text's formation, rather than to that of the original events to which the text points, and which it would be wrong to accept as an 'unmediated' reality in their own right. Not that Strauss considers them as being without any historical foundation 'as they stand'; but their 'substantial' or spiritual significance is 'identical' with the philosophy which mediates between the content and form of Scripture and shows them to be one. The Bible demands then neither supernatural belief nor historical verification but critical understanding.

This suggests again a similarity between the reading of the Bible and the reading of literature. Strauss is one of the heirs, be it remembered, of the Romantic idealization of art, which rested on the same philosophical grounds as had inspired Hegel's philosophy (who was himself much influenced by it). His analysis of the mythological transformation of fact in the Gospels reveals anew the spiritual power of the imagination and fresh reasons for believing in the metaphysical significance of literature. And there are indeed marked points of resemblance between artistic and religious experience, especially if the latter is regarded anyway in an aesthetic light, as many Romantics believed it should be. The truth of an artistic or of a religious experience can be described as the apprehension of a unifying spirit which resolves disparate things into a whole. Analysis can distinguish between the content and the unifying form, but a complete criticism must end by restoring what has been put asunder. The work of art persuades us of its 'truth' by the power with which this inner, unifying spirit is felt to operate, rather than by reference to the world outside its text or canvas, which it assumes into itself and transforms— including the personality of the spectator, to the point where the latter loses his sense of separate identity. The same could be said of religious experience, which does not convince the believer by argument or evidence 'of' something quite other than himself, but converts him 'into' something by revealing his inner identity with the spirit which works in him and all things. And if we say, with regard to the Bible, that there form and fact, reality and idea are ideally one, we shall be uttering a familiar Romantic criterion of artistic truth, the source of much poetic aspiration—and disappointment. This is the doctrine of the poetic symbol which Coleridge, for example, brought back from Germany with him and which was intuitively understood by so many poets of the generation of Goethe and Wordsworth, whether or not they had been reading idealist philosophy. In looking at a picture or a play, just as in entering into the spirit of a metaphor or poem, we can understand what it means to say that (here) the being of the thing is identical with its meaning. We are in a position then to glimpse what that mysterious Hegelian ideal is: the identity of thought and being. It is an ideal we encounter more frequently and conventionally in aesthetics as a harmony of form and content.

No matter, then, what fabrications and figures of speech the first actors or authors of the Biblical story may have adopted in order to express their essentially spiritual inspiration, such illusory objectivity is the necessary condition of artistic expression, and indeed of all forms of spiritual communication, which is never free of metaphor, is always a 'manner of speaking'. We, the spectators of art always know that what we are looking at is an illusion, the historical foundation of which is irrelevant to its meaning, while of the whole we often say just what Strauss says of the Bible: that it 'contains a great deal of truth'. The actors in a story or play cannot, of course, themselves take this double view, which it is the task of criticism to explore, for to do this they would have to be both inside and outside their story at the same time—though again here it may be recalled that many of Strauss's Romantic predecessors were fascinated by the possibility of circumventing the conditions of literature in this way. 'Irony' they called it then, and it has persisted in many guises since, as literature has grown increasingly self-conscious about its relationship to life; however this modern literary tendency is called, it goes beyond mere play with technique to induce thoughts of circumventing the conditions of life altogether. Critical philosophy itself might be described as an attempt at a similar kind of circumvention of the limits of knowledge. But the hazards of such an enterprise are often only too clear in the art which has tried to transcend its own conventions, by processes very like dialectic or annulment, refusing (for instance) to allow the reader to accept in 'good faith' any representation—whether of persons or objects or utterances—as relating directly to the world, and insisting instead on the artificiality of such seeming 'objectivities'. The result has appeared often enough, to author and spectator alike, to express not so much a transcendence of old-fashioned faith as a crisis of faith, not higher certainty but an abyss of uncertainty.

This was still far from being the mood, of course, of the earlier generations of higher critics and believers. To appreciate the imaginative appeal latent in a literary reading of the Bible, before criticism had directed attention away from the wealth of its content to the purely ideal—and finally quite empty—significance of its form, it is worth glancing at the work of Herder. He had a remarkable aesthetic sensibility to all aspects of literature, life and learning, but virtually no philosophical-critical apparatus (a happy accident perhaps of his date of birth: 1744). His work on the Old Testament was known to Strauss, who acknowledged him as 'one of the first to break through the limitations of the eighteenth century and prepare the way for the nineteenth'[25]—a cultural transition which, as we have seen, meant for Strauss a passing beyond the old impasse of truth and history. For Herder it passed via poetry.

Herder's books *On the Spirit of Hebrew Poetry* and *The Oldest Document of the Human Race* form part of a much larger, unsystematic, but spiritually consistent group of writings on poetry, especially early poetry, on the origins of language, and on the unity and evolution of human consciousness. He enthused about the initial wholeness of experience (doubtless influenced in this by his reading of Rousseau), which he believed came most clearly to expression in poetry, was now largely lost due to the tendency of modern civilization to conceive truth solely in scientific terms, but which a truly imaginative sense of history should now recover. For history he saw as an expression of the spirit of man—the term *Zeitgeist* is his—that would finally reveal to humanity the image of itself. It was like a continuous *Heilsgeschichte* from the time of Adam and the patriarchs to the present day, and it was compounded of events, social customs and moral values, religious rites and political institutions, artistic and practical achievements: in a word, it was culture, a form of organic growth. Each cultural epoch revealed as a whole a phase in the growth of the human spirit, bearing man from his earliest, intuitive intimacy with things to the detached superiority of thought. Was not this entire spectacle likely to appear, however, as a movement in the wrong direction, away from creative awareness towards sterile knowledge, away from the revelation of God towards the materialistic worldliness of modern Europe? Precisely this doubt haunts Herder's rambling, excited writings, which sound often like an amateur venture without proper equipment into the vast realms of speculation that only Hegel's System could claim to conquer—and then at a much higher level of abstract speculation. Herder's own attempts at a philosophy of history break off in confusion.

They certainly do not begin in confusion, however, but in a wonderfully lucid and luminous evocation of the spirit of the first biblical age. Herder undertakes something more difficult than Strauss—namely, to show the shaping power of the mythological imagination in producing the primal history of the human race in Genesis. Moreover, he does not keep half an eye on the lack of proper historical validity in the narrative, as Strauss was to do for the purpose of showing up the product of an unenlightened religious mentality by the light of his own critical understanding of that mentality. Herder begins to think dialectically, in that he continually contrasts primitive, imaginative modes of understanding with rationalistic ones; but he states the contrast to the simple detriment of the latter and does not resolve it into anything higher than his belief in the superior wisdom of the former. For Herder, there can be no spiritually truer history of how the world and man came into being, no fuller revelation of what in truth they are, than is given in this biblical story—a conviction that is made easier for him perhaps by the fact that in German the word for 'history' is the same as the one for 'story'. Herder does not hide behind this pun, but confronts the issue directly by posing the question whether Genesis should be regarded as *only* a 'fable'. His answer is that the very question betrays the disastrously divided character of modern intelligence, which seeks truth in abstraction from the form of its expression, communication, and reception, thus destroying the living unity of fact and meaning as they present themselves together in experience—the living unity, indeed, of mind and body, of sensation, feeling, motive, conscience and thought which constitutes the totality of human life. All allegorical readings break up the text in this way, and Herder (claiming Luther as an ally) will have none of them. For him, every detail, including speaking with serpents, seeing oneself naked, and so on are literally—or perhaps we should say 'literarily'—true. He finds himself in some embarrassment, of course, with regard to the evils of allegory, which he knows to have been practised since ancient times; but he makes a distinction between prophetic interpretations of Scripture which preserve a foundation for their poetic images in history or at least in personal experience, and rationalistic interpretations which do not. In calling the former *Typik*, Herder adumbrates the now widely recognized difference between typology and allegory.[26]

For Herder, the aesthetic quality of the Old Testament *is* its truth, and our anxious concern for other meanings, discriminations of fact from fantasy, or text redaction show only that we have grown deaf to its poetry:

> If we still had poetic souls; were we still the young people of the race, in the childhood of the world, ignorant of a wisdom learnt from mute, dead writings . . . ;if we were still one of those listening communal choirs whose curiosity was not yet accustomed to any education except from a prophet, a holy man raising them up to new truths in the tones of a harp and of a godly song: Ah! then I would not bother to utter a word. I would say: Listen to the song of creation and of the Sabbath! . . .
>
> But now we are no longer in that dawn of the world, and in the busy, burdened days in which we are hustled about, the voice of that early poetry sounds but faintly and confused; the air and our ear are grown dull; our soul is filled with other impressions, and we do not know what it is we hear in the distance.[27]

Herder follows the same method in his writings on the Bible and on the poetry of primeval times: alternately warning against the insensitivity of modern intelligence, removed from all that is natural by social

habit and abstract knowledge, and then evoking the mentality of the
nomadic, desert tribes (or of some other primitive people), who stood
so much nearer to the primal things of creation: to the earth they felt
beneath their feet, and the sky they beheld and breathed, to night and
day, sun and moon, and all manner of living things, plants and animals.
These things were not concepts, but the 'real' substance of their
thoughts. There can be no question of 'reconciling' their account of the
foundations of the world with later, sophisticated theories in philosophy or science, for that would be to destroy the essential virtue of
Genesis and the subsequent books of the Bible, a virtue Herder
repeatedly calls 'poetic'. He uses the word so often that he almost
dissipates its meaning, but broadly speaking it signifies for him a spirit
of unity. He discovers this first in the seven days of creation and in the
simplicity or *Einfalt*—a word having overtones of unity—of the original
people whose lives were based on daily awareness of what their God
had created, including themselves and the Sabbath which completes
the unity in rest and contemplation. The spirit of unity then reveals
itself through the tribe and the feeling of racial oneness even in
separation. 'The spirit of Hebrew poetry' is in effect the spirit of Israel,
and this in two mutually complementary senses: that the feeling of
being one nation under God gives the completeness of a living whole
to the many varied stories—Herder is fond of organic metaphors to
convey this idea—and also that the wholeness of the Book gives to the
Jewish nation its sense of unity.

Herder is a good Hebraist and knows how the imagery of the Bible
recurs, and how reference to earlier incidents, or prophecies of future
ones, are woven into the text. He claims that Hebrew itself is a
peculiarly poetic language, as distinct from a logical one, because it is
rooted in verbs, expressive of the living process of the world—'a sea of
waves, where one action surges into the next'—and therefore not
connecting subject and predicate by means of the fixed abstract
relationship of the copula. He expands on theories current in his time:
that of Brown concerning poetry and music, which gives Herder
grounds for imagining national festivals[28] (rather in the Greek
manner—another idealized early people) where everyone would be
united in reciting, singing, and dancing in unison their sacred
Scripture. Or again, he develops Lowth's celebrated insights into the
parallelism of biblical style,[29] to argue that it symbolizes a parallelism
between heaven and earth, as well as of things past and present.
Mankind's youthful feeling for life's wholeness is contained in and
created by this form: Herder never thinks of an idea in isolation from
the means of its expression; his conception of language and thought is a
fundamentally creative one. Parallelism is one manifestation of that
unifying spirit which made possible later, more specialized forms of
unitary consciousness in philosophy, science, and art. The poetry of
the Bible, 'by representing everywhere the eye of God watching over
the progress of mankind, brought the same unity and simplicity

[*Einfalt*] into the history of the world as it also revealed in the phenomena of nature'.[30]

In conclusion, we must return to the paradox which casts its shadow over this kind of Romantic enthusiasm for past 'poetic' ages, which Herder's critical condemnations of modernity fail to dispel, and which shows up even more darkly in other Romantic enthusiasts. The more passionate their evocation of earlier periods of immediacy and faith, the more different and remote must seem one's own by contrast. The dialectical element cannot be eradicated from this manner of thinking: it is the secret of its imaginative sympathies as well as of its own sense of actual alienation. The immense distance at which we in the present now stand is Herder's chief premise, as we noted, and it is subtly reiterated with every word of encouragement he utters to read the Old Testament with ancient, oriental eyes. Precisely the claim that the spirit of that world was a poetic one, makes us aware that the spirit of our own is not, and that our relationship to Scripture is that of an aesthetic spectator. Herder avoids confronting theoretically the implications of his own situation; yet for all his stylistic liveliness in dealing with biblical texts, he does not escape the irony which afflicts the scholarly labours of his idealistic contemporaries and followers. This irony can be felt in their philological research into the primal roots of words back across centuries of morphological distortion to find the word-thing itself; and in their history, which sought the substantial reality, not an intellectual abstract, of what had actually been; and above all in their philosophy, which tried to reintegrate the structures of thought with the structures of being. Their efforts intensified the condition they longed to overcome: that separation of thought and being, experience and knowledge, whose unity seemed so tantalizingly near in every work of art (especially of music, the greatest art of the period), and also for Herder in the poetry of the Bible. The only philosopher who made of the impossibility of the task a step, as we have seen, towards its fulfilment was Hegel, whose extraordinary logic claimed to effect 'a transition from faith to knowledge, the alteration, the transfiguration of faith into philosophy'. And that without losing 'the content of religion—except for the more specific content of external nature and finite spirit which does not fall into the sphere of religion'.[31]

But, alas, external nature and finite 'mind' do form part of the Bible, just as they do of actual experience. The grand accommodation of the Bible within the frame of knowledge, like the Romantic dream of a life as whole and beautiful as art, were hopes that could not last. The task of disentangling the Bible again from aesthetics on the one hand, and on the other from Hegelian philosophy fell first to Kierkegaard; and the problem of demythologizing the text has haunted Protestant theology until today. The Bible makes a unique claim upon us just because its content does not match its form. It is not sealed off, ended and resolved, as a work of literature is, leaving us 'all passion spent'. It is more like literature than it is like either history or philosophy, but it opens a door through which the inscrutable odours of reality reach us, not merely the perfected perfumes of poetry. The history of criticism, both of the lower and the higher kind, reminds us that its strange stories may not be taken literally perhaps—for who knows exactly what 'literally' means?—but not just as literature either. They indicate but do not finalize the meaning of something that undoubtedly happened.

Notes

1 Calvin, *Institutes*, I, 7, i.
2 *Ibid.*, III, 19, xv.
3 N. A. Boulanger (1766), *l'Antiquité dévoilée*, Paris, for example Book IV.
4 C. F. Dupuis (1794), *De l'Origine de tous les cultes*, Paris, for example Book I.
5 E. R. Curtius (1953) *European Literature in the Latin Middle Ages* (trans W. Trask), New York p. 47. But see p. 37: '*Ars* must be rigorously distinguished from "art" in the modern sense'.
6 Calvin, *op. cit.*, I, 8, i.
7 *Op. cit.*, A. S. Pringle-Pattison (ed). (1924), Oxford, p. 4.
8 *Ibid.*, IV, 19, xiii.
9 In his edition of these essays Professor I. T. Ramsey argues that it is one. See his introduction to I. T. Ramsey (ed.) (1958), *The Reasonableness of Christianity*, London.
10 The phrase has become famous from the English title of Albert Schweitzer's *Von Reimarus zu Wrede. Eine Geschichte der Leben-Jesu-Forschung*, translated as A. Schweitzer (1910), *The Quest of the Historical Jesus*, London.
11 B. Smalley (1952), *The Study of the Bible in the Middle Ages*, Oxford p. 97.
12 Voltaire, *Oeuvres complètes*, Moland (ed.) XXIV, p. 526.
13 D. F. Strauss (1862), *H. S. Reimarus und seine Schutzschrift*, Leipzig, § 40.
14 D. F. Strauss (1840), *Das Leben Jesu*, Tübingen 1840, trans George Eliot, (1846), *The Life of Jesus*, London, Preface.
15 H. Nohl (ed.) (1907), *Die Positivität der christlichen Religion*, Tübingen, § 7.
16 H. Nohl (ed.) (1907), *Der Geist des Christentums*, p. 332.
17 *Ibid.*, p. 334.
18 *Ibid.*, p. 334.
19 *Ibid.*, p. 341.
20 J. B. Baillie (trans) (1931), *Die Phänomenologie des Geistes*, London, p. 93.
21 D. F. Strauss (1840), *op. cit.*, § 144.
22 *Ibid.*, § 151.
23 *Ibid.*, § 144.
24 D. F. Strauss (1862), *op. cit.*, § 40.
25 *Ibid.*, § 39.
26 See in this connection R. P. C. Hanson (1959), *Allegory and Event*, London.
27 J. G. Herder (1827), *Aelteste Urkunde des Menschengeschlechts*, Cotta ed., I, p. 29.
28 *Vom Geist der ebräischen Poesie, op. cit.*, II, 2, vii.
29 R. Lowth (1753), *De sacra poesi Hebraeorum*, trans G. Gregory (1787), New York.
30 *Vom Geist der ebräischen Poesie, op. cit.*, I, 1, vii; see also i and ii.
31 *Enzyklopaedie der philosophischen Wissenschaften*, 1817, revised 1827 and 1830, Preface and § 573.

PART III

TRANSLATION AND CULTURE PATTERNS

Jewish gnostics argued that the Hebrew of the Torah was God's undoubted idiom, though man no longer understood its full esoteric meaning.
G. Steiner in *After Babel, Aspects of Language and Translation*, Oxford 1975, p. 59.

Multae terricolis linguae, coelestibus una
(Motto printed in the Bagster Bibles, first published in 1794—quoted in C. F. D. Moule: *The Holy Spirit*, Oxford 1978, p. 88)

6 TOWARDS A REDISCOVERY OF THE BIBLE: THE PROBLEM OF THE STILL SMALL VOICE

Stephen Prickett

I WANT to start with two quotations from biblical critics. The first is from Coleridge:

I take up this work with the purpose to read it for the first time as I should any other work,—as far at least as I can or dare. For I neither can, nor dare, throw off a strong and awful prepossession in its favour—certain as I am that a large part of the light and life, in and by which I see, love, and embrace the truths and the strengths co-organized into a living body of faith and knowledge . . . has been directly or indirectly derived to me from this sacred volume,—and unable to determine what I do not owe to its influences.[1]

The second quotation is from a far more respectable source in its own time than was Coleridge's controversial *Confessions of an Inquiring Spirit*: the Preface to the *Good News Bible* of 1976:

The primary concern of the translators has been to provide a faithful translation of the Hebrew, Aramaic, and Greek texts. Their first task was to understand correctly the meaning of the original . . . the translators' next task was to express that meaning in a manner and form easily understood by the readers . . . . Every effort has been made to use language that is natural, clear, simple, and unambiguous.[2]

Now an observer from another culture—let us say, the man on the Peking omnibus—might be forgiven for assuming that the tone of breezy confidence exuded by the translators of the Good News in 1976 came from their having understood and resolved the problem that worried Coleridge. Where he was forced to be hesitant, tentative and uncertain, they, carried forward by the march of scholarship in the intervening 150 years, could be authoritative and precise. The progress of learning clarifies and illuminates the relation between cultures. Yet, as we all know, the baffled Peking everyman would once again have been deceived by the inscrutable occident.

Coleridge's hesitancy was in face of a particular and very real problem: that of cultural relativity—in perhaps its most extreme form. He was acutely conscious that not merely were many of his basic assumptions derived from the Bible, but that even the very system of critical values by which he might hope to weigh and assess those assumptions was itself drawn from the same source. He was aware of having come to consciousness within a society which, while it was clearly very different from anything to be found in either the Old or New Testaments, had taken many of its most basic pre-suppositions from them. In the last resort, he was 'unable to determine' what he did 'not owe to its influences'. In attempting to read the Bible as he would

105

any other work, he was already enmeshed in an almost insoluble tangle of likeness and unlikeness, extending from the simplest equivalencies down to the most complex unconscious premises. But that, as he goes on to argue in the *Confessions*, is no reason for not attempting such a critical enquiry: on the contrary, it makes it the more important. 'In the Bible', he affirms, 'there is more that *finds* me than in all other books put together'.[3] To read the Bible intelligently and critically is to perform an act of self-examination.

Yet in so saying, Coleridge declares himself to us, with hindsight, to be at a moment of peculiar historical transition. The series of 'letters' written during the 1820s, but only published six years after his death, in 1840, as *The Confessions of an Inquiring Spirit*, reveal him poised between two apparently antithetical intellectual worlds. Behind him lay nearly a century of quite remarkable progress in biblical criticism both in England and Germany. In the 1790s he had belonged as a Unitarian to some of the most advanced critical circles of his day in England. Such men as William Frend, a fellow member of Jesus College, Cambridge and Thomas Beddoes from Oxford (both of whom were to be expelled from their Fellowships for their views) had introduced him to the ideas of the new wave of German critics and historians such as Eichhorn, Lessing and Herder. It was on Beddoes' advice that while in Germany in 1798 Coleridge read Eichhorn and attended his lectures at Gottingen, and his notebooks during the time he was writing the *Confessions* in the 1820s are studded with references not merely to Eichhorn, but to all the leading German critics. He also became familiar with the work of Belsham and Lardner, and via his friendship with Godwin, of all people, he met the extraordinary Alexander Geddes, a Scottish Roman Catholic priest who by the 1790s was himself a leading Higher Critic with a wide circle of correspondents and readers in Germany.[4] Coleridge, however, did not accept their ideas uncritically. For instance, to Eichhorn's rationalist temperament the visions of Ezekiel were no more than deliberate fabrications: in the phrase so dear to Enlightenment scholars, they were a 'pious fraud'. To Coleridge, this was simply obtuse.

It perplexes me to understand how a Man of Eichhorn's Sense, Learning, and Acquaintance with Psychology could form, or attach belief to, so cold-blooded an hypothesis. That in Ezekiel's Visions Ideas or Spiritual Entities are presented in visual Symbols, I never doubted; but as little can I doubt, that such Symbols did present themselves to Ezekiel in Visions—and by a Law closely connected with, if not contained in, that by which Sensations are organized into Images and Mental Sounds in our ordinary sleep.[5]

In this psychological objection to Eichhorn's sweeping iconoclasm Coleridge stands with the later generation of German Historical Critics for whom such notions would also have seemed implausible and crude. But Niebuhr's classic study of Livy in his *History of Rome*, which was to prove a model for so many later biblical critics, though it avoids the simple dogmatism of Eichhorn's method of scriptural exegesis, is, of course, ultimately no less rationalistic in tone— pointing forward to the methods of such people as Feuerbach and Strauss. Coleridge's hesitant literary balance between religious self-searching and openness to the Higher Criticism was, by contrast, as alien to the world of George Eliot and Matthew Arnold as it was to that of his own eighteenth-century predecessors.

The intellectual *Zeitgeist* of advanced biblical critics in the middle of the second half of the nineteenth century is probably best reflected not in works like *Literature and Dogma* and its sequels, but in a fascinating and much-neglected novel by Arnold's niece, Mrs Humphry Ward. Robert Elsmere, in her novel of that name, is a brilliant young clergyman who begins to study initially, not the Scriptures, but the lives of the saints:

Hitherto he had been under the guidance of men of his own day, of the nineteenth century historian, who refashions the past on the lines of his own mind, who gives it rationality, coherence, and, as it were, modernness, so that the main impression he produces on us, so long as we look on that past through him only, is on the whole an impression of *continuity* and *resemblance*.

Whereas, on the contrary, the first impression left on a man by the attempt to plunge into the materials of history for himself is almost always an extraordinarily sharp impression of *difference* or *contrast*. Ultimately, of course, he sees that these men and women whose letters and biographies, whose creeds and general conceptions he is investigating, are in truth his ancestors, bone of his bone, flesh of his flesh. But . . . what motives, what beliefs, what embryonic processes of thought and morals, what bizarre combinations of ignorance and knowledge, of the highest sanctity with the lowest credulity or falsehood; what extraordinary prepossessions, born with a man and tainting his whole ways of seeing and thinking from childhood to the grave!
. . . Then he sees what it is makes the difference, digs the gulf. *'Science'*, the mind cries, *'ordered knowledge'*. And so for the first time the modern recognises what the accumulations of his forefathers have done for him. He takes the torch which man has been so long and patiently fashioning to his hand, and turns it on the past, and at every step the sight grows stranger, and yet more moving, more pathetic. The darkness into which he penetrates does but make him grasp his own guiding light the more closely. And yet, bit by bit, it has been prepared for him by these groping half-conscious generations, and the scrutiny which began in repulsion and laughter ends in a marvelling gratitude.[6]

The conclusion of such studies is inescapable. The implications for the biblical critic are clear:

Testimony like every other human product has *developed*. Man's power of apprehending and recording what he sees and hears has grown from less to more, from weaker to stronger, like any other of his faculties, just as the reasoning powers of the cave-dweller have developed into the reasoning powers of a Kant . . . .

To plunge into the Christian period without having first cleared the mind as to what is meant in history and literature by 'the critical method' which in history may be defined as the 'science of what is credible' and in literature as 'the science of what is rational' is to invite fiasco. The theologian in such a state sees no obstacle to accepting an arbitrary list of documents with all the strange stuff they may contain, and declaring them to be sound historical material, while he applies to all the strange stuff of a similar kind surrounding them the most rigorous principles of modern science. Or he has to make believe that the reasoning processes exhibited in the speeches of the Acts, in certain passages of St Paul's Epistles, or in the Old Testament quotations in the Gospels, have a validity for the mind of the nineteenth century, when in truth they are the imperfect, half-childish products of the mind of the first century, of quite insignificant or indirect value to the historian of fact, of enormous value to the historian of *testimony* and its varieties.[7]

Though, it is true, such an approach, with its Arnoldian stress on *Aberglaube*, makes much play with the 'poetic' nature of the biblical narratives, we find nevertheless that the word 'poetic' itself in such contexts has undergone a semantic shift increasingly common in the nineteenth century, sounding less and less as if it refers to a work of art, and increasingly as if it denotes the outpourings of a Jungian Collective Unconscious. This impression is reinforced by the latent evolutionary images, and by the assumption that the 'strangeness' of so many parts of the narratives is a clue to its primitive nature. Such an approach, for all its evident critical value, does not however provide a sympathetic framework for an examination of Hebrew poetry or prose in aesthetic terms, or for the notion that there might conceivably be problems in biblical texts accessible neither to improved linguistic scholarship, nor to the assumptions of Higher Criticism. Yet, as Coleridge, for instance, was well aware, the development of German Higher Criticism had depended in the first place upon earlier, more purely literary, discoveries that had originated in England during the eighteenth century.

Probably the most important single event had been the publication of Bishop Lowth's Oxford Poetry Lectures, on *The Sacred Poetry of the Hebrews*, in 1753.[8] To Lowth we owe above all the rediscovery of the principles of Hebrew prosody. That the Old Testament contained much that was 'poetic' was clear, but in spite of the ingenuity of Hebrew grammarians such as Bishop Hare it was difficult to find, even in such obvious songs as the Psalms, any sign of rhyme or regular metre. Lowth demonstrated for the first time that, so far from depending on such European forms as rhyme and metre, the poetry of the Psalms and prophetic books depended upon what he called 'parallelism'.[9] This 'correspondence of one verse or line with another' provided, Lowth suggested, the basis of Hebrew poetry,[10] and took its origins from the antiphonal choruses we find mentioned at various places in the Old Testament. As David returned victorious from battle with the Philistines, for instance, the women sang 'Saul hath smote his thousands' and were answered by a second chorus with the words 'And David his ten thousands'.[11] This simple, rhythmic, antiphonal structure of statement and counter-statement, set in either repetition or contrast, provided the Hebrew psalmists and prophets with a basic pattern of extraordinary flexibility. Lowth himself distinguishes no less than eight different types of parallelism. With it, the formal devices of European poetry were unnecessary. From the simplest forms of reiteration and echo it could move through various forms of comparison and contrast (which were not lost on Saul, for instance, in the example just quoted) to antithesis and even dialectic. Moreover, as Lowth and others observed, this structure of parallelism, whether fortuitous or providential, had left its mark printed indelibly on the whole pattern of Hebrew thought. The characteristic biblical mode of encounter with God is not, as one might expect, submission, but *argument*. Wrestling Jacob, or Abraham pleading for the cities of the plain with his disingenuous 'Peradventure for ten righteous men . . .' sets the tone for book after book of the Old Testament—culminating, perhaps, in the great debates of Job. Moreover, it is a tradition of which God seems to approve. Abraham, Jacob, Elijah and Job are all men whose passion for arguing with God finds favour and reward. It provided a pattern that was to shape the whole subsequent development of Jewish thought right down to our own day. A rabbi in the recent television programme on different Faiths, *The Long Search*, actually defined Judaism as an argument with God in progress over the past 3,500 years. There is an apocryphal version of the famous 'trial of God' in Auschwitz in which, after the verdict of 'Guilty' is brought in on God, a Great Voice is heard from the heavens exclaiming '*This* time O rabbis, you have gone too far!'. Prostrate with terror, the leading rabbi was nonetheless heard to mutter, 'You also, O Nameless One. You also!'.

Lowth's rediscovery of the principles of Hebrew parallelism also pointed the way towards two other conclusions scarcely less significant for the history of biblical criticism. The first is that the Hebrew prophets were also the *poets* of Israel.[12] In spite of their mixed and often obscure social backgrounds, they were not rustics, but men whose religious training was also simultaneously an aesthetic and technical training in the art of verse.[13] They were masters of the dialectical skills of their craft, and the inheritors of a highly sophisticated intellectual tradition. Unlike European poets, however, they did not belong to an isolated courtly circle, but remained, often in opposition to the political establishment, in close touch with the rural and pastoral life of the ordinary people, using in their verse the metaphors of agriculture and everyday life. Though Lowth's rediscovery of Hebrew prosody led directly to a revival of primitivism in English poetry during the latter part of the eighteenth century, the writers of Isaiah or Job were themselves no more 'primitives' than those, like Smart, Cowper, Blake, or Wordsworth, whom they inspired. To talk of language that is 'simple, clear, and unambiguous' in the case of the biblical writers is as incongruous as it would be of the latter poets. When the eighteenth century saw an 'oriental sublimity' in the language of the Old Testament it was with admiration, not condescension. The second conclusion arose directly from this. Though writers like Addison, before Lowth's time, had admired the poetic power of the Old Testament, it was only in the wake of Lowth's *Lectures* that it could be seen how little of Hebrew poetry was lost through the normal linguistic problems of translating poetry. Whereas contemporary European poetry, heavily dependent on rhyme and metre, was extremely difficult to render in another language with any real equivalence of feeling, Hebrew poetry was almost all translatable. As Hugh Blair, a Scottish disciple of Lowth put it:

It is owing, in a great measure, to this form of composition, that our version, though in prose, retains so much of a poetical cast. For the version being strictly word for word after the original, the form and order of the original sentence are preserved; which by this artificial structure, this regular alternation and correspondence of parts, makes the ear sensible of a departure from the common style and tone of prose.[14]

Blair might have added that it is one of the peculiar strengths of the Authorized Version that it consistently attempts the most literal translation possible, at the risk of unintelligibility or even nonsense. Though considerable difficulties could and did remain in the English Bible, they were difficulties inherent in the language and concepts involved—usually, in effect, real theological difficulties—rather than accidents of rhyme or verse-structure.

Thus in taking up the Bible to read it for the first time as he might any other book, Coleridge is writing against a background not merely of his knowledge of the German Higher Criticism, but also of his sense of the peculiar poetic richness of the language and intellectual tradition he was encountering. Indeed, in many cases his sensitivity to that tradition exceeded that of the German critics.[15] His confession of what 'found him' in the pages of the Bible was a response of the whole man. It was, in short, the response of a poet to some of the greatest masters of his own craft.

In contrast, the brisk common sense tone of the modern translators seems to stem from their capacity to ignore both the problems of translations from one culture to a different, yet related one, and the peculiar inwardness of the experiences described. One of the most complex and self-searching acts of consciousness has been somehow reduced to a matter of linguistics. To understand what their effort to 'use language that is natural, clear, simple, and unambiguous', has produced, a single, fairly detailed example should suffice. To take one of many, I quote from the Authorized Version part of a story from the Elijah cycle of an individual's argument with God:

And he arose, and did eat and drink, and went in the strength of that meat forty days and forty nights unto Horeb the mount of God. And he came thither unto a cave, and lodged there; and, behold, the word of the Lord came to him, and he said unto him, What doest thou here Elijah? And he said, I have been very zealous for the Lord God of hosts: for the children of Israel have forsaken thy covenant, thrown down thine altars, and slain thy prophets with the sword; and I, even I only, am left; and they seek my life, to take it away. And he said, Go forth and stand upon the mount before the Lord. And, behold, the Lord passed by, and a great and strong wind rent the mountains, and brake in pieces the rocks before the Lord; but the Lord was not in the wind: and after the wind an earthquake; but the Lord was not in the earthquake: and after the earthquake a fire; but the Lord was not in the fire: and after the fire a still small voice.

I Kings 19. 8–12

Two opposite things are likely to strike a modern reader about this story of Elijah on Horeb. The first is how bare and stark the biblical narrative is. We are not given any answers to the obvious circumstantial and naturalistic questions. What, for instance, *was* this 'fire'? Was it a bush fire? Was it connected with the earthquake? What, in any case, did it burn? Stripped of any foreground[16] detail, the story is strangely enigmatic in its concentration on the central theme: Elijah's encounter with God. Our second reaction is the opposite of this: we begin to suspect this bare account of harbouring extreme complexity. Elijah's long-delayed meeting with God turns out to be not at all what he had expected. Instead, his original assumptions are disconfirmed by a revelation so ambiguous as to resist any attempt to reduce it to a direct simple statement. This is the essence of the translator's problem.

Translation, especially from one period of time to another, is not just a matter of finding the nearest equivalents for words or syntactic structures. In addition it involves altering the fine network of unconscious or half-conscious pre-suppositions that underlie the actual words or phrases, and which differentiate the climate of thought and feeling of one age from that of another. For example, pre-nineteenth-century commentaries on this passage concentrate almost exclusively on its figurative meaning. Dr Leonard Howard in his commentary to *The Royal Bible* of 1761 explains that: '*after the fire*, that is, after the storms, thunders, lightnings, and earthquakes, which attended the promulgation of the law; *came a still voice*, that is, the gospel, wherein God spoke to us by his son, with the greatest lenity and sweetness, using the most convincing arguments, and the most soft and gentle persuasions'. As late as 1806, Mrs Trimmer, that formidable engine of the SPCK Tract Society in her *Help to the Unlearned in the Study of the Holy Scriptures* could still tell her readers that: 'The LORD's *speaking in a small still voice*, was a sign that He was graciously disposed to show lenity and forbearance towards the idolatrous people of Israel, and to preserve the land of Israel for those who had not yet bowed the knee to Baal . . .'.[17]

It would be a mistake to assume that modern translators and commentators are less subject to the spirit of their age than their predecessors. For instance, one noticeable feature of modern English that separates it from the past is its tendency towards a single 'focus' or field of reference. Increasingly (though still not inevitably) it implies explanations at only one level of our experience. Thus, in the case of the Elijah story, what he hears after the earthquake, the wind, and the fire, may be literally translated from the Hebrew as 'a voice of thin silence'. As we have seen, the King James version renders this curious oxymoron into English as the well-known 'still small voice'. Bearing in mind that in Elizabethan English 'small' could still mean 'thin' (as in the case of 'small beer') this is a remarkably accurate translation. In so far as it is obscure and ambiguous, it is an obscurity and ambiguity that is faithful to the original. Something very odd has happened to Elijah.

Modern translations, however, seem to be almost unanimous in rejecting the ambiguity of the original. The New English Bible translates it as 'a low murmuring sound'. The Good News Bible remains naturalistic, but goes for the opposite interpretation, telling us that it was 'the soft whisper of a voice'. It seems clear, in short, that neither group of translators had the faintest grasp of the implications of what they were doing. The Authorized Version's 'still small voice' retains much of the odd, boundary-breaking quality of the Hebrew which prevents us from applying to it modern, and essentially un-biblical distinctions between what we (but not the Hebrews) might call 'inner' and 'outer' experiences. Is the event visionary or miraculous? Natural or supernatural? We are not told, for these are not biblical categories of thought. Yet in the New English Bible we are given the 'low murmuring sound' as an apparently *natural* phenomenon. There is nothing peculiar or odd about low murmuring sounds, after all. They are entirely natural, like winds, earthquakes, and fires—they just happen to be a little less noisy. 'The soft whisper of a voice' from the Good News Bible is little better. Though, like the New English Bible, it has arbitrarily chosen a particular interpretation, this time implying personal speech, its suggestions are still entirely naturalistic. There is no inherent peculiarity about the event to indicate that what follows may turn out to be a quite new kind of experience. Yet that is what the story is about. In contrast to the new translations, the 1611 version remains as stubbornly paradoxical as the original Hebrew, and it is precisely that oddity or paradox of the original text that the modern translators, themselves responding to the unstated assumptions of the intervening scientific revolution, found either untranslatable, or, more probably, unacceptable. Since our distinctions between 'inner' and 'outer' are un-biblical categories (so the argument seems to run) we can only be 'modern' by treating the whole story *at one level*. Yet this is plainly as false to the original meaning as it would be to try to introduce the modern distinctions into the narrative. What is quite clear from the story is that the paradoxical 'voice of thin silence', which is the true manifestation of Yahweh, does not belong to the same associative 'set' as earthquakes. Though there there is no word for 'Nature' in Hebrew, since all natural phenomena were seen as being as much the result of God's direct action as the most startling miracle,[18] it is nevertheless clear that there is a fundamental discontinuity between the cyclical world of nature-mysticism (in the cult of Baal) and the world of meaningful change, and therefore of History, into which Yahweh was bringing his people. It is this fundamental discontinuity that is the point of the story.

The account of Elijah's experiences on Horeb is given a very specific historical setting. After the rout and slaughter of the prophets of Baal, Jezebel the Queen has threatened his life, and Elijah, believing himself to be the sole survivor of the faithful, has fled to Horeb. The full force of the dramatic disconfirmation that follows depends on our recognizing that Horeb is traditionally associated with Sinai the 'mountain of the Lord', where Moses himself had encountered God before the burning bush. Elijah has come to Horeb with certain expectations precisely because of that sense of history that was already distinctively the mark of the men of God. Before the assembled prophets of Baal he had already vindicated Yahweh in pyrotechnics—proving once again the power of the God who had traditionally manifested himself in fire. Now he has come to receive the divine revelation for which he believes himself to have been spared, and for which he has been preparing himself. What follows is the more unexpected. Paradoxically, his idea of Yahweh is disconfirmed by a greater display of natural violence than any yet. But Yahweh is not a fire God. His presence, when at last it is found, is experienced as something mysteriously apart from the world of natural phenomena. It comes in the form of a simple question: 'What doest thou here, Elijah?' He had come expecting one thing, and found another—entirely different. For a start, his own report is quite untrue: there are yet 7,000 in Israel who have not bowed the knee to Baal. Elijah is instructed to return and organize no less than two separate *coups d'état*. Hazael is to be made King of Syria, and Jehu King of Israel. History is yet again to be reshaped by revelation, just as long before Moses had been sent back by God to lead his people out of Egypt. Finally—and ominously—he is ordered to appoint his own successor.

At every level the ambiguous discontinuity persists. Any attempt at 'explaining' the contrast between the fire and the voice of thin silence is in danger of losing that sense of an immediate but unstated connection between the two that is emphasized even by the very act of dissociation. Yahweh is not a fire God—or one of winds and earthquakes—yet from whom, if not from him, did these things come? Moreover, what about these modern categories in which, it is true, we cannot help thinking: are we to interpret Elijah's experience as a 'miracle' (like, say, Moses' burning bush) or are we to understand it as a 'vision' (in the same category as Isaiah's vision of the Lord in the Temple, when he, too, is purged by fire)? We are poised between two different kinds of event in a story that cannot, and must not, be told in any other way without destroying the meaning—just as Kierkegaard discovered in *Fear and Trembling* that the story of Abraham and Isaac could not be 'interpreted' and retold. The whole effect of Elijah's mysterious experience seems to be to deny, *and* simultaneously affirm, certain connections. Thus Yahweh *is*, and *is not*, a God of natural phenomena (a paradox we are more familiar with in the theological terms of 'immanence' and 'transcendence'); revelation is both 'miraculous' and 'natural'; God is concerned with both the individual and the shaping of history. The story seems to insist that at each level these two modes are both completely discontinuous and yet inseparable.

I could go on: the passage is a rich and fascinating one, but there is surely no need. I have taken one example at some length because it

shows better than any theoretical introduction the kind of fundamental theological confusion that seems to have gripped almost all the
modern translators. It is simply not possible, in the words of the
Preface to the Good News Bible, 'to use language that is natural, clear,
simple, and unambiguous' about something that is as complex and
mysterious as human religious experience. It is not about things that
are natural, clear, simple and unambiguous. Moreover I submit that
those theologians who think it is do not know the basics of their own
calling. Even outside the confines of the Bible they would have lined
against them the witness of generations of poets, sages, saints and
divines of all persuasions. We are, in short, confronted by a very
strange phenomenon: a generation of biblical critics and scholars at
once sceptical and naïve, straining at gnats and swallowing camels.
What is at stake here is fundamentally a matter of *integrity*—in the full
meaning of the word.

Though this phenomenon is not primarily a matter of particular
doctrinal beliefs, it can be seen most strikingly at points where older
beliefs, belonging to a different mental and world-picture, are
innocently 'translated' into modern ones. The Elijah story, as we have
seen, is a case in point. Another example can be found outside the Bible
in C. S. Lewis's Narnia stories. Those familiar with them will probably
have experienced the same mixture of delight and unease in them that
I have. The unease comes to me, for instance, when Aslan substitutes
himself for Edmund as the White Witch's lawful victim, is killed, and
rises again because of 'deep magic from before the dawn of time'.[19]
This is an allegory of the substitutionary theory of the atonement, and
illustrates more strikingly than anything else I know the difficulty of
'translating' this theory into modern terms. Try as we may, I doubt if
many of us can really enter into a mental set that sees Christ's
salvation of man in terms of a 'ransom' paid to the Devil, or as the
result of a 'bargain' of any kind (a bargain, moreover, that in Lewis's
case is struck and then immediately broken because the Witch does not
seem to know the hidden ground rules and can therefore be cheated).
The example is a useful one, since it clarifies this question of 'integrity'
in a non-biblical and therefore less inherently controversial context.
The problem, of course, concerns not the depth of Lewis's own
convictions (entirely a matter between him and his Maker) but the
wholeness or integrity of his *artistic* vision. At this key point in the
story he has allowed his narrative to be controlled by a belief that
simply does not fit into the total moral structure. His artistic sense of
the whole has been over-ridden by his commitment to a particular
dogma that belongs to a different mental set. Lewis was in many ways
a refreshingly humble man; he himself was to castigate vigorously the
Bultmann School of criticism in his essay *Fern-Seeds and Elephants*;[20] here,
untypically, he is too certain about things in whose very constituency
there is an inherent uncertainty.

Yet this, of course, *is* a biblical problem. Figure after figure in the

Old and New Testaments alike is humbled for thinking he knows too many of the answers. Elijah's dogmatic certainties about his role and purpose are broken open by a revelation of a wider whole. But perhaps the classic example of such a disconfirmation is that of the Book of Job. I do not think we understand the debate in Job aright unless we realise that, within the terms of the conventional theology of the day, Job's Comforters are *right*. They are good sound men of doctrine, and in the moral confidence that that engenders, they are applying the solid certainties of human logic to the greatest mystery of human experience—that of undeserved suffering. I can never read the story without being half-persuaded by them: Job is clearly behaving quite impossibly. Yet when the Lord finally, and unexpectedly, *does* reply to Job out of the whirlwind, using many of the arguments previously advanced by the discomforted Comforters, it is to justify Job and denounce his friends for apparently this very lack of integrity over which we have been puzzling. Job's baffled arguing from the depths of his misery is preferred to the most sophisticated theologising.

Job's Comforters, however, were at least competent theologians within their own terms. Their confidence may have been ill-founded, but it was backed by the received wisdom of the day. They were conscious of their own theological tradition. The same does not seem to be true of the translators of the Good News or New English Bibles, whose received wisdom appears to be that of a narrow specialism, insulated from the broader vision of what the Bible is about. The translators of the King James Bible because they believed they were handling the literally inspired Word of God, took care, so far as they could, not to 'interpret' it, or make it more easily understood for the masses. The modern translators seem to have no such inhibitions. They should perhaps reread John Wesley's famous comment on those who would 'improve' his hymns:

Many gentlemen have done my brother and me . . . the honour to reprint many of our hymns. Now they are perfectly welcome so to do provided they print them just as they are. But I desire they would not attempt to mend them: for they really are not able . . . . Therefore, I must beg of them one of these two favours: either to let them stand just as they are, to take them for better or worse; or to add the true reading in the margin, or at the bottom of the page; that we may no longer be accountable either for the nonsense or for the doggerel of other men.[21]

The most noticeable thing about the modern 'improvements' to the story of Elijah, for instance, is that the story now makes *less* sense, is less charged with meaning than in the Hebrew or the Authorized Versions. If the Bible is the record of Israel's experience of God, then where that record is difficult or obscure there is at least a good chance, especially when we are dealing with poetry, that what it is recording is itself difficult or obscure for us to come to grips with. Much as I admire the scholarship of those responsible for the new translations, I cannot help the suspicion that many of them have simply never been trained in the discipline of close reading of difficult or ambiguous texts, where ambiguities and cruces are themselves often important parts of the argument. We give to Kant's *Critiques* or *King Lear* a verbal respect that we now are prepared to deny to the Bible.

Put very briefly, then, my case is this. For reasons apparently contingent, and not of historical necessity, round about 1800 there occurred a disastrous split in the critical thinking of biblical scholars. On the one hand, the revisionists, in their efforts to accommodate the essence of Christianity to what was then conceived of as scientific and historical truth, tended to see the books of the Bible as multi-layered palimpsests, the creation of a 'tradition' rather than individual writers, or even the work of a kind of Jungian Collective Unconscious; on the other, the defenders of biblical inspiration, for whom the actual words remained of paramount importance, tended to retreat towards an increasingly narrow fundamentalism. For neither group were the older skills of the cultured literary critic particularly relevant. The erstwhile cultural breadth that enabled Robert Lowth, Hugh Blair, or even Coleridge to move freely in the course of a few sentences from a discussion of Hebrew customs and social context to questions of cross-cultural influences via an investigation of prosody and aesthetics was all but lost by the mid-years of the nineteenth century. Questions of the influence of Isaiah on Virgil's Fourth Eclogue, or of Genesis on the influential Roman critic Longinus, which fascinated the earlier critics, concerned as they were with the interaction of the classical and biblical worlds, are lost in discussions of mythology. Since Coleridge's time, biblical and literary criticism have been increasingly separated—to the detriment of both. What is now needed is not greater technical or linguistic expertise, but a return to the sense of the complexity of the whole that gives meaning to the minutiae of scholarship; a return to the awareness of a Lowth or a Coleridge. As Coleridge himself wrote in one of his notebooks, the gifts needed for a Biblical scholar are remarkable:

Great and wide Erudition, with curious research; a philosophic imagination quick to seize hold of analogies; an emancipation from prejudice, and a servile subjection to the prejudices of great names; a faith that shutteth out fear; a freedom from the superstition which assumed an absolute *sui generis* in every word of the O. and N. Testaments, and is for ever craving after the supernatural; a sound and profound Psychology—these are the principal requisites.[22]

Notes

1 S. T. Coleridge (1849), *Confessions of an Inquiring Spirit*, London, p. 9.
2 (1976), *The Good News Bible*, London.
3 S. T. Coleridge (1849), *op. cit.*, p. 13.
4 See E. S. Shaffer (1975) *'Kubla Khan' and 'The Fall of Jerusalem'*, Cambridge, pp. 26–8.
5 E. S. Shaffer (1975), *ibid.*, p. 89.

6 Mrs H. Ward (1890), *Robert Elsmere*, London, pp. 276–7.
7 Mrs H. Ward (1890), *ibid.*, p. 317.
8 R. Lowth (1758), *De sacra poesi Hebraeorum*, trans G. Gregory (1787), London. Based on lectures, first delivered in 1741.
9 'The correspondence of one verse or line, with another, I call *parallelism*. When a proposition is delivered, and a second is subjoined to it, or drawn under it, equivalent, or contrasted with it in sense; or similar to it in the form of grammatical construction; these I call parallel lines; and the words or phrases, answering one to another in the corresponding lines, parallel terms.' R. Lowth (1753), *ibid.*, Vol. II, p. 32.
10 R. Lowth (1753), *ibid.*, Vol. II, p. 53.
11 R. Lowth (1753), *ibid.*, Vol. II, pp. 27–9.
12 'From all these testimonies it is sufficiently evident, that the prophetic office had a most strict connexion with the poetic art. They had one common name, one common origin, one common author, the Holy Spirit. Those in particular were called to the exercise of the prophetic office, who were previously conversant with the sacred poetry. It was equally part of their duty to compose verses for the service of the church, and to declare the oracles of God.' R. Lowth (1753), *ibid.*, Vol. II, p. 18.
13 R. Lowth (1753), *ibid.*, Vol. II, p. 12.
14 H. Blair (1820), *Lectures on Rhetoric and Belles Lettres* Vol. II, Edinburgh, pp. 270–71.
15 See S. Prickett (1976), *Romanticism and Religion*, Cambridge, chapter 2; also E. S. Shaffer (1975), *op. cit.*
16 For the use of the terms 'foreground' and 'background' in biblical narrative, see E. Auerbach (1968), *Mimesis*, Princeton, chapter 1, p. 3. ff.
17 Mrs Trimmer (1806), *Help to the Unlearned in the Study of the Holy Scriptures*, London, p. 196.
18 See H. Wheeler Robinson (1962), *Inspiration and Revelation in the Old Testament*, Oxford, p. 34.
19 C. S. Lewis (1950), *The Lion, the Witch and the Wardrobe*, London, chapter XV.
20 C. S. Lewis (1975), *Fern-Seeds and Elephants*, Glasgow.
21 (1933) *The Methodist Hymn Book*, London, p. viii.
22 S. T. Coleridge (n.d.), Notebook No. 41, pp. 34–5.

7 BIBLICAL INTERPRETATION AND CULTURAL RELATIVISM

Duncan Forrester

MOST children brought up, as I was, in a Christian home encounter the Bible long before they can read it themselves. I heard it read in Church, and at home, I had Bible stories read to me; a great deal of biblical language flowed over my head and eddied around my awakening consciousness before I was given my first simplified book of Bible stories and, somewhat later, a blue-bound Authorized Version in bold print so that I should not strain my eyes. Cumulatively all this gave me the impression that the Bible was different from other books, the most important of all books, the one book that the child and his parents, and grandparents, and all sorts of people had in common. Like the stories from the Bible, my parents told me or read me the stories of Goldilocks, and Beauty and the Beast, but I was conscious that even if they enjoyed reading fairy stories to me they did not read them themselves, and that although I might savour Rumplestiltskin, grown-ups were not really interested in discussing *that* story, but would happily talk with me about Joseph or the marriage at Cana of Galilee. It seemed that the adults with whom I was in most immediate contact felt they were still exploring the meaning of a book I was just starting to discover for myself; and felt that meaning to be important to me as to them; for unlike almost all the other books they read and then put back on the shelves, this one was constantly thumbed, and divided into short portions to be wrestled with day by day.

Every child knows that good stories may be, indeed must be, told over and over again; Bible stories are not peculiar in this regard. I remember, for instance, pestering my mother almost every day as we passed a certain old house on our way to the shops to tell me the story of Willie Douglas, who once, many years before, had lived there—or so we believed. As a boy, Willie Douglas had been page to Mary Queen of Scots, and had attended her while she was imprisoned in Loch Leven castle. He it was who had stolen the key from the Governor while he was in his cups, and ushered the Queen out to the waiting boat, throwing the key into the depths of the loch, from which it had been dredged up centuries later. Why did I insist on that story being told me so constantly that it must have driven my mother, imaginative story-teller though she was, half demented? The answer I think, looking back, is quite simple: it answered my questions, Who am I? Where do I belong? Where do I come from? In dramatic and vivid fashion, it gave me a history in a way Beauty and the Beast, for all the profundity of its meaning, never could. And the same is true of Bible stories when told or read in this kind of context, which is as it were the natural setting for a sacred book, in which the text and the reader enter into a particular kind of urgent, if repetitive dialogue.

Repetition is, of course, a prominent characteristic of ritual, and I am suggesting that when the Bible is read within the believing community we have a ritual way of reading which is a special kind of dialogue between the reader and the text. This is made unusually explicit in the Passover Haggadah within Judaism, in which, soon after the start of the rite, the youngest child present asks four questions:

'Why does this night differ from all other nights? For on all other nights we eat either leavened or unleavened bread; why on this night only unleavened bread?

On all other nights we eat all kinds of herbs; why on this night only bitter herbs?

On all other nights we need not dip our herbs even once; why on this night must we dip them twice?

On all other nights we eat either sitting or reclining; why on this night do we all recline?'

To which the response is:

'We were Pharoah's slaves in Egypt, and the Lord our God brought us forth with a mighty hand and an outstretched arm. And if the Holy One, Blessed be He, had not brought our forefathers forth from Egypt, then we, our children, and our children's children would still be slaves in Egypt.

So, even though all of us were wise, all of us full of understanding, all of us elders, all of us knowing the Torah, we should still be under the commandment to tell the story of the departure from Egypt. And the more one tells the story of the departure from Egypt, the more praiseworthy he is'.[1]

And then they do just that—reading and discussing passages of the Bible and all sorts of rabbinic stories which have a bearing upon the deliverance from bondage, from which gradually emerge answers to the child's questions, which are also the perennial questions of the adults present.

I have dwelt upon the Passover ritual for a variety of reasons. It illustrates the point I made earlier that biblical stories have a bearing, sometimes oblique, sometimes direct, upon fundamental questions of identity, and their repetition within the believing community confirms and strengthens the answers to these questions. But the context within which the stories are told and told again is a ritual context, that is, things are done as well as said, and the whole is charged with a depth of symbolic meaning. The context generates the questions, shapes the answers, and gives plausibility to the whole way of reading. This may most clearly be obvious in the Passover or in the Lord's Supper, but my point is that biblical stories told within the believing community can never be totally detached from the representation of the central acts of salvation in ritual. This means that the believing community is affirming in the strongest possible way that these stories are *their* history, that they understand themselves in the light of them; but also that they are *present* now, in their re-enactment: *we* experience deliverance from bondage in Egypt, the Lord makes himself known to *us*, now, in the breaking of the bread. The story of Willie Douglas was important to me because it was about a boy, because it was history, *my* history, however highly embroidered, because the house in which he had lived was there, close by the house in which I lived. We belonged together within the same community, constant in place and continuous over time; and I felt no insuperable difficulty in entering into his experience any more than in encountering Jesus in story and in ritual.

All this, of course, bristles with problems, to some of which we will return later. There is a perhaps terribly naïve confidence in the possibility not only of communicating across vast periods of time, but even of making the past present today, which simply sidesteps the difficulty of historical understanding. There is a singular lack of interest in drawing any hard and fast distinction between history and myth. There is a breathtaking confidence in the continuity and sameness of the believing community across the ages. There is a conviction that history, stories, are the heart of the Bible, to which the myths and parables and ethics and doctrine and poetry and proverbs are all in a sense ancillary. And binding all these presuppositions together is the conviction that the Bible is the *Holy* Bible, different from, and more important than, all other books.

As a student I encountered a different sort of book, and was trained in reading philosophical texts like Plato's *Republic*. A book such as this was presented for our study over many weeks on the assumption, made perfectly explicit to us, that this was a work of genius, with a subtlety and profundity of meaning which made it hard to understand, but ultimately worth the intellectual effort required. The problem was not essentially that it had been written many centuries ago, and that Athens was clearly a very different kind of community from St Andrews; it was that the mind of a genius moved on a higher plane: it was hard for us to understand Plato because we were not geniuses rather than because we were twentieth-century undergraduates. The techniques of interpretation, it is true, were of more general application, but this particular text had been chosen for us not just as the focus for a new way of reading, but because its matter was assumed to have some perennial relevance and importance, although just how this might be the case was left to us to discover. It was dinned into us that it is hard, but not impossible, to understand the *Republic* and we were encouraged to apply ourselves in detail to Plato's words, if possible in the original Greek. We were advised to beware of commentaries and secondary works, and were given the minimum of contextual material, probably lest the effort to understand might be frustrated by glib attempts to explain a superficial account of Plato's teaching as a reflection of class conflicts in ancient Athens, or the psychological quirks of the author's personality. We were warned not to neglect the possibility that there might be some perennial teaching in the book by interpreting it as a tract for the times and nothing more.

Above all, we were taught to be modest in our approach to the text:

because Plato wrote many centuries before, we cannot assume that his thought has been superseded. Modesty involved as far as possible setting aside one's own presuppositions and untutored questions, and in particular struggling to make sure that one understood what Plato was saying, and why, and how it all hung together before one dared to criticize or ask questions about relevance. And we were given the impression that few, if any, among us would ever be in a position actually to enter into dialogue with Plato; it was enough, for the present, if we penetrated into an understanding of what the text was saying. The modesty before the text with which we were inculcated was no doubt excessive, but to a degree it was necessary if the reader were to be properly open to the text with an awareness that it must be read in a different way from an Agatha Christie detective story, and it was not *toto coelo* different from the reverence with which I had learned to approach Scripture. Neither modesty nor reverence, unless taken to ridiculous extremes, impedes a scholarly reading.

Neither for the Bible nor for the *Republic* was there felt to be any basic problem involved in lifting a text from one century and reading it in a very different setting; in both cases the reading of the text was seen as presenting the possibility of a critical stance towards the spirit of one's own age—by no means a bad thing, if it can be achieved. The two books belonged in different communities: the *Republic* was a book for the mature and for an intellectual elite, for Guardians, an academic text; the Bible was a book for everyone, even for children, a book to be made available for all, a book which must not be confined to the Academy or withheld from the masses. Each had shaped a community and, if only for that reason, merited attention.

But the Bible had, and has, a place, if a rather strange and problematic one, in the Academy as well as in the Church, as I was to discover when I proceeded to read theology. Here we found the Bible presented to us as an authoritative text much as Plato's *Republic* had been, rather than as a book presupposed to be sacred. The distinction may be a hard one to maintain, for as I have suggested modesty, even reverence, in one's approach to an authoritative text need not inhibit scholarship, and indeed may be the condition for a proper reading. But the student who was already familiar with the Bible as a sacred text, who had been brought up in an atmosphere saturated with the Bible, who had in all probability memorized a variety of passages, read the Bible daily, and used it in his prayers, had now to learn a new way of reading a well-known text. He had to learn to address a different sort of question to the text, suspending as far as he was able his earlier conclusions about what the Bible says in order to read it afresh, as if it were a new and unfamiliar book. This process often enough resulted in confusion and dismay; certainly the transition in ways of reading was frequently profoundly unsettling, as it was realised that there were substantial discrepancies between the old reading and the new.

The situation was further complicated by problems of motivation.

Most students who study Plato's *Republic* do so because they have to, or because they find the book interesting and stimulating; few, I imagine, read it as a key to how to become a successful politician, or as a relevant blue-print for social and political reform today; they read it to sharpen their wits rather than their political skills. But although there are those who study the Bible in universities because of its intrinsic interest or its literary and cultural significance, most students still come to it as 'the supreme rule of life and doctrine', a book on which to build their prayers, their preaching, and their lives—in other words, a sacred book, the Holy Bible. And such students often find that the older type of exegesis which was clearly a function of the community of faith and dealt with Scripture unashamedly as a holy book is more congenial by far than the newer biblical criticism which seems to them 'academic' (in the bad sense, as being detached from, and irrelevant to, real life), and sometimes positively subversive to faith. There is a real dilemma here: the modern biblical scholar may respond to his students' unease by saying that faithfulness to the text is destructive only of belief which is based on a naïve view of Scripture, to which the student is fully entitled to reply that it is strange that only now, after 2,000 years, do we possess the critical techniques necessary for a correct reading of the Bible; and if these techniques have made redundant the exegesis of all earlier commentators, perhaps they have destroyed or questioned the very features of the text which make it significant enough to justify so much study.

Our problems are now beginning clearly to emerge. There is, at least potentially, a conflict between the study of the Bible as a holy book within the Church, and the study of the Bible as an important ancient text within the university. There are significant differences in approach, techniques and motives for study, as well as in the uses to which the results of study are put. The contrast is a real one, although I have undoubtedly simplified the issues in order to present a clear polarity. It is no part of my present concern to enquire which way of reading is the better, the more useful, or the more faithful to the text. I do not wish to take sides with Kierkegaard in attacking biblical scholarship (although I must admit to a certain sympathy with him!) when he argues:

Suppose that in the New Testament it were written, for example (a thing which we can at least suppose), that every man should have $100,000 . . . do you believe that then there would be any question of a commentary?—or not rather that every one would say: That is easy enough to understand, there is absolutely no need of a commentary, for God's sake, let us be delivered from any commentary . . . .

But what actually is written in the New Testament (about the narrow way, about dying to the world) is not a bit more difficult to understand than that about the $100,000. The difficulty lies elsewhere, in the fact that it is not to our liking—and therefore we must have commentaries and professors and commentaries. It is to get rid of doing God's will that we have invented learning . . . we shield ourselves by hiding behind tomes.[2]

Kierkegaard certainly has a point, but his presupposition that there is a simple, faithful, and responsive way of reading the Bible, which gives immediate access to the meaning of the text, cannot be accepted as it stands. On the other hand, the assumption that only now has academic study rescued the Bible from churchly obscurantism so that its true meaning may for the first time be dredged up from beneath the pious imaginings with which it has been overlaid carries little conviction. My real sympathies are with the Jewish student training to be a rabbi who had great problems in his first encounter with modern biblical criticism, but eventually won through to a conviction that this kind of study provided positive help to him in his reading of the Bible. And going from university to study in a Yeshiva in Jerusalem, where students devoted themselves entirely to the traditional rabbinic study of the Torah as the Law in which their whole being delighted, he found there a different, but no less useful and illuminating, way of studying the Bible.

What is of primary interest to us in this essay is the fact that the two ways of reading the Bible arise in different social contexts, the university and the believing community, and that to a large extent it is the social context which determines the questions which are posed and the general approach to the text. But if it is admitted that the social context influences the way a text is read, three issues call out for clarification: first, what we mean by a social context; secondly, how the social context influences the reading of a text; and, finally, what the relation is between various ways of reading arising from different social contexts. Is there any way of judging between different ways of reading, or are we in a realm of total relativity, in which even the words of the text themselves provide no objective criterion for rival interpretations?

The two social contexts we have already distinguished have, of course, an area of overlap, and both are set within the broader social and cultural context of the modern West. Thus there are those who belong both to the university and to the believing community, and see no fundamental incompatibility in the ways of reading and inter-preting the Bible characteristic of the pulpit and the lecture room. But perhaps this is simply because they are twentieth-century men whose exposition in Church and Academy is more influenced by the basic presuppositions of modern western culture than by anything else. Of course, this simply pushes the problem of what we mean by a social and cultural context to a different level. Dennis Nineham borrows from Troeltsch and other German thinkers the concept of 'cultural totalities', by which he means unified and coherent complexes, any aspect of which can only be understood in relation to the whole.[3] He is primarily (indeed, I suspect, exclusively) interested in totalities which occur in different ages rather than in totalities which exist simultaneously, like the contexts of Church and university which we have just discussed. These also serve to remind us of the facts of interaction and overlap which make it impossible for us to speak of Church and university as self-contained totalities, or even to regard modern western culture as a totality since it has such complex and fascinating contacts with other modern cultures and with its own past. Nineham's over-hasty acceptance of the concept of totality, and his emphatic insistence upon the difficulty of communicating between one age and another, lead him to a rather despairing picture of modern man as encapsulated within his age, incapable of questioning the underlying assumptions of his contemporaries, or communicating in any real sense with those of other ages or cultures. This view of man as isolated within his own age and culture naturally leads on to regarding the thought-forms of our age—our old friend, the *Zeitgeist*—as in some sense absolute, the peak of human achievement. The modern age, together with the ways of reading the Bible which it has developed, is placed beyond question.

It is not, however, necessary to go to such an extreme in order to make a proper allowance for the influence of the social and cultural context, in all its fascinating diversity, upon the way in which a text is read and interpreted. Communication, between one context and another very different one, is no doubt difficult and bristles with problems, but it is a counsel of despair to assume that it is virtually impossible, precisely because this assumes an absolutizing of one's own culture and the dominant forms of understanding and interpretation in that culture. Nineham's book is haunted by a shadowy 'visiting anthropologist' who is never formally introduced to the reader, and remains anonymous; which is just as well, for no serious anthropologist of whom I am aware would countenance Nineham's gloomy conclusions about the inaccessibility of other cultures, or support his neat escape from total relativism by absolutizing the present moment. The anthropologist appears also as the typical modern man, since his function is to present 'the strange world of the Bible' which Karl Barth discovered to be so exciting that it forced modernity into crisis, as not only infinitely strange, but quaint, naïve and impenetrable by the modern mind. The language of Canaan cannot be translated into modern speech; it is a code beyond our power to break. Collingwood may have been rather too optimistic about the ability of the careful historian to enter into the mind of Julius Caesar as he hesitated on the bank of the Rubicon, but he was surely quite realistic in believing that, given effort, eagerness, and sympathy, one may understand a radically different cultural context and learn from it. It is not helpful to reify 'cultural totalities' after the style of German Romanticism, and then voluntarily imprison oneself in one's own.

Our second question, concerning the influence of a cultural context on the reading of a text, we have already dealt with in part. Particular questions arise from the context, and are addressed to the text; and here as elsewhere, the questions you ask largely determine the answers you get. A text is used in different ways, depending on the context. The Bible is perhaps pre-eminently a book which questions the reader, and often rejects or reshapes the questions he brings to his reading, putting him and his context into question. It relativizes the relativizer, in other words, thereby inducing a proper modesty before the text. It is no escape from this to say that there are two ways of reading, the one seeking as objective as possible an understanding of what the writer really meant, the other concerning itself with the application of the teaching of an authoritative text to a fresh situation. Karl Popper's account of the *Republic* as the foundation document of totalitarian oppression was not simply a criticism of the modern *use* of the *Republic*, but a fresh reading of the meaning and intention of the text itself. He did not argue that the book was being misused or wrongly understood, but that its teaching was objectively malignant and morally repulsive. Modern totalitarianism had underlined the true, and dangerous, meaning of the text. In a not dissimilar way, Nineham cannot but recognize that the Bible is the foundation document of the Church. But he argues that 'modern man' (that elusive figure with whom some contemporary theologians have such intimate acquaintance, and to whose conjectural opinions they accord such authority) can no longer read the Bible as a sacred book.[4] This is so, because Nineham believes there is no longer a slot within our cultural totality for sacred books, so that the whole concept does not make sense. Closely allied to this is his rejection of the canon, leaving the Christian free to seek illumination where he will—from other books, from sermons, and from the liturgy, provided sermons and liturgy are freed from 'what has rightly been called "the curse of the canon"'.[5] Precisely why it is no longer appropriate or possible to read the Bible as a sacred text is nowhere spelled out, and we are left to conjecture that it is simply because the majority of people do not regard it as such. What is, of course, abundantly clear is that if Nineham and his like won the day the Bible would soon lose its strange capacity to question the reader and relativize his modern preconceptions, and could never merit a Popperian onslaught since biblical scholars would be seen as having lost confidence in its authority, relevance and indeed intelligibility.

Our third problem concerns the possibility of discriminating between various ways of reading the Bible. Traditional exegesis has, as we know, distinguished various types of meaning in biblical passages— literal, spiritual, allegorical, and so on—and has often sought to arrange them in some kind of hierarchy of meanings, under the ultimate control of the text itself. The modern scholar is also aware of diversities of meaning and interpretation, and relates many of them not unilluminatingly to variable social and cultural circumstances. Whereas the traditional exegete tried (with what measure of success is immaterial to present purposes) to test interpretations against the text, the modern scholar of the school of Nineham judges an interpretation by its compatibility or otherwise with 'modernity', rather loosely defined. It is rather like the student who demands immediate relevance in everything he studies. Christians of past ages may have been rather naïve in their belief that they had direct access to the world of the Bible, and could draw directly from the Scriptures perennially relevant patterns of faith and behaviour; but at least they did not feel themselves imprisoned in the present moment, and drew from the Bible tools for the refashioning of themselves, their Church, and their society. If the choice is between absolutizing the Bible or absolutizing modernity we are indeed in a sorry state. But the dilemma is false. Other possibilities are before us.

'Day unto day uttereth speech, and night unto night sheweth knowledge': Nineham has provoked us into giving perhaps excessive attention to matters concerning interpretation across time. There are problems and possibilities relating to interpretation from one contemporary culture to another, one social context to another, which are of no less interest and which have the capability of enriching and deepening ways of reading the Bible, and teaching a proper modesty through relativizing the relativizers. The process of translation, dialogue—and sometimes conflict—between those who read the Bible in different ways relating to their varying cultural background can be most illuminating as well as frustrating. My initial contact with India helped me immediately to understand certain biblical passages more clearly. Seeing daily flocks of indistinguishable sheep and goats running together, and gradually discovering that the only reliable differentiating sign was that the sheep's tails hung down, while the goats' pointed heavenwards, helped me to understand why the separation of sheep and goats was regarded as not altogether a simple operation in the Bible. In studying the Gospels with students who had come straight from the villages I found my rather tortuous attempts to explain, or rather explain away, the miracle stories met with amazed incredulity; miracles as such were not problematic for them as they were for me, since many of them had seen people possessed by demons healed through prayer and the laying on of hands, and accordingly found my scepticism quite implausible prejudice—which perhaps it was. Virtually all my friends and students had a clear idea of what a sacred text was, and well-defined notions of how best it should be read, which were in many respects far different from mine. Hindu students opted to take courses on the Bible in large numbers not just because it is an important work of literature but because they and their parents, while remaining Hindus, regarded the Bible as a holy book, from which they derived spiritual nourishment. They brought, of course, their own presuppositions to the reading of the text. The more philosophically inclined among them, for instance, would interpret the New Testament—John's Gospel in particular—in a monist way, centering their reading on sayings such as 'I and the Father are one' and the high priestly prayer 'that they may all be one; even as thou, Father, art in me, and I in thee, that they also may be in us . . . that they may become perfectly one'. Such encounters forced me to re-examine and explain, and sometimes modify, my own reading of some passages, and made others which I had found virtually unintelligible spring vividly to life. The whole process of translation and communication from one culture to another can provide extraordinary illumination of the text. I am intrigued, for instance, at the way in which Protestant missionaries in India throughout the nineteenth century read the New Testament as a charter of equality, so that their converts had to renounce caste and demonstrate their willingness to accept as brothers those who were, within the caste system, regarded as irremediably polluting. But when these converts argued that the same New Testament passages raised question marks against denominational barriers among Christians, put class as well as caste under judgement, and disallowed the practice of racial superiority, these same missionaries were horrified and commonly found their converts' way of reading the Bible quite unacceptable.

There is a story, which I hope is true, of a group of Buddhists and Christians who decided they would study the Bible together. They started, appropriately enough, with John's Gospel. 'In the beginning was the Word', was read out, and immediately an aged Buddhist monk groaned, 'Even in the very beginning was there no silence in your religion?' The story does not relate how the Christians talked themselves out of that one; but I am sure the effort to explain in itself enriched their reading of the text. I remember once preparing to preach on the passage in Romans 8 about the whole creation groaning in travail together until it will be set free from its bondage to decay and obtain the glorious liberty of the children of God. I consulted, as I have been trained to do, a number of commentaries. All save one seemed highly embarrassed by Paul's talk of cosmic redemption and treated it as a kind of spiritualized picture of the salvation of individuals which had little to do with the material universe. Only the commentary by F. F. Bruce, a biblical scholar who is embarrassingly close to being a fundamentalist, seemed to take what Paul was clearly saying about nature seriously, and thereby highlighted deficiencies in the liberal scholarly reading of the other commentators. A similar illumination comes, I believe, from a series of essays such as this, in which literary critics, biblical scholars and theologians, Christians and non-Christians, challenge each other with their differing ways of reading the Bible.

I have consciously kept from discussing the politics of differing ways of reading the Bible although a political dimension has been latent in much of what I have said. I have done this partly because the political hermeneutic which is coming today mainly from Latin America is, in my opinion, so important that it deserves more extensive treatment than I can afford here; but also because it should be obvious that every social and cultural context which affects reading is also a political context. Kierkegaard is surely right in suggesting that we are reluctant to read, or unable to understand, what we do not want to know in a text, we are unwilling often enough to be questioned by a book. We interpret away or tone down the unacceptable parts, or become deaf to their significance through constant reiteration. I remember in the early years of my ministry sometimes having a horror in the middle of reading the Bible in Church either because the passage seemed to call in question the person who was reading so blandly and authoritatively, or because I felt it so offensive to the congregation that they must surely walk out. But they never did, and I now rarely find it threatening to read the Bible aloud. Which suggests, I believe, that ritual repetition and over-familiarity can distance one from the meaning even as one delights in the words. It would be good for those of us who, in our comfortable and rather self-indulgent society enjoy—among other things—chanting the Magnificat, if we could sit with the peasants in Solentiname, studying the same passage, as recounted by Ernesto Cardenal:

I asked what they thought Herod would have said if he had known that a woman of the people had sung that God had pulled down the mighty and raised up the humble, filled the hungry with good things and left the rich with nothing.
     Natalia laughed and said, 'He'd say she was crazy.'
     Rosita: 'That she was a communist.'
     Laureano: 'The point isn't that he would just say the Virgin was a communist. She was a communist.'
     'And what would they say in Nicaragua if they heard what we are saying here in Solentiname?'
     Several voices: 'That we're communists.'
     Some one asked: 'That part about filling the hungry with good things?'
     A young man answered: 'The hungry are going to eat.'
     And another: 'The Revolution,'
     Laureano: 'That is the Revolution. The rich person or the mighty is brought down and the poor person, the one who was down, is raised up.'
     Still another: 'If God is against the mighty, then he has to be on the side of the poor.'
     Andrea, Oscar's wife, asked: 'That promise that the poor would have those good things, was it for them, for Mary's time, or would it happen in our time? I ask because I don't know.'
     One of the young people answered: 'She spoke for the future, it seems to me, because we are just barely beginning to see the liberation she announces.'[6]

I, for one, find it impossible to deny that this represents a way of reading the Magnificat from which we can easily be excluded if we become imprisoned in our own immediate context. But if we are truly open to a plurality of ways of reading it can liberate us for new and better understanding of the Bible. What I am saying cannot be better summed up than in the words of Pastor John Robinson in 1620 as he bade farewell to those of his congregation in Leiden who were joining the Pilgrim Fathers to sail in the *Mayflower* from one context, seeking another that was new and free for the faithful reading of the Bible:

He charged us, before God and his blessed angels, to follow him no further than he followed Christ; and if God should reveal anything to us by any other instrument of his to be as ready to receive it, as ever we were to receive any truth by his ministry. For he was very confident that the Lord had more truth and light yet to break forth out of his Holy Word.[7]

Notes

1 N. N. Glatzer (ed.) (1969), *The Passover Haggadah, with English Translation, Introduction and Commentary*, New York, pp. 21–3.
2 S. Kierkegaard, *Efterladte Papirer*. Vol. X1, p. 389, cited in W. Lowrie (1962), *Kierkegaard*. New York, p. 539.
3 D. E. Nineham (1976), *The Use and Abuse of the Bible*. London, pp. 15 and 27.
4 D. E. Nineham (1976), *ibid.*, p. 229.
5 D. E. Nineham (1976), *ibid.*, p. 230.
6 E. Cardenal (1977), *Love in Practice: The Gospel in Solentiname*. New York, pp. 30–31.
7 E. Winslow (1953), cited in *Companion to Congregational Praise*, London, p. 128.

PART IV

SPEECH AND ACTION

One of the basic truths put forward in the Bible as a whole is not merely that God is always right and man is always wrong, but that God and man can face each other in an authentic dialogue.
(T. Merton, in *Opening the Bible*, London 1972, p. 34)

> Dic ubi Salomon, olim tam nobilis?
> Aut Samson ubi est, dux invincibilis,
> Aut pulcher Absalom, vultu mirabilis,
> Aut dulcis Ionathas, multum amabilis?
>   (Anonymous Franciscan poem)

8 THE BIBLE: DIALOGUE AND DISTANCE

Gabriel Josipovici

Friendliness is not the abolishing of distance but the bringing of distance to life.
(Walter Benjamin)

Part I

WHEN stories are read to us in childhood we accept them without
question. Spoken as they are by someone we love and who forms part
of the world into which we have come, they seem to us as natural and
inevitable as that world itself. As we grow up we leave many of these
stories behind us, never to be thought of again until we in turn read
them to our children, but a few we find ourselves reading on our own.
When that happens it is sometimes difficult to relate the pages before
us to our memories of the stories, though these memories inevitably
direct and condition our later reading. The tales of Arthur and his
knights, it turns out, all fit together in a long and complex book
written by a fifteenth-century Englishman; the stories of Scheherezade
and of Sinbad the Sailor come from a book called *The Thousand and One
Nights*; the stories of Moses and the plagues are to be found in a book
called the Bible.

Our relation to these stories can no longer be the unproblematic one
of our childhood. Because we now read instead of simply listening, a
whole range of questions present itself which had never troubled
us before: Who was King Arthur? Did he really exist? When did
Moses live? Did the plagues really happen? And, if not, what do the
stories mean? Gradually we discover that there is a complex see-saw
movement at work in the process of reading: we try to assimilate the
books we love to ourselves, indeed, we love them because they speak
to our condition, but we also love them because they are other than us,
because they guide us out of ourselves towards the world at large. This
double process, which is at the basis of all reading, is easier to discern in
its aberrations than in its normal functioning. Clearly a book is being
misread if a person assimilates it so entirely to himself that he twists
what it has to say in order to make it fit in with his own needs; and
equally clearly it is being misread if it is so emphatically placed in its
historical and cultural context that any link with our present needs is
rigorously denied. To give an example: the reader of *Hamlet* who
insists that Claudius is really the hero, or that all that is wrong with
Hamlet is that he is suffering from an Oedipus complex, is not really
reading the play before him; but then so is the person who denies that

we can identify at all with Hamlet because we cannot will ourselves into a belief in ghosts or in Hell and Purgatory.

This problem of right reading is of course multiplied one thousand fold when the book in question is a sacred text. For on the one hand there is the very strong impulse to preserve the text in its pristine state: not one word, not one letter, must be altered, for all of it is sacred; on the other hand there is the impulse of each person to make the text his own, to discover its relevance *to himself*. Indeed, the history of both Judaism and Christianity can best be seen perhaps as a perpetual conflict between these two attitudes to the sacred text, and the triumph now of the one and now of the other.

It is important to realise, however, that, no matter how firmly we insist on the otherness of a text and on its objective status, we inevitably, by the simple act of reading, assimilate it to ourselves and our own desires and thought processes. This is because there is no such thing as a fundamental literal meaning, which is there *in* the text for all to see, prior to any human interpretation. All language requires deciphering and so all reading is translation: simply to 'make sense' of a phrase requires acting upon it so as to make it a part of the world of our consciousness. It is thus extremely hard not to distort a text, especially if it is an ancient text with unfamiliar thought-patterns, so as to make it fit our world. With the Bible we can see this process at work from the very beginning. The earliest versions and translations make every effort to be absolutely faithful, but inevitably, in the course of adapting a given text to another language and other patterns of speech, they cannot help harmonizing and explaining, and thus, in however small a way, altering what is there.

Let me give two tiny examples of this process at work. In the Hebrew text of the story of Noah we are told: 'And he sent forth a raven, which went forth to and fro, until the waters were dried up from off the earth. Also he sent forth a dove from him to see if the waters were abated from off the face of the ground.' (Genesis 8. 7–8).[1] The purpose for which Noah sent the raven forth is not expressly stated, as it is in the case of the dove. The Septuagint adds 'to see if the waters had subsided' after the first sentence as well as the second, and most commentators follow it in asserting that the object was clearly the same in both instances. But if the two birds had been sent forth for exactly the same reason it would have been indicated in connection with the first bird rather than the second. By putting it the way it does the text is perhaps indicating that Noah first sent forth the raven without any specific intention, just to see how it would act, and since he learnt nothing from it he then sent forth the dove.[2]

Again, in Genesis 11, the chapter concerned with the descendants of Shem, we have very close parallels with Genesis 5 which was concerned with the descendants of Adam. However, where each paragraph of chapter 5 recorded the total number of years of the father's life and ended with the words 'and he died' (except in the case

of Enoch, though here there is a parallel expression), in chapter 11 this
is left out in all cases except in that of Terah in the Hebrew text
established by the Masoretes (11. 32). The Samaritan Recension of the
Pentateuch, however, gives the total number of years at the end of
each paragraph here too, thus harmonizing chapters 5 and 11, but at
the cost of losing the special significance of Terah, who is, after all,
Abraham's father.[3]

These might seem to be trivial alterations, but they are of crucial
importance for our purposes. The desire of the translators is natural
enough. The very telling of a story implies the bringing of order into
chaos, the turning of a number of discrete and therefore meaningless
facts into a sequence and thereby imbuing them with meaning. The
significance of our examples lies in the fact that the little changes made
by the Pentateuch and the Samaritan Recension are just like the
myriads of little changes we unconsciously make all the time in order
simply to assimilate what we read. The danger lies in the fact that
enough of these little changes can add up to a total mis-reading, and it
is against this that we need to guard ourselves. The problem is not an
easy one to deal with, and it is compounded by the fact that in any
ancient text there are obvious lacunae and corruptions. However,
there should be no need to despair. It is only the rather naïve belief that
we can if we try hard enough achieve absolute certainty that causes us
difficulties. The literary student frequently comes across such problems, and he has learnt how to deal with them. For example, there is
evident doubt about the correct ordering of the individual tales in *The
Canterbury Tales*, but that does not mean that we cannot reach a pretty
good idea of Chaucer's overall design and of his central concerns in
that work.[4] Again, it is obvious that *Pericles* is not all the work of
Shakespeare. But, rather than trying by quasi-scientific methods to
discover exactly what is and what is not by Shakespeare, critics and
scholars have tended in recent years to adopt a more easy-going
attitude: they put aside questions which cannot in the nature of things
be answered and concentrate on the more interesting and amenable
problems of what it is the play seems to be about, what light is thrown
on it by other late Shakespeare plays, and what light it in turn sheds on
Shakespeare's art. These questions can be answered perfectly well
even if we do not have any absolute certainty about how much of
Pericles is by Shakespeare and how much by other hands.

Similarly with the Bible: while there can be no doubt about the
enormous value of much of the work of that branch of scholarship
which seeks to separate the different strands to be found in the biblical
books, we should recognize that even if there was complete agreement
among scholars, not only will we never be able to arrive at absolute
certainty, but the quest for such certainty distracts us from the more
important task of understanding what we have before us. The quest
for origins and the quest for certainty (which are inextricably allied)
clearly belong to certain nineteenth-century modes of thought which,

in other disciplines, have come to be seen as a barrier rather than an incentive to progress. But because the desire to get at *the* truth is so potent a factor in our psychological make-up, it is extremely difficult to get rid of it. It is, however, an effort we must make. The quest for absolute certainty is a chimera. Understanding is a human activity and there is no way in which we can by-pass the human reader, with his doubts, hesitations, partial responses, flashes of insight and inevitable blind spots. The best we can do is to be wary about too easy an assimilation of the text to our own presuppositions and too great a confidence in so-called scientific methods of reaching conclusions.

There is a further, very important, factor about the application of these general remarks to the Bible. When we remind ourselves of the general truths I have been outlining above, we are not merely making preliminary methodological points about reading and interpretation, which we can then apply to the Bible. All that I have said so far actually constitutes a central theme of the Bible, from Genesis right through to the New Testament. In what follows I would like to draw out this theme and explore its implications.

Part II

From the very start of the Bible we are presented with a God who is both utterly other than man and a God who speaks as men speak. To speak is to divide the envelope of silence, and the Bible opens with God, through speech, dividing one thing from another in order to form a world from chaos: 'God said, Let there be light: and there was light. And God saw the light, that it was good: and God divided the light from the darkness' (Genesis 1. 3–4). Adam is then in his turn given the task of naming the animals, thus continuing the work of God, in whose image he has just been made.

But naming is not really typical of speech. Speech implies another, and it is in dialogue with man that God reveals his complete difference from the gods of the other peoples of the ancient world. For it is one of the characteristics of dialogue that it both maintains distance between the two people engaged in it, and bridges that distance. In the words of Walter Benjamin 'it does not abolish distance but brings it to life'.[5] Or rather, it can, if both partners wish it to, do that. But it is always possible for one partner in dialogue to refuse to take part, and there are many examples of such refusal in the Bible. Indeed, the best way of approaching the complex nature of dialogue is to look at an example or two of its negation.

One of these occurs straight away. We are told that when Adam had eaten of the tree of knowledge he became self-conscious and wished to cover up his nakedness. When he heard 'the voice of the Lord God walking in the garden in the cool[6] of the day' (Genesis 3. 8) he hid himself. Why? Because speech implies coming face to face with the person to whom one is speaking. Adam hides himself because he cannot face God. When God finds him—and the ensuing dialogue is wonderfully airy, unlocalized, yet direct, so that we do not know if Adam and God still do not see each other—when God finds him we can imagine that he bowed his face to the ground in shame and could not look God in the eye.

This tells us something important about dialogue, which we could describe in the words of a later exchange: 'The voice is Jacob's voice, but the hands are the hands of Esau (Genesis 27. 22)'. It is possible to conceal ones appearance, even the feel of one's body—remember the blind Isaac's groping fingers—but a person's *voice* conveys his uniqueness as nothing else can. But note the multiple ironies of the episode of the blessing of Jacob. Jacob says to his blind father: 'I am Esau'. And Isaac has no option but to believe him. In other words there is always a tension, which can occasionally, as here, become an outright contradiction, between *voice* and *speech*. The word can be creative, as with God and Adam naming the world and the animals, but it can also be decreative, a lie. And that is one of the characteristics of language, not an aberration. For language does not close a gap, as physical force would do; it only functions because of this essential freedom to lie. Voice is embodied in words, and the voice cannot be concealed; but words convey meaning and so can convey lies as well as truth. That is one of the paradoxes of speech.

The story of Jacob's lie is not over yet, however. The exchange I have just quoted is followed by the actual blessing. Now this, the story tells us, once given, even if in error, cannot be taken back. This follows naturally from the fact that while voice is natural, language is conventional; because falsehoods such as Jacob's are possible, it is also possible for there to be promises, covenants, blessings, that is, certain forms of language which are guaranteed to be free from falsehood not by anything inherent in them but by agreement between two individuals or two communities, or, as with God and Israel, an individual and a community.

I will return to this in a moment, but first I want to look at one other example of dialogue refused:

'Now the word of the Lord came unto Jonah the son of Amittai, saying, Arise, go to Nineveh, that great city, and cry against it; for their wickedness is come up before me. But Jonah rose up to flee to Tarshish from the presence of the Lord. . . .'

                                                                    Jonah 1. 1–3

Rather than talk to God face to face (or mouth to mouth, as the Old Testament often puts it), Jonah tries to flee. He enters a ship going to Tarshish—Tartessos in Spain, the very limit of the known world—but God finds him out, even there. It is interesting to note that when the mariners, desperate because of the storm God has raised up, rouse Jonah, he is sleeping in the very bowels of the ship, and the word the

Bible uses for his deep sleep (Jonah 1. 5) comes from the same Hebrew root as *tardemah*, the word used for the sleep which comes upon Adam when Eve is drawn out of his side by God (Genesis 2. 21). In other words, it is a loss of consciousness which in this case one can only feel to be willed—a reversion, as the story makes clear, to the womb, to the time before man was called upon to speak, when he could claim that he was still unformed, still a part of someone else. Jonah's transference to the whale's belly is thus only a confirmation of his state. However, miraculously, inside the fish's belly, after three days and three nights, Jonah suddenly finds it in himself to *give voice*: he calls out to God, and God, as always when someone calls to him, answers back:

Then Jonah prayed unto the Lord his God out of the fish's belly, And said, I cried by reason of mine affliction unto the Lord, and he heard me; out of the belly of hell cried I, and thou heardest my voice. . . . And the Lord spake unto the fish, and it vomited out Jonah upon the dry land, And the word of the Lord came unto Jonah the second time, saying, Arise, go unto Nineveh. . . .
Jonah 2. 1–2, 10 and 3. 1–2

There is, then, no escape from dialogue in the Bible. This is recognized by all the main figures who are called by God: Noah, Abraham, Moses, Samuel, Isaiah, Jeremiah. When God first calls them their response is usually: 'Please, leave me alone. I don't want to speak to you. I am not worthy. I can't do it.' Nevertheless, they answer, and God strengthens them, telling them that he 'will be with them' or 'with their mouth'. Moses is a good example:

And when the Lord saw that he turned aside to see, God called unto him out of the midst of the bush, and said, Moses, Moses. And he said, Here am I. And he said, Draw not nigh hither: put off thy shoes from off thy feet, for the place whereon thou standest is holy ground. . . . And Moses said unto God, Who am I, that I should go unto Pharaoh, and that I should bring forth the children of Israel out of Egypt? And he said, Certainly I will be with thee.

Exodus 3. 4–5, 11–12

The same elements are found in the calling of Jeremiah:

Then the word of the Lord came unto me, saying, Before I formed thee in the belly I knew thee; and before thou camest forth out of the womb I sanctified thee; and I ordained thee a prophet unto the nations. Then said I, Ah, Lord God! behold, I cannot speak: for I am a child. But the Lord said unto me, Say not, I am a child, for thou shalt go to all that I shall send thee, and whatsoever I command thee thou shalt speak. Be not afraid of their faces: for I am with thee to deliver thee, saith the Lord. Then the Lord put forth his hand, and touched my mouth. And the Lord said unto me, Behold, I have put my words in thy mouth.

Jeremiah 1. 4–9

The words in the two instances are almost identical, and they occur again and again whenever dialogue is instituted with God: Here am I, *hineni* in the Hebrew. It is worth pausing over this phrase and over the drama within which it occurs.

I use the word 'drama' advizedly. The talk of theologians about the primacy of event in the Bible can make us forget that dialogue too is a form of event. In the Old Testament the call of God and the answer *hineni* constitute moments of particular dramatic significance. J. L. Austen has drawn attention to what he calls 'performative utterances'.[7] Linguists as well as philosophers have been quick to pick this up, but what he has to say has profound bearings on literature too, and on our immediate subject in particular.

A performative utterance is a form of words in which the speaker is not just saying something about an action, but is actually performing the action by uttering the sentence. If I say: 'Here is an apple' or 'Tomorrow I am going swimming', it is not really very important if I use a different form of words or simply hand you an apple or take my swimming trunks out of a drawer and point to them, making a gesture which signifies 'tomorrow', as I may do if I have a piece of cake in my mouth and you are in a hurry to depart. But if I say: 'I bet you it will rain tomorrow' or 'I apologize for the error' or 'I promise you to try harder', it is the saying itself that constitutes the act. Now *hineni* does not simply mean 'present', which could just as well be expressed by holding up the hand. The speaker is in effect saying: 'Here I am, in this spot and no other, attentive to you and to no other; and by saying "Here I am" I accept the responsibility for myself and for whatever tasks you will impose on me.'

It is important to note that though this is the common response to the call of God, it is not used uniquely of the conversations between men and God. And in this it is typical of the Bible: the language of dialogue between man and God is the same as that between man and man. In the episode of the blessing of Jacob it is significant that Esau says *hineni* to his father, and Isaac to Jacob, but that Jacob never uses it himself. He cannot, of course, because he only gets the blessing by denying himself. Again, in Genesis 22. 1, 7 and 11 we read:

And it came to pass after these things, that God did tempt Abraham, and said unto him, Abraham: and he said, Behold, here I am. . . . And Isaac spake unto Abraham his father, and said, My father: and he said, Here am I, my son. . . . And the angel of the Lord called unto him out of heaven, and said, Abraham, Abraham: and he said, Here am I. . . .

Here, by contrast, Abraham, the angel and God all use the same form of words, so that we sense a relationship of trust between Isaac and Abraham similar to that between Abraham and God. An even clearer example of the naturalness of the use of the term is provided by the story of the calling of Samuel. Samuel, it will be remembered, ministered to the Lord before Eli, and when he lay down to sleep 'the Lord called Samuel: and he answered, Here am I. And he ran unto Eli, and said, Here am I; for thou calledst me. And he said, I called not; lie down again.' (I Samuel 3. 4–6) This happens three times. Finally Eli understands what is going on: 'Therefore Eli said unto Samuel, Go, lie down: and it shall be, if he call thee, that thou shalt say, Speak, Lord; for thy servant heareth' (I Samuel 3. 9).

I think we find it hard to understand the notion of a performative utterance because for us words tend to be merely counters; certainly we tend to think of them as internal, having to do with thought rather than action, and when we think of them as expressive it is of an individual character, a secret self. Thus when we speak of the power of the word of God in Scripture we tend to think of it as something quite outside the normal range of experience; we think of mystical visions and of such stories as that of the rash young man who was consumed with fire for having dared to read the first chapter of Ezekiel.[8] But it is important to remember that the world of the Old Testament is on the whole the world of everyday life, of people talking, quarrelling, cheating, lying and helping each other, just as they do in normal life. And it is in this mundane context that God chooses to speak to men.

I pointed out earlier that Jacob gets his blessing by trickery, but that once Isaac has spoken he cannot take back his words. For his blessing of Jacob is a performative utterance: there is not on the one hand speech and on the other a thing, the blessing. Note how the words of Genesis 27. 26–30 themselves grow out of the whole scene:

And his father Isaac said unto him, Come near now, and kiss me, my son. And he came near, and kissed him: and he smelled the smell of his raiment, and blessed him, and said, See, the smell of my son is as the smell of a field which the Lord hath blessed: Therefore God give thee of the dew of heaven, and the fatness of the earth, and plenty of corn and wine: Let people serve thee, and nations bow down to thee: be lord over thy brethren, and let thy mother's sons bow down to thee: cursed be every one that curseth thee, and blessed be he that blesseth thee. And it came to pass, as soon as Isaac had made an end of blessing Jacob. . . .

that Esau arrived, and the trick was discovered:

And Isaac trembled very exceedingly, and said, Who? where is he that hath taken venison, and brought it me, and I have eaten of all before thou camest, and have blessed him? yea, and he shall be blessed. And when Esau heard the words of his father, he cried with a great and exceeding bitter cry, and said unto his father, Bless me, even me also, O my father. And he said, Thy brother came with subtilty, and hath taken away thy blessing.

Genesis 27. 33–35

Once the blessing has been given, the words spoken, it cannot be taken back.

There is an even more terrible example of the irreversibility of words solemnly spoken in the story of Jephthah, one of the leaders of Israel in the early days of raids on the communities inhabiting Palestine. In Judges 11. 30–31 we read:

And Jephthah vowed a vow unto the Lord, and said, If thou shalt without fail deliver the children of Ammon into mine hands, Then it shall be, that whatsoever cometh forth of the doors of my house to meet me, when I return in peace from the children of Ammon, shall surely be the Lord's, and I will offer it up for a burnt offering.

He goes out to fight and returns in triumph, to be met by his only daughter coming to greet him, 'with timbrels and with dances':

'. . . it came to pass, when he saw her, that he rent his clothes, and said, Alas, my daughter! thou hast brought me very low, and thou art one of them that trouble me: for I have opened my mouth unto the Lord, and I cannot go back.'

Judges 11. 35

Speech takes place in time and, like time, it cannot be wound back. Once again the Bible brings out into the open something which is usually concealed, the tension that always exists between speech as an acoustic phenomenon, a stream, and speech as mere purveyor of meaning. The meaning here, as in the story of the blessing of Jacob, is bound up with the physical act of speech itself.

The story of Jephthah of course has its parallels in ancient Greek literature, and this should alert us to the fact that much of our difficulty with the Bible comes from the fact that it simply belongs to a very ancient culture, where the distinctions between inner and outer, thought and action, were not as clear-cut as they appear to be today. John Jones, for example, in his brilliant book on Greek tragedy, has pointed out that when Aeschylus makes Agamemnon walk on the red carpet at the turning point of the first play of the *Oresteia*, our tendency is immediately to turn this carpet into a symbol of the king's pride. But the real way to read the action is in a much more mundane and literal sense: such carpets were part of the actual wealth of the house, and by making the head of the house trample on it Klytemnestra is quite literally asking him to trample his wealth underfoot.[9] Even when we are reminded of such things, however, it is very hard for us not to feel that somehow, somewhere, there must be more than the literal, that something symbolic must be meant. What we cannot grasp is the horror that the literal desecration of the rich carpet would arouse. A similar adjustment is required in our reading of the Old Testament. We must constantly renew the effort not to translate tacitly what we read into our own terms, but to try and grasp it in the terms in which it is presented.

The form of language is the form of life, as Wittgenstein puts it. What then is the form of life that emerges out of the predominantly performative mode of speech of the Old Testament? This is the question that Erich Auerbach tried to answer in his now classic analysis of the story of Abraham and Isaac, and all readers of the Bible owe him a great debt.[10] But even Auerbach is, I feel, betrayed by the presuppositions of his own culture—a German Protestant one—and is consequently guilty of subtle but crucial misreadings.

Auerbach almost certainly chose Genesis 22 as his example of Old Testament narrative because of Kierkegaard. In *Fear and Trembling* Kierkegaard attempted to give his generation back a sense of the power and strangeness of the Old Testament by showing how impossible it was to reduce what happens in that episode to any of our known terms or categories. Auerbach pressed this insight further when he contrasted the world of Genesis 22, a world of crisis, 'fraught with background',[11] as he put it, with the gentle and sunny world of the Odyssey. But I must confess to some unease with phrases like 'fraught with background', 'crisis' and 'tension', when applied to this episode. It seems to me that they betray an insufficient sympathy with what I have called the everyday world of the Old Testament. If we look at the story as a whole we must be struck by the way that the key phrase, 'Here am I', is used by Abraham both to God and to Isaac. I believe that we read tension and crisis into the story because we desperately want to fill the gaps which seem to exist in it, even if it is only with words which will sum up our sense of how big those gaps are. But here, as elsewhere in the Bible, the weight of utterance is sufficient unto itself. There is no interiority into which Abraham and Isaac retreat. The narrative does not move towards a crisis. Each sentence has a weight equal to all the others. This is a narrative which takes great events in its stride and moves on without fuss. It does this because the narrative itself trusts that all will be well, or rather, does not even question the fact that all will be well. Our problems only arise if we stop the continuity of the story and ask: What is Abraham feeling? Why is God doing this? But the narrative does not stop. And what drives it forward is confidence in the created world and in God's relation to it. It is the same confidence that we find expressed, for example, in Isaiah 58. 9: 'Then shalt thou call, and the Lord shall answer; thou shalt cry, and he shall say, Here I am (*hineni*)'. Or in Psalm 22. 24: 'For He hath not despised nor abhorred the affliction of the afflicted; neither hath he hid his face from him; but when he cried unto him, he heard'. It is the same confidence, the same unquestioning certainty that all will be well in the end that I suggested we experience in childhood, when a parent reads a story out loud to us before we go to sleep.

Every action has an aim, but such trust has no aim. Action connects what is not yet with what will be; trust is entirely of today because what has been and what will be can be taken for granted.[12] God seems to be taking the future away from Abraham when He claims his only son, but the story runs on without seeming to sense in this any crisis; it at least has confidence in the outcome. And it is right. God restores Isaac to Abraham, and we move on to Isaac himself in the following chapters, and then to his sons, and then to the sons of his sons. Thus even the extraction of this episode for analysis, out of the continuum of the Bible, is an act which is far from neutral, one which unconsciously falsifies our response. For it is a central fact about this book that it is not a collection of stories, though there are many stories contained within it. But they form part of a chain, a continuum in time. Genealogy and dialogue are the twin pillars on which this book is built.

'And the Lord spake unto you out of the midst of the fire,' we read in Deuteronomy 4. 12, 'ye heard the voice of the words but saw no similitude; only ye heard a voice'.[13] Immediately after this follows the central commandment: 'Take ye therefore good heed unto yourselves; for ye saw no manner of similitude on the day that the Lord spake unto you in Horeb out of the midst of the fire; Lest ye corrupt yourselves, and make you a graven image, the similitude of any figure. . . .' (Deuteronomy 4. 15–16).' There follows a list of such similitudes, and then Moses reminds the people: 'But the Lord hath taken you, and brought you forth out of the iron furnace, even out of Egypt, to be unto him a people of inheritance, as ye are this day' (Deuteronomy 4. 20). God spoke, and God acted. What is important is not what he looked like, but *that* he spoke, and *that* he acted.

We can now see why the central commandment must be that you shall make to yourselves no graven images. The fear of idols is not simply the fear of the gods of the nations in the midst of which Israel finds herself. It springs from the sense Israel has of two radically opposed views of the world. In one view idols are to be worshipped, for idols are objects in which magical powers reside. The object belongs to you, and you can keep it in your house, under your bed, inside your clothes; but you also in a sense belong to it. For Israel, on the other hand, God is not a possession. He is a person with whom one can talk. The fear of Him is not the magical fear of an object that possesses occult power, but stems from the realisation that to be called by God means having to respond to Him, and that is never an easy or a painless thing.

Nor is it ever final. Dialogue, as I have repeatedly stressed, takes place in time: 'I have opened my mouth unto the Lord and I cannot go back'. Promises and covenants are only an extension of dialogue. They too depend on the acceptance of time as beneficial. The Bible spends much time listing genealogies because the relation of man to God is seen as something that unfolds in time. The meaning of Israel's destiny, like that of each individual, is not something that is given once and for all, but something that grows and changes and develops, just as the meaning of any exchange of words between two people does not reside in any one word or any one sentence (which it is therefore crucial to decipher), but in the whole encounter.

Dialogue, however, can be frustrating. Men hunger for the certainties which speech will always deny. The Bible recognizes this hunger and its dangers, and so it shows us both the primacy of dialogue and the frequent refusal of dialogue. Two episodes in particular show us idolatry taking on truly cosmic proportions. What the episode of the Tower of Babel shows us is the attempt of men to by-pass dialogue and its uncertainties and to reach up to heaven not through words but through the erection of a giant tower which, they feel, will close up for ever the gap that exists between heaven and earth. As a result of this they are dispersed over the earth and their language is fragmented into mutually incomprehensible tongues. Dante, following midrashic tradition,[14] tells us that the giant Nimrod was the builder of the tower, and his punishment in Hell consists in his being cut off entirely from the speech of men (*Inferno* XXXI). For to speak, to enter into dialogue, implies the acceptance of distance and of limitation; it depends, in a sense, on a voluntary giving up of a part of the self. What Nimrod tried to do, Dante suggests, was to speak a purely private language, the language of his immediate feelings. He refused to abide by the rules of speech, which we have to observe if we wish to be understood by others. And this attempt at total freedom is of course a fall into bondage, the bondage to one's private whims and fantasies; whereas, paradoxically, the acceptance of language, of limitation, leads us back into the outside world.

There is of course one other place in the Bible where men try to by-pass the process of dialogue and to become God instead of being content to speak to Him: that is the episode of the eating of the forbidden fruit. The temptation offered by the serpent is simple, and it is a perpetual one: eat and you won't need to talk *to* God any more, for you will *be* God. We can perhaps now finally understand the full irony of Adam's shamed attempt to hide himself from God when God calls out to him in the cool of the day: he who tried to overcome speech has forfeited speech: when God calls out to him he can only hide.

Part III

Things are constantly changing in the course of this book. Everyone knows that in Genesis myth becomes saga and saga legend as we move from Adam to Abraham and from Abraham to Joseph. If only we would not look at these things from a position of supposed superiority, imposing our own notions of what a book ought to be, or even of what historical development ought to be. It is easy enough to say that it is a fact of cultural history that myth comes first and is followed by saga and then by more realistic narratives. The danger with this is that we cease to be surprised by the fact that all three exist in perfect harmony in one book of the Bible. But it is a fact about the Bible, in contrast with most books, that it is both one and constantly changing.

History, the history of Israel, is meaningful. Every event that takes place seems to have a meaning. But that does not necessarily imply that the precise meaning can be spelt out. We sense that the binding of Isaac is meaningful, but our way of asserting this is not to dissect it but to *repeat* it. Events here are not so much interpreted as lovingly recalled and retold. Why now and not sooner? Why here and not elsewhere? Why me and not another? These questions may be raised but there will not be any great urgency to answer them. That God spoke, that he acted, this is what is important. Events in the historical books of the Old Testament happen the way they do because the world in which they take place goes easy on interpretation, so to speak: event, whether it is the Exodus from Egypt or the binding of Isaac, is primary. We invoke such events, remember them in wonder, question them.

But a question is never meant to throw up an answer, only another question. The book of Job is of course the greatest example of this in action. It ends not with an answer to Job's agonizing questions, but with God asking a few questions in his turn:

Gird up now thy loins like a man;
For I will demand of thee, and answer thou me.
Where wast thou when I laid the foundations of the earth?
Declare, if thou hast understanding.
Who hath laid the measures thereof, if thou knowest? (Job 38. 3–5)
. . . .
. . . . . . who shut up the sea with doors,
When it brake forth, as if it had issued out of the womb? (38. 8)
. . . .
Canst thou draw out leviathan with an hook?
Or his tongue with a cord which thou lettest down? (41. 1)

As time went by, however, the tone changed. Though the change can already be found in parts of the books of Kings, it is most clearly seen in the prophetic books.[15] Moses, of course, was a prophet, but he acted as well as speaking: he led Israel out of Egypt. By the time we get to the so-called writing prophets certain doors have been closed, certain arteries have hardened. The antagonism of Hosea for Jacob is well known: What had such a trickster to do with our faith? he asks (Hosea 12) But, as I tried to suggest earlier, the stories of Jacob have everything to do with the faith of the Old Testament. In the prophets, however, we see a new will at work: there is a positive attempt to interpret, and meaning becomes primary, event secondary. The prophets no longer speak to God, except to insist on their weakness. They do not argue, as Abraham and Job argued; rather, God speaks through them. It is as if the weight of the dialogue had become too great for the nation. It splits into two camps: those who commit idolatry and those who denounce it.

'I am not eloquent' (Exodus 4. 10), Moses had said when God called him, and God had answered: 'I will be with your mouth' (Exodus 4. 12). When Jeremiah answers in the same way God makes a similar reply: 'Behold, I have put my words in your mouth' (Jeremiah 1. 9). But in Jeremiah's case, as in that of the other prophets, the word is withdrawn from its natural context in everyday dialogue. It is now a roaring, says Amos; it has an almost physical weight for Isaiah; Ezekiel eats the very scroll on which the writing is to be found. The word of God is so heavy that it overflows the natural boundaries of language. It enters the bodies of the prophets and affects them like an illness. The passages in which this is described are often overlooked, and the prophets thought of only in terms of what they say. But the prophetic books are made up of more than laments or diatribes, and it is these other portions that we need to examine.

There is an interesting story in Herodotus about the message sent by a certain Thrasybulus of Miletus to Periander of Corinth. Periander[16]

sent a representative to the court of this despot, to ask his opinion on how best and most safely to govern his city. Thrasybulus invited the man to walk with him from the city to a field where corn was growing. As he passed through this cornfield, continually asking questions about why the messenger had come to him from Corinth, he kept cutting off all the tallest ears of wheat which he could see, until the finest and best-grown part of the crop was ruined. In this way he went right through the field, and then sent the messenger away without a word. On his return to Corinth, Periander was eager to hear what advice Thrasybulus had given, and the man replied that he had not given any at all, adding that he was surprised at being sent to visit such a person, who was evidently mad and a wanton destroyer of his own property—and then he described what he had seen Thrasybulus do. Periander seized the point at once; it was perfectly plain to him that Thrasybulus recommended the murder of all the people in the city who were outstanding in influence or ability.

The message is not sent in words but in sign language. This serves two purposes: it keeps the messenger from understanding it, and it also drives it home more deeply into the mind of the one who does understand it. However, it also has certain obvious disadvantages in relation to ordinary language.

In the prophetic books we find a whole range of these actions which speak louder than words. First of all there is the simple emblematic or allegorical vision, such as this from Jeremiah:

The Lord showed me, and, behold, two baskets of figs were set before the temple of the Lord. . . . One basket had very good figs, even like the figs that are first ripe: and the other basket had very naughty [*ra'ot*, bad] figs, which could not be eaten, they were so bad. Then said the Lord unto me, What seest thou, Jeremiah? And I said, Figs; the good figs, very good, and the evil, very evil, that cannot be eaten, they are so evil. Again the word of the Lord came unto me, saying, Thus saith the Lord, the God of Israel: Like these good figs, so will I acknowledge them that are carried away captive of Judah. . . . And as the evil figs, which cannot be eaten, they are so evil; surely thus saith the Lord, So will I give Zedekiah the King of Judah, and his princes, and the residue of Jerusalem that remain in this land, and them that dwell in the land of Egypt: And I will deliver them to be removed into all the kingdoms of the earth, for their hurt, to be a reproach and a proverb, a taunt and a curse, in all places whither I shall drive them.

Jeremiah 24. 1–5 and 8–9

A little more complex is the incident described in chapter 19. God orders Jeremiah to take an earthen pot and, with the elders of the people and the priests, to go to a certain spot, and there exhort them and tell them that God will destroy them because they have forsaken him. Having done so, he must break the pot in front of them: 'And [thou] shalt say unto them, Thus saith the Lord of hosts; Even so will I break this people and this city, as one breaketh a potter's vessel, that cannot be made whole again.' (Jeremiah 19. 11). Here, though we still have the visual equivalent to an action, the prophet himself is involved and the vision is no longer static but dramatic. It is but a short step from this to God's command to Isaiah in Isaiah 20. 2–4:

At the same time spake the Lord by Isaiah the son of Amoz, saying, Go and loose the sackcloth from off thy loins, and put off thy shoe from thy foot. And he did so, walking naked and barefoot . . . three years for a sign and wonder upon Egypt and upon Ethiopia; so shall the king of Assyria lead away the Egyptians prisoners, and the Ethiopians captives, young and old, naked and barefoot, even with their buttocks uncovered, to the shame of Egypt. . . .

This is disturbing because it is no longer simply emblematic. Since Isaiah has to act like this for three years it suggests that he somehow takes the suffering and shame of Egypt upon himself. And we get the same feeling from the extraordinary episodes described in chapters 27 and 28 of Jeremiah:

In the beginning of the reign of Jehoiakim the son of Josiah king of Judah came this word unto Jeremiah from the Lord, saying, Thus saith the Lord to me; Make thee bonds and yokes, and put them upon thy neck. . . . And it shall come to pass, that the nation and kingdom which will not serve the same Nebuchadnezzar the king of Babylon, and that will not put their neck under the yoke of the king of Babylon, that nation will I punish, saith the Lord. . . .

Jeremiah 27. 1-2, 8

However, the (false) prophet Hananiah will have none of this. He takes the yoke from the neck of Jeremiah and breaks it: 'And Hananiah spake in the presence of all the people, saying, Thus saith the Lord; Even so will I break the yoke of Nebuchadnezzar king of Babylon from the neck of all nations. . . .' (28. 11). The Lord, however, admonishes Jeremiah: 'Go and tell Hananiah, saying, Thus saith the Lord; Thou hast broken the yokes of wood; but thou shalt make for them yokes of iron.' (28. 13) It is as though language had become insufficient: not only must every statement be accompanied by a visual image, but even argument itself is reduced to dumb show, giving it a curious ritualistic quality.

We are dealing with something more than symbols or emblems. Isaiah walking barefoot for three years, Jeremiah yoking himself like a beast of burden—something very strange is going on here. The drive towards total identification with the nation, even to the point of taking its sins and pains into one's own body, is most evident perhaps in Ezekiel 4. 4-8:

Lie thou also upon thy left side, and lay the iniquity of the house of Israel upon it: according to the number of the days that thou shalt lie upon it thou shalt bear their iniquity. . . . And when thou hast accomplished them, lie again on thy right side. . . . And, behold, I will lay bands upon thee, and thou shalt not turn thee from one side to another, till thou hast ended the days of thy siege.

Such behaviour is not just supplementary to language, it swamps it completely. One senses in all these prophets a terrible longing to escape from the limited, contingency-bound use of words, to some absolute. This is so important to them that they are willing to sacrifice themselves in order to show upon their very bodies the meaning of the events that are occurring around them and which the people refuse to acknowledge. Hosea takes a whore to wife as a sign of Israel's whoredoms, and calls his children 'No mercy' and 'Not my people', as though the very identity of those nearest and dearest to him must also be subsumed in the over-riding need to convey a message. Even more striking is the passage in Ezekiel 24. 15–24 which tells of the death of the prophet's wife:

Also the word of the Lord came unto me, saying, Son of man, behold, I take away from thee the desire of thine eyes with a stroke: yet neither shalt thou mourn nor weep, neither shall thy tears run down. Forbear to cry, make no mourning for the dead, bind the tire of thine head upon thee, and put on thy shoes upon thy feet, and cover not thy lips, and eat not the bread of men. So I spake unto the people in the morning: and at even my wife died; and I did in the morning as I was commanded. And the people said unto me, Wilt thou not tell us what these things are to us, that thou doest so? Then I answered them, The word of the Lord came unto me, saying, Speak unto the house of Israel, Thus saith the Lord God; Behold, I will profane my sanctuary, the excellency of your strength, the desire of your eyes, and that which your soul pitieth; and your sons and your daughters whom ye have left shall fall by the sword. And ye shall do as I have done: ye shall not cover your lips, nor eat the bread of men. And your tires shall be upon your heads, and your shoes upon your feet: ye shall not mourn nor weep; but ye shall pine away for your iniquities, and mourn one toward another. Thus Ezekiel is unto you a sign: according to all that he hath done shall ye do: and when this cometh, ye shall know that I am the Lord God. . . .

Clearly we are in touch with something very primitive here. The preponderance of lamentation in the work of the prophets suggests that they are to some extent fulfilling a role of ritual mourning. We should beware of taking too personally the self-lacerations I have been describing. Nevertheless, the very fact that the Bible asserts that we are not dealing here with nameless *nebiim* but with men who are named and whose deeds are lovingly recorded, makes it necessary for us to see in their actions a particular *personal* response to the tragedy that is befalling Israel. Indeed, one might feel that their responses are *too* personal, too excessive. It may be helpful, in order to understand what is going on here, to turn away from ancient sources and to seek help in what might at first sight seem an unlikely place: Freud's *Studies on Hysteria*.[17]

This is an early work of Freud's, but the case histories and analyses he gives of five women suffering from various forms of hysterical paralysis are as suggestive as anything in his later writings. There is not the space here to enter into his argument in detail, but the basic point he makes is this: these women are often paralysed in places which are physiologically impossible. Their bodies, Freud suggests, are taking revenge on them for their suppression from their consciousness of elements which nevertheless have to find expression. Thus the body itself 'talks', as Freud says, and talks in such a way that the conscious subject is able to deny awareness of what is said while going on saying it even more emphatically than it ever could in words.

This insight of Freud's must immediately remind the student of literature of something very similar which was in the air in the arts of the time: 'One might almost say, her body thought' was the phrase of Donne[18] that haunted Yeats, and he, like so many of the Symbolists, was looking for a language more necessary, more absolute, than the brittle and arbitrary medium of words:

> O chestnut-tree, great-rooted blossomer,
> Are you the leaf, the blossom or the bole?
> O body swayed to music, O brightening glance,
> How can we know the dancer from the dance?
>
> 'Among School Children'

I am not sure that we have to choose between Freud and Yeats, between neurosis and the truth of art. I am not sure that the awe we feel at the thought that 'her body thought' does not transcend our divisions and distinctions. In any case, I have no wish to place the prophets in a pigeon-hole marked 'neurosis' or 'poetic truth'; I only want to draw attention to the strange metamorphosis of the concept of speech from Genesis to Ezekiel. The underlying element of trust that I suggested formed the foundation of the calm which characterizes the story of the binding of Isaac has gone. Voices are more strident, they have to carry across a greater distance. Instead of trust we are confronted with doubt and despair. Language, at such times, seems thin and inadequate, while the distance that separates two people engaged in dialogue becomes something intolerable, something that must be bridged at all costs.

Part IV

In the historical books of the Old Testament we find a combination of dialogue and event. The two spring from the same ground. Event is meditated upon and meanings attach themselves to such events as God's appearance to Abraham or the Exodus from Egypt. In the prophets it is as if the grounds of trust have gone. At the same time event and speech have contracted into one: *I* do this, and in so doing *I* become a sign. The sign signifies, meaning is attached to event. In the historical books we see God talking to man and man answering. Some men or groups of men refuse to speak, but that is all right, for they too are part of the story. We are shown God's purpose both revealed and partially concealed in the course of an enormous span of time, from the creation of Adam to the destruction of the Temple. In the prophets we see history contracted into one man: God does this to Jeremiah and Ezekiel, and it is a sign that *X* or *Y* will happen. In the Gospels we see a coming together of these two strands.

The world of the Gospels is very different from that of the Old Testament. The Old Testament presented us with a world of everyday, normal life; the New Testament presents us with a world in crisis. Crowds rush about, hysterics and epileptics abound—we are closer to the world of Dostoevsky than to that of Abraham, a world of startling peripeties and terrifying heights and depths. People talk, but not to each other; they talk to hide themselves from one another. Jesus himself speaks in strange incomprehensible ways, not answering questions directly but following his own line of thought. Nevertheless, his speech is potent: he need only say 'Come forth' or 'Arise' and the sick are cured, the dead rise up.

In the Old Testament the prophets had been interpreters of tradition: as God led our fathers forth out of Egyptian bondage, so will He lead us forth out of Babylon. In the New Testament too Christ is an interpreter, but what happens here is much stranger: He does not talk about the great events of the day, he talks *about himself*: 'But as the days of Noe were, so shall also the coming of the Son of man be' (Matthew 24. 37). And again in Matthew 12. 38–40:

Then certain of the scribes and of the Pharisees answered, saying, Master, we would see a sign from thee. But he answered and said unto them, An evil and adulterous generation seeketh after a sign; and there shall no sign be given to it, but the sign of the prophet Jonas: for as Jonas was three days and three nights in the whale's belly; so shall the Son of man be three days and three nights in the heart of the earth.

Ezekiel too, we saw, presented himself to the people as a sign. But it was a sign of something else. Jesus presents the something else as a sign of himself.

I do not think we have seen quite how extraordinary this is. It is not enough to say, as scholars have recently been doing that Jesus or the Gospel writers use midrash much as the rabbis would have done.[19] The rabbis are always pluralistic, under their hands the text of Scripture flies open in a thousand different directions. Jesus, on the other hand is obsessionally concerned with only one story and everything is done to lead his listener or reader to concentrate on that story. In interpreting the events of the Old Testament he selects a specific range of meanings and texts and leaves many others unmentioned. He then acts out a drama which will set the seal on his chosen interpretation and cut out for ever all other possible ways of seeing God's relations to man as described in the course of the Old Testament. He does this carefully and, it seems to me, consciously. And, because the final seal is nothing less than his own death, the conviction carried by this particular interpretation is enormous. Let us look at the nature of his achievement a little more closely.

There is a story by Borges that is apposite here. It is called 'The Theme of the Traitor and the Hero'. The action takes place in Ireland. The narrator, Ryan, is the great-grandson of Fergus Kilpatrick, the heroic leader assassinated in his prime, on the eve of a victorious revolt. Ryan is fascinated by the circumstances of his ancestor's death. Like Lincoln, Kilpatrick was assassinated in a theatre; other aspects of his murder have affinities with the killing of Julius Caesar, especially with Shakespeare's version of that event. All this makes Ryan at first suppose that there exists 'a secret form of time, a pattern of repeated lines'. But somehow the parallelisms not just with other historical murders, but even with fictional ones, are too numerous. Ryan grows suspicious. He investigates further. Eventually he discovers the following facts: Kilpatrick was not a hero but a traitor; his fellow-conspirators found this out just in time and condemned him to death. But in order to further their cause they so contrived it that Kilpatrick's guilt would never be known and it would look as though he had been shot by the English enemy and died a hero and martyr to the cause. The new leader, James Nolan, plans it all:

Nolan, urged on by time, was not able to invent all the circumstances of the . . . execution; he had to plagiarise another dramatist, the English enemy, William Shakespeare. He repeated scenes from *Macbeth*, from *Julius Caesar*. The public and secret enactment comprised various days. The condemned man entered Dublin, discussed, acted, prayed, reproved, uttered words of pathos, and each of these gestures, to be reflected in his glory, had been pre-established by Nolan. . . . Kilpatrick was killed in a theatre, but the entire city was a theatre as well, and the actors were legion, and the drama crowned by his death extended over many days and many nights.[20]

Jesus is both Nolan and Kilpatrick. We feel that all the other characters in the Gospels are actors in a play which Jesus (and the reader) grasps, but of which they are at best only vaguely aware and at worst totally ignorant. But Jesus does more than simply 'grasp' it mentally. He actually manipulates it so that, as the Gospels tell us, 'it may be fulfilled'. 'Thinkest thou', Jesus says when he is captured, 'that I cannot now pray to my Father, and he shall presently give me more than twelve legions of angels? But how then shall the scriptures be fulfilled, that thus it must be?' (Matthew, 26. 53-4).

The climax of the play occurs on the cross. We expect a man's last words to be uniquely his, but here an amazing thing happens: Jesus speaks not his own words, but those of Psalm 22. The effect of this is truly astonishing. Jesus seems in that moment to give up not just his life, but something which is perhaps even more precious, the right to speak what he feels. At this moment the whole vast book which began with the creation of the world is turned inside out: instead of Jesus being reduced to a cipher by his self-denial, it is all that has gone before (including Psalm 22) which is turned into an expression of his being. Jesus at this moment has appended his signature to the book, so to speak. It is *his* book, the whole Bible. By his death he has given it a meaning, a centre, an end and therefore a beginning. John's gospel is thus not at all radically different from the other three; it only makes explicit what we feel implicitly as we read the others.

In the Old Testament there are many centres: Abraham and his journey from Ur, Moses and the Exodus, David and Jerusalem. There are also many meanings, some of which do not tally with others. That does not matter, however, for in trust life goes on, meaningful, though we cannot quite fathom the meaning. In the Gospels *the* meaning is spelt out, *the* signature appended. And this imperialism of meaning is taken even further in the other books of the New Testament. In the Epistle to the Romans especially, one can sense the hunger for an end, for an *absolute* meaning, which will have no truck with the uncertainties of dialogue. The images are all stark contrasts: from sleep to waking, from darkness to light, from death to life. Cursed be the Law, the time of Redemption is at hand. The Epistles testify to the success of Jesus's achievement in closing the book, concluding the dialogue, abolishing uncertainty, all the doubts and misunderstandings inherent in speech. The Book of Revelation merely adds the ultimate full stop.

And yet. And yet. For one thing, there are four gospels, not one. This already acts as a brake on centralization, on the establishment of a single absolute meaning. For another, in contrast to the pseudo-gospels and the saints' lives, which sacrifice all for the sake of the single meaning, the Gospels do leave us with a strong sense of that distance and that primacy of dialogue which we saw to be so integral a part of the historical books of the Old Testament. Where this occurs most strongly is, ironically, in the place where, for perhaps the first time in the entire book, God is called but does not answer:

And he went forward a little, and fell on the ground, and prayed that, if it were possible, the hour might pass from him. And he said, 'Abba, Father, all things are possible unto thee; take away this cup from me; nevertheless, not what I will, but what thou wilt.' And he cometh, and findeth them sleeping. . . .
Mark 14. 36–7

God's silence presses in upon one as one reads this, asserting His presence as no speech could ever do. Such a passage should make even the most confident of us, confident in our faith or our scepticism, think again: the book remains open, distance is re-established.

Notes

1 I use the Authorized Version throughout.
2 See U. Cassuto (1964) *A Commentary on the Book of Genesis* (trans I. Abrahams), Jerusalem, Part II, p. 109.
3 U. Cassuto (1964), *ibid.*, p. 251.
4 See D. R. Howard (1976), *The Idea of the Canterbury Tales*, California, especially chapter I, 'The idea of an idea'.
5 W. Benjamin (1977), *Understanding Brecht*, (trans A. Bostock), London.
6 The Hebrew has *ruah*, the breath or spirit of the day.
7 J. L. Austen (1962), *How to do Things with Words*, Oxford, *passim*.
8 Babylonian Talmud, Hagigah 13a. See G. Scholem (1961), *Major Trends in Jewish Mysticism*, New York, first Schocken ed., pp. 40ff.
9 J. Jones (1962), *On Aristotle and Greek Tragedy*, London, pp. 84–96.
10 E. Auerbach (1968), *Mimesis* (trans W. R. Trask), Princeton, chapter I.
11 E. Auerbach (1968), *ibid.*, pp. 9–10.

12 I am indebted here to Ignaz Maybaum's fine lecture, 'The binding of Isaac'.

13 *kōl devarim*, 'the voice of the words'—is it the voice that is heard or the words? It is worth pondering the question.

14 See J. Bowker (1969), *The Targums and Rabbinic Literature, An Introduction to Jewish Interpretations of Scripture*, Cambridge, pp. 179–89.

15 Job is quite probably written after many of the prophetic books. It seems to me, however, that it remains closer to the world of the patriarchs in spirit than to that of the prophets.

16 In A. de Sélincourt (trans) (1972) *Herodotus, The Histories*, Harmondsworth, pp. 376–7.

17 See J. Breuer and S. Freud (1974), *Studies on Hysteria* (trans J. and A. Strachey) Harmondsworth.

18 In 'The Second Anniversary'.

19 See especially M. D. Goulder (1974), *Midrash and Lection in Matthew*, London; and J. Drury (1976), *Tradition and Design in Luke's Gospel*, London.

20 J. L. Borges (1970), *Labyrinths* (trans J. Irby), Harmondsworth.

9 SAMSON AND THE HEROIC

Ulrich Simon

Mais je suis pleine de respect pour le héros, dit la princesse sur un ton légèrement ironique. . . .
(Proust, *Du Côté de chez Swann*, p. 404)

THERE are many good reasons why one should not tackle the heroic in a book concerned with the Bible. Even those unfamiliar with the New Testament feel it in their blood that Jesus is not a hero in the commonly accepted sense. He did not go into battle and he did not die in a battle. Indeed, if the Crucifixion were a heroic death we would not trouble about the Christian religion. There have been too many 'heroes' during the ages to pay special homage to one. Moreover, we now live in an age when heroics are at a discount, and when the anti-hero is more popular. The hero has become a stock-in-trade, cheapened on screen and in fiction. Our political history in the West has undermined belief in a world fit for heroes to live in, and though we hear echoes of the fame of great explorers and soldiers we bring a healthy scepticism to the whole subject. Like Thomas Carlyle, who wrote *Heroes, Hero-Worship, Heroism in History* in 1898, and hated to give these lectures (he wanted the money though it meant 'feeling like a man to be hanged'), we are also very muddled as to what we mean by the theme. He mixed up the divine, the prophetic, the poetic, the cultic, the man of letters, and kingship, and by a fantastic mixture of names, from Muḥammad to Napoleon, presented a fanciful, inconsistent, monotonous, and useless picture of the Hero.

The intellectual confusion arises, however, out of the subject. In 1936 L. Raglan[1] sifted twenty-two characteristics pertaining to the subject; even a few stress the lack of system to be contended with. The hero has a virgin mother, is sired by a father king, is a son of god because of his unusual conception, is spirited away after attempts to kill him, reared by foster-parents, claims his kingdom, wins victories, is crowned and enacts laws, suffers loss of favour and is driven away, dies on top of a hill, has no burial, and is succeeded by no children. But this is not all, for his tomb becomes the central place of a cult, and relics are kept by the devotees. The hero becomes divine and he protects the city and even responds to the people who pray to him. Yet the hero is always as self-centred and self-willed as he is self-made. However varied his place and history, the hero is a free man, exalted and exalting.[2]

The biblical stories in Genesis are remarkably free from this pattern of heroism. The compilers either did not cherish heroics at all, or the sources of the narrative material simply did not offer such traditions in Israel. The antediluvian episodes, from Adam to the tower of Babel, contain a wide range of experiences, but none of them are heroic. Adam is Man in the Garden and then expelled. Cain is a murderer, the giants are hybrid offspring, and Noah is boat-builder and wine-dresser. The patriarchs are semi-nomadic owners of cattle, and only once does it appear that Abraham is drawn into conflict and takes his share in a victorious battle. The saga is one of movement in search of pastures and peace. Even Jacob, the victim of tremendous ordeals, avoids armed conflict and, though lamed in a supernatural struggle, becomes Israel against his will. This 'fighter of God' excels in a special and new manner of greatness, and his son Joseph, the dreamer, rises to power by prophetic interpretation and action. Even more astonishingly, the greatest of all, the liberator Moses, is already past the age of heroism when he returns from Midian to lead his enslaved people to freedom. True, he becomes their mediator with God and suffers on their behalf, and it is as their Lawgiver that he continues to be present in their history. But Moses is prophet, not hero.

Now it may be thought that later editors suppressed the heroic material, which must have existed, as it did, for example, in Asia Minor and Greece, and as it has become immortalized in Homer.[3] To a certain extent this may in fact be the case, but it does not explain why somewhat unexpectedly the heroic streak pervades the stories of the conquest. But even here the heroic is still muted, as for example in the case of Moses' successor, Joshua. Since the Lord is the conqueror and Joshua acts as his vassal the military exploits are hardly on a Herculean scale. Rahab the harlot betrays Jericho, and Jericho is duly taken. But in the book of Judges we listen to a different tenor. The narrator insists that these 'lawless' events took place after Joshua's death. Be that as it may, there are Canaanites in the country, and the tribes of Israel find themselves in a desperate plight and in need of a 'saviour'. Deborah ranks as an outstanding leader, but she cannot be called a heroine. Nor can Jael, who kills Sisera in a treacherous manner. Moral standards, of course, do not affect our judgement of heroes. Gideon is an ideal soldier and even something of a dreamer, combining strategic common sense with a mystical awareness. No doubt the Epistle to the Hebrews mentions these captains of the faith as remarkable links in the chain of deliverance because they had become, after many centuries, types of witnesses of the faith, even heroic martyrs in the battle for the righteous cause. But when we read these stories as they stand, they resist this typological interpretation, for they pin-point earthy events of almost trivial proportions. Jephthah is no more a hero than Abimelech, but his daughter, whose name we do not know, approaches the heroic stature of an Iphigenia. Jephthah's daughter 'bewailed her virginity upon the mountains' (Judges 11. 38) before the father's vow was kept and the girl sacrificed. She was a heroine in acceptance, and the cultic memory stirred the generations which followed.[4]

Thus in the middle of the Book of Judges the innocent reader suddenly enters upon the tragic dimension of heroism. It is not tragedy in the accepted sense, for the narrative remains just that, prosaic, matter of fact, with an ordered, though episodic, arrangement of factual events. The absence of poetry is most marked. There is no development towards Greek tragedy, no chorus, and no actors who can take the stage. Instead the omniscient narrator tells his tale, not like a bard at court, but as a chronicler in the village. These stories do not bear the imprint of royal etiquette, and one wonders if David, for example, had heard of them. Saul and David certainly figure later on as *gibborim*, valiant men among the valiant, fighters with daring exploits, and striving after honour. But none of them are comparable to Samson, the *Gibbor par excellence*. Not even in failure!

The narrator allows himself much space to introduce his hero. Compared to the brief vignettes and silences in Genesis (see chapter 22!) there is in Judges 13 an almost leisured style. The barren woman is promised a son who is destined to become a Nazirite. No explanation is vouchsafed, except that the unborn child is to be dedicated to God and to abstain from the razor, drink, and women. An ascetic is to be born by supernatural-natural means. The angelic encounter before conception stresses the *mysterium*. The boy is born, and his name Shimshon adumbrates his special mission. He is to act like the Sun (Shemesh), he is a figure of light, possessed by the Spirit. The birth of this ecstatic hero must be understood in contrast to the bands of ranting drunkards and naked prophets, who induce their madness by toxic means. Shimshon is a Nazirite, consecrated by God and to God.

Biblical stories, however, never proceed according to a predictable pattern. If you expect Samson to be 'moved by the Spirit of the Lord' you are hardly prepared for the adventures which follow. They hardly remind you of a sun hero and the classical images are far away. No labours of Heracles for Samson the Nazirite! Nevertheless, the narrator always sees a divine purpose behind the most trivial events, such as Samson's courting of a woman in Timnath. He meets with a young lion and kills him (one labour of Heracles), and later finds a swarm of bees in the carcass, from which he removes the honey, keeping father and mother in ignorance (Judges 14. 5– 9). Everything is done in a low key, as if to keep the mythological at bay. The scene is domestic. The element of conflict and treachery is also local and personal.

The narrator dwells upon his hero's innocent stupidity, which makes him vulnerable to his first wife's tricks. Samson is clever at the contest of riddles, but he cannot win because she, the Philistine, bullies him into disclosing the answer (14. 15–18). The Philistine sovereignty over the tribes of Israel is the historical dimension which Samson does not understand at all. Nevertheless, he is being used by God in the ensuing skirmishes. Alienated from his wife and dispossessed, he avenges himself in gangster fashion. The destruction of the standing corn by setting the foxes' tails alight (15. 1–7) has its parallels outside Israelite tradition. It is a theme which entertains the public, for at a distance this cruel hooliganism sounds comical. Indeed, the whole of this episode is probably meant to appeal to (our?) sense of humour. But there is also a great seriousness in the advancement of the plot: 'Binding Samson' spells out the fearful threat. But Samson is not a Prometheus to be bound by a tyrannical Zeus. He himself will enmesh his freedom in cords. For the moment he retains his freedom by his strength, and this physical power is so immense, ecstatic, beyond control, that the narrator ascribes it to the Spirit.

The episodic nature of the narrative almost defeats a chronological understanding of the exploits. Heroes do not live according to the calendar, and in that respect Samson's career is heroic. Nevertheless, the careful reader must raise an eyebrow when he reads that Samson was a 'judge', and judged Israel for twenty years (Judges 16. 31). Even making allowances for the word to 'judge', and bestowing upon it the meaning 'deliver' in a martial sense, one hesitates to credit Samson with so much stability, for he is not a stable character. Could he be schizophrenic, as we say today? The man who dies for thirst and then receives water in an almost sacramental manner (15. 18–19) has little in common with the Samson who goes down to Gaza, sleeps with a harlot, frustrates his enemies, and carries the city gates on his shoulders to the top of the hill (16. 1–3). Now it seems that his brains are addled in inverse proportion to his gigantic strength. Delilah who entices him may, like Samson, evoke a mythological role, for her name is linked to the stem meaning *night*.[5] Thus the farcical love affair and the intrigue are being played out on two levels, between a potent man and a woman of many parts, and between two cosmic poles, namely of light and darkness. The narrator would fail in his task if he now turned didactic on such matters. The story, and the story alone, carries the centre of gravity. The build-up of tension is conventional enough. Samson mocks Delilah until after three times he discloses the secret of his strength: it is the Nazirite vow (16. 4–22). The hair is cut, the Lord has departed from the hero, and the Israelite gangster captain will not escape again. He is bound with fetters of brass. The humiliation of the strong man is the climax of the narrative. This blind man, who is enslaved by the enemy and must work for them, seems to end the heroic tale. He suffers for no good cause. Therein lies his significance, especially for the modern reader whose world is peopled with victims without a cause.

Samson's humiliation is reversed in death. Indeed, he only becomes a hero in the resolve to be avenged of the Philistines. The climax of the story discloses the 'suspension of the ethical', as Kierkegaard called it, and which, alas, Christians have tended to neglect for so long that they appear mealy mouthed and moralistic to the point of boredom.[6] The Samson narrative should always provide the antidote to this particular form of poison. The story teller remains wholly in control of the material and there is a complete absence of hysterical feeling. The blinded and defenceless hero is exposed to the final degree of degradation: 'Call Samson, that he may make sport for us' (16. 25). One enters the arena and hears the laughter which must greet the tumbling giant. All the notables are present to watch the circus. Three factors have escaped the jailors' eyes: their captive's hair has grown, he is almost a Nazirite (16. 22); the fool has conceived a plan, for he asks to feel the pillars to lean on them (16. 26); lastly, he offers a prayer for strength, he is God's man and instrument (16. 28). Thus he enters the world of heroism, for he offers his life freely (16. 29–31). Is this suicide? Is he to be condemned for his intention, which is one of total destruction, as far as it is in his power? What is to be our evaluation of such a senseless piece of slaughter, seeing that it produced no lasting effect? The true liberation from the Philistine oppression had to wait for the kind of social and political alignment which came to a head under Samuel, suffered a setback under Saul, and then triumphed under David. Samson is a hero in death, whose example can hardly be cited in realistic terms as progressive or useful. On the contrary, the tragic dimension of Samson must be found outside the world which we are pleased to think of as real.

Hence interpretation becomes part of the story. The heroic tale, more than any other, does not live in the past. What has been called the after-life of the story excels the actual content of it, analysed down to its bare bones, as to what 'really' happened, and how, and when, and where. The Samson story has indeed an earthiness, as we have seen, which removes it from mythology. However tempting the Sun-and-Night ingredient in the story, it does not offer archetypal themes directly, if only because the place names—Dan, Timnath, Lehi, En-hakkore, Zorah, Eshtaol—give a local colour to memories of 'real' events. But whatever the intention behind this local colour, the after-life ignores them and strict historical placing. It is, of course, Samson the ambiguous hero who casts his shadow into the future, and what he has become, and is still turning out to be, even in our own day, arrests our attention.

I am not concerned to give here a summary of the interpretation of the story throughout the ages. Needless to say the Jews looked upon Samson as a typical representative of their misfortunes and their persistent endurance, in which their enemies often perished alongside them. Strangely enough, the Old Testament provided here no precedent, for the story circulated in pre-exilic and in post-exilic Israel without comment. Even the great prophecies in Isaiah, of the child miraculously born, and of the Servant, chosen, beaten, humiliated and vindicated—either in or after death—do not overtly refer back to Samson. It is only in the post-Christian *midrashim* that he, in common with other outstanding personages is celebrated as superhuman, though it is stressed that he was not without unselfishness and blame when in prison. This unworthy leader of the tribe of Dan is nevertheless projected as an eschatological saviour figure; he is recompensed for one eye now, but it is in the future that his other eye will be paid for.[7]

The Christian *kerygma* has no place for Samson, for not only is he not part of the Messianic tradition, but also his character, which is neither that of lawgiver nor that of mystic or prophet, makes him quite unsuitable for a role similar to that of Moses, David, or Jeremiah. Moreover, his quite obvious Herculean traits, which were already noticed in antiquity, would hardly be welcome in an anti-pagan stance. However, the riches of Christian interpretation, which may sometimes be called wilful, were not averse to incorporating Samson as a pre-figuration of Jesus Christ. As we have already noted, the writer of the Epistle to the Hebrews had presented a whole range of the heroes of faith in the famous chapter 11. If Rahab the harlot is to be numbered as a member of the great cloud of witnesses, why should not Samson be included? The writer, who follows the Alexandrian tradition of typology, whose master was Philo, is daringly original in the tremendous sweep of figures before Christ. They have this in common, that they suffered, resisted the easier way of compromise, and altogether heroically endured the ordeals of temptation, tyranny and despair. Samson rightly belongs here also, because he is not so much an emblem of perfection as of a man to be made perfect through suffering. Here is an example of a foolish giant who fails and whose loss is his gain, for Grace crowns nature. The idealization is justified once he is seen as one of the precursors of Christ, who, like the contemporaries of the writer, suffer and 'look to Jesus' as the author and finisher of their faith.

Christian art developed the Samson theme in the course of its great iconographical growth. The fourth-century bas-relief in marble at Naples (Santa Restitute Chapel) blazes the trail. The manuscripts of the thirteenth, fourteenth and fifteenth centuries certainly glory in Samson as a forerunner of Christ. The sculptures celebrate in him the victor who breaks the jaws of hell.

It would go beyond the scope of our investigation to dwell upon the amazing inspiration which lies behind the Samson motif in painters like Mantegna, Rubens and van Dyck. But, while ignoring the modern return to the theme, no one can withhold admiration from, and deep spiritual responses to, Rembrandt's miraculous portraitures in Dresden and Berlin. The texts which are here eternalized are Judges 14. 10 ('And his father went down to the woman, and Samson made a feast there; for so the young men used to do'), and Samson's encounter with his father-in-law. Thus from beginning to end the story of Samson enshrines the human pilgrimage, the external events symbolizing the internal struggles.

This spiritual dialectic enters our Western literary heritage. Hans Sachs, the poet of Wagner's Meistersingers, wrote a tragedy called

Samson, and there were many plays depicting these events on a popular level. But it is during the Reformation and afterwards in the struggle against Rome that Protestant writers see themselves mirrored in Samson. Rowley and Jewby are now largely forgotten,[8] but Milton's *Samson Agonistes* bestows the classical stamp on the interpretation of Samson as the Christian protagonist of freedom against tyranny. This work rounds off the most remarkable career of a genius, who was at the same time a supporter of revolution, regicide, English patriotism, strength, and expansion, and possibly a sympathizer even with that underground ('third') culture, which included all sorts of anti-orthodox fanatics, pacifists, utopians and the like. Samson Agonistes becomes a universal testament for defeated militants. Though personal to the point of the victim's real blindness, Milton's affliction is projected through this tragedy into the realm of the modern quest: how is it that God forsakes his servants, and what is to be expected from the unshakeable stand for truth?

The strangeness of Samson's new life in European culture, which can best be gauged by listening to Handel's oratorio, can hardly be exaggerated and helps us to understand a great deal of the after-life and inherent vigour of the biblical narrative. One can easily grasp the heroic in the Davidic tradition, especially if the slain Goliath lies at the feet of the young idealized warrior. But Samson is not young. The pathos of the narrative, now in European languages and therefore somewhat removed from the original, centres in the peculiar destiny with which we begin to identify. In some respects Milton's tragedy can never be surpassed, although it must be said that it is hardly ever performed (except on radio). There is an undeniable monotony of style, and even the few departures from the original narrative are not sufficiently interesting to hold our attention. As to the monotony it seems that we, the hearers, have lost the necessary sensitivity, for in his foreward Milton deliberately draws attention to the measure of the verse as 'of all sorts'. The ancient rule of the unity of space and time reminds us of the formality of Racine rather than the freedom of Shakespeare.

The Argument makes it clear from the start that Milton pursues a special aim, but what this is remains in dispute. According to Hill we have here the defiant answer of one defeated politically and staking out a new hope, a glorious hope, a utopian escape from the consequences of the Restoration in 1660.[9] Others espy something resembling Christian resignation, which, of course, is not a negative emotion, as Hill wrongly supposes. The fall of the hero is the central theme, whatever one's sentiments: 'The Sun to me is dark and silent as the Moon. . . .' (lines 86–7). Milton surely does not spare himself and may be called penitent: 'My self, my Sepulcher, a moving Grave, Buried. . . .' (102–3). Slowly he works his way to the recognition that he is his own affliction, as the Chorus prepares us: 'Can this be he, That Heroic, That Renowned, Irresistable Samson?' (124–6).

The danger is self-pity. A survey of the glorious past can bring new temptations, for the 'might have been' is too awful to contemplate. But the heroic is precisely reborn in the sober recognition of things as they really are. Even the horrors of humiliation recede when the victim sees himself as 'a foolish Pilot' who has shipwrecked the vessel entrusted to him from above. Fools and folly! Key words to articulate the moral torpor which yields to flattery and intoxication. Milton knows that the inspired is abnormally vulnerable. Otherwise how account for Dalila ('that specious monster') and the ease with which she turns his inner fortifications? The absurdity of the tale agrees with the madness of men. We are not reasonable, least of all the inspired hero, but 'just are the ways of God, and justifiable to men' (293–4), once they know God and his laws.

Manoa's visit to his son exposes all the pitfalls of the human condition. It is always the same: 'Might have been'. Too late the understanding dawns, and there can be no escape from the consequences. The hero cannot be ransomed, for he has sold himself: 'Spare that proposal, Father, spare the trouble. . . .' (487). Penitence and pardon look more promising, but what is to be done? 'My hopes all flat' (595) pleads the slave, in the suicidal mood. There is no remedy, only speedy death. The Chorus, however, alters the mood with the tremendous: 'God of our Fathers, what is man!' (667).

The saving action lies in a kind of replay, which is not in the biblical narrative. Once again Delilah approaches, in a light-hearted 'forgive-and-forget' mood, with a sincere desire to make amends, as it seems. But now the hero falls no more into the trap of appearances. He is, as she finds out, implacable, even though 'beauty, though injurious, hath strange power' (1003). Samson has killed the pleasure principle, the vain desire for gratification. He is ready to meet the real enemy.

The giant Harapha of Gath follows Delilah. He disdains combat with the blinded prisoner, who now has matured, knows no spells, uses no forbidden arts. Samson has become the protagonist of the true God, albeit in his humiliated state. The Chorus fear the giant's 'malicious counsel', but Samson need no longer fear: the worst, namely death, is no longer the worst, but the best. This is the 'invincible might' of the spirit against which tyrannic power rages in vain, and the Chorus expresses our deep-seated faith: 'Oh how comely it is and how reviving to the Spirits of just men long oppresst!' (1268–9). Patience is needed to see the outcome, as Samson is bidden to the great Feast, where 'gymnic artists, wrestlers, riders, runners, jugglers, and dancers' engage in their antics (1324–5), and the man of God is to add a spice of amusement. But the spurned invitation induces in Samson 'something extraordinary', rousing motions of freedom. Now the Spirit which rushed on him will be efficacious, and while the father touchingly endeavours to work for the son's freedom by paying the ransom, the great deed is done and now reported—'evil news rides post, while good news baits' (1538). Is it good news, or bad? All the sons of Gaza are fallen, overwhelmed in a moment, but Samson is dead. Now death has paid the ransom, and though it looks like suicide, destroying and destroyed, the final act must not be interpreted thus. When he tugged and shook and pulled down the same destruction on himself it was a dearly bought revenge, but it was also the vindication of truth: 'virtue given for lost, depressed and overthrown' (1697–8) has risen like a phoenix from the ashes.

The hero is dead, but leaves no years of mourning: 'No time for lamentation now!' The father intones no dirge but rejoices that Samson has quit himself like Samson. Never has the tongue of poet more gloriously created the voice of Christian triumphalism: 'Nothing is here for tears, nothing to wail' (1721). He frees heroics from hysteria; peace, consolation, and calm of mind seal the exaltation.

The era of European expansion could easily feed on the heroic style of Milton, Corneille, Racine and Schiller. But never could it free the idealism of the Samson tradition from the military abuse of the figure of the hero. In the endless wars soldiers and sailors were naturally expected to behave like heroes or, when dead, were placed on the pedestal of heroism. There is something infinitely touching about the young who die in battle, and the Horatian sentiment *Dulce et decorum est pro patria mori* becomes inseparable from the biblical tradition. This secularization of Samson means that he is a hero in his own right, and not a reflection or representative of the Lord, the true *Gibbor*. The Romantic imagination gave the figure a new twist. In German poetry we have the conventional picture of the fallen rider, dying in the field of battle, clasping the flag which he defends to the last, watched over sadly by his horse, while the sun sets in the west. It must be remembered that such scenes were not as sentimental as they appear to us. There really were camps or bivouacs, with fires at night, and bugle calls in the evening and in the morning. Goethe, by no means a sentimentalist, gives a description of the campaigns in France when the revolutionary armies proved irresistible and soon, under Napoleon, swept east and south over Europe. But it is precisely in the 1790s that heroism may first be said to breathe its last, for the new battle tactics and use of explosives terminate the significance of the individual officer and his men. From now on the horse is more likely to be killed before its rider, and even if the conventional picture lasts into the twentieth century, perhaps for purposes of propaganda, it is known not to be true. A great disenchantment comes over the Romantics: 'Where are the heroes now?' asks Hölderlin. What has become of the sacred rites? The eagle is captured.

The hero's passing may perhaps still be seen in the light of Samson, whose death is greater than his life, and who reaches the dimension of the classical apotheosis through his resolution to die. Before the heroic age closes, Beethoven gives lasting expression to the aspiration of a new heroism, a kind of idealism which deliberately eschews military pomp and nationalistic arrogance. The *Eroica* of 1803 belongs to the full flow of Napoleonic imperialism and the resultant disenchantment which put an end to the Storm-and-Stress (*Sturm und Drang*) enthusiasm of the preceding decades. As Wordsworth distanced himself from the events in Paris, and as Hölderlin parted company with the adulation of warriors and the revolutionary armies, so Beethoven withdrew the original dedication to Napoleon, for he who had been expected to bring freedom had made himself Emperor. Thus the symphony was dedicated to an unknown hero, perhaps the composer himself and those, who like him, would probe beneath the veneer of heroic attitudes to find the true hero, the unique One. Hölderlin called the Christ the brother of Heracles and Dionysus, for the Christ ends the counterfeit which mocks heroism.

Music cannot be interpreted narrowly as a text, but undeniably Beethoven conceives of the hero as having died in a supreme battle of the spirit. Handel had already set the pattern with the Dead March in *Saul*, and now Beethoven gives funereal grandeur to the hero on his way to eternity. The hero has nothing in common with the flag-waving and swash-buckling officer, but his true colours derive from a nobility of character and a moral determination. Perhaps the ideal is set too high, for it leaves out the human fallibility which the Samson story enshrines. Beethoven's hero could never play the trick of the foxes' tails.

Until the outbreak of the First World War the image of the hero remains alive. It is impossible to evaluate its strength in daily life and among ordinary people. Nowadays the tendency prevails to belittle the force of self-sacrifice in public life. Certainly the literature of the nineteenth century discloses a critical attitude towards official hero worship. Tolstoy's pacifism expresses notions about war which leave little room to the Samson-Christ figure on the battle field. Precisely because Tolstoy was a soldier and experienced the beginnings of modern warfare, his realistic portrayal of army leaders, officers and men de-romanticizes the hollow and blown-up idol of the hero. The Czar and the generals, no less than the ordinary soldiers, have no illusions about losses, wounds, gangrene, amputations and death. Yet at the same time Tolstoy not only allows his chief character, Prince Andrei, to retain a nimbus of greatness, but also demonstrates that after his hero's death, in peace time, life is boring and altogether questionable. The dashing young Pietra's self-oblation seems more worthwhile than the lingering prolongation of existence. Tolstoy, almost in spite of himself, states the problem of heroism.

But war is not the only place fit for heroic action. The missionary movement of the Christian Churches in the nineteenth century afforded countless examples of self-giving. A glance at memorial tablets shows how many of the young idealists gave their lives in the swamps of India and elsewhere. They were neither imperialists nor Samsons, for nothing could have been further from their intentions than to bring the roof down over the enemy. Their goal, perhaps mistakenly, was to raise a roof over impoverished friends. A tragic awareness can dominate only a fighter against the Philistines, and these missionaries did not wish to kill the Philistines of their day, if the word may be stretched to mean what the modern term implies. Just as Samson is not what Samson once was, so the enemies of Samson have also changed beyond recognition.

Yet, despite the enormous social and technical upheavals of the industrial societies, the heroic tradition, whether Christian or secular, or both, by no means died in Europe. The Civil War in America could have ended it, for never was up till then so much blood shed for so much profit and unscrupulous profiteering. Shaw certainly imported into England a healthy scepticism about war and exploitation. Without total cynicism his Major Barbara, for example, lay bare the comic and tragic interactions of idealism and materialism. Chivalry, bravery, and moral excellence could hardly survive the tone of the Edwardian era in England. More important, Socialist ideology exposed bourgeois heroism as unfit for the masses and condemned especially military action as in any way virtuous. If heroic action was called for, it had to be in the interest of class warfare. But men do not live by ideology alone, and the instinct for hero worship remained alive.

When the trumpets and drums proclaimed in 1914 the outbreak of war they met with a ready response among the youthful volunteers. After years of peace, maintained by skilful diplomacy, so that crisis after crisis had been resolved by compromise, the murder of the Archduke Ferdinand in Sarajevo had triggered off the inevitable cataclysm. The house of European security collapsed like the proverbial house of cards, and the young men responded to the call of duty and sacrifice. One has to rely upon individual witnesses to portray the scene and comprehend it in all its strangeness. Carl Zuckmayer, for example, in his perfect autobiography[10] fills in all the details of an incredible complex of emotions, ambitions, inhibitions and intellectual sophistication. It is a mistake to assume that these youths in their last year at school did not know what they were letting themselves in for, although they could not, any more than their elders, anticipate the nature of the mass slaughter.

August 1914[11] saw the revival of the Samson psyche on a vast and international scale. These young men, often driven on by their sweethearts, longed for freedom, though they had it in good measure. They had a romantic inner propulsion, which eschewed fear. At the same time, they had hidden motives and actions, especially in brothels, which gave a negative impetus to be away and out of it all. Their generosity knew no bounds, for they really wanted to serve their country. They were political animals in an only very restricted sense, and easily persuaded that they were fighting for their king or in a sacred cause. Hence they also released in themselves a religious sentiment which had already died in the Western world. Even the young who had imbibed some Socialist conviction and were dedicated to a pacifistic rule of life could not help responding to the call to arms. The flags fluttered in the breeze, the drums sounded, the men marched, and the forming solidarity in death was set in motion.

Many writers, including Zuckmayer, have shown how soon disillusionment set in. Once arrived in the front line, after tedious training under repulsive NCOs, these babies had to become men. The professionals were sometimes kind to them, but more often gruff and cynical. Thus even before the guns fired and decimated the ranks of the newly arrived volunteers they had suffered a spiritual shock from which they could not recover again. There were no heroes, no bloody heroes, and if you wanted to be one you were a crazy idiot. The vast literature about the war depicts this collapse of the mental strife. Yet, curiously enough, it also bears witness to the astounding deeds of self-sacrifice, of Samson-like actions, which occurred despite machine-guns and later tanks and gas. Passchendaele, the Somme, Vimy, Verdun remain names associated for ever with a tragedy which recalls some ancient qualities.

They survived the war, despite the onslaught of anti-heroism. I belong to a generation which still remembers war memorials, religious services of remembrance, armistice days, the sounding of the last post. For a boy these ceremonies conveyed a deep stratum of spiritual reality. The fallen were in death like Samson. Yet as one grew up one perceived the ambiguity of the stuff, and no one helped one to a clearer approach than Shakespeare. A comparison between *Henry V* and *Henry IV* developed a mature dialectic. These plays gave one distance from the confusing documentation in newspapers. On the one hand, there is the hero, the one of the few, who chooses to fight, who regards this hour as memorable, who places his trust in being remembered by future generations, who leads in the name of God and for God's cause, who embodies the true pathos of sacrifice; and on the other, there is the sick world of blunted enterprises, of treacheries and plots, and the bloated face of a Falstaff leading a platoon of nobodies into a useless battle in order to make money, to buy drink and harlots. What is honour, and what is valour, if Falstaff be our guide?

This double approach is already implicit, I think, in the Samson narrative, just because the hero is also the anti-hero among the mob. Samson becomes Samson, and Prince Hal becomes Henry V. But the years between the wars did not support this theme. On the one hand, Brechtian alienation mocked at the whole concept and revived only a Falstaffian mode, and on the other, political extremists continued to foster their own brand of military and totalitarian heroism. Thus heroes of the Soviet Union were made while millions were enslaved by their despots, and the Hitler war machine spun again the web of war romanticism, as if the trenches and flame-throwers were the sacraments of sacrifice 'pro patria'.

This chapter in our history is far from finished. Orwell held that 'in the face of pain there are no heroes'[12] after what he had seen during the Spanish Civil War, but human beings have to surmount, as he did himself, the 'miserable machine—heroically, one must force it on'.[13] The Second World War has left a legacy of total enslavement and destruction as well as of unprecedented individual heroism, and the post-war literature abounds with examples of both the self-seeking swine and the born hero.[14] This radical confrontation has become a stereotype in films and fictional narrative. Such cheapening or vulgarization seems to have come to stay, but it does not really provide a guide to reality.

We are left with the ambivalence of the Samson story, both in our individual experience and as a political fact. As individuals we play with total self-sacrifice, with desperate remedies in frustration, with a religious dedication to our ideal, and yet we endeavour to secure pleasure and gratification of the senses. But when the crisis of life demands it, the true Samson in us prevails, if all goes well. In public life the issues are far more complex, for the Samson may be drawn upon for terrible purposes of destruction. The Nazi holocaust is a warning against a sacrificial interpretation of useless suffering, but it also utters a voice from the past which declares that so much evil can only be met with by a total readiness to give a life for life. In the present the threat continues, for it seems that our whole history moves inexorably to a clash of wills, in which those liable to be defeated will use the ultimate weapon, and, like Samson, destroy themselves to destroy the enemy. Thus strength and weakness still meet in the final denouement, when the roof falls in. The ultimate question, then, concerns Samson's identity and whether he can still be thought of in terms of Christ, the Cross, and the Christian hope.

The biblical narrative has therefore not spent its power yet. It not only engages the reader and brings deep and dormant feelings to the surface, and vitalizes a spirit of penitence in adversity and generosity as the occasion affords it, but it also confronts him with the necessity of taking sides in an interminable conflict between right and wrong. The Samson story is wrongly understood if it throws a blanket of indifferentism over all suicide pilots or bomb-carrying terrorists. Rather, its abiding theme is the propriety of violence and the ultimate justification of self-sacrifice. The young fighter pilots of England, who were 'the few', rose to the sky in the true spirit which they inherited from the Bible, Shakespeare and Milton. Without that brand of godly heroism a race is doomed.

Notes

1 L. Raglan (1936), *The Hero; a study in Tradition, Myth and Drama*, London.
2 The Epic of Gilgamesh is a far better introduction to the subject than any analytical

summary. See N. K. Sandars (1972), *The Epic of Gilgamesh. An English version with an Introduction*, Harmondsworth, and J. Campbell (1949), *The Hero with a Thousand Faces*, New York.

3 See C. Gordon (1962), *Before the Bible: the Common Background of Greek and Hebrew Civilizations*, London, where the connections between Homer and the older parts of the Old Testament are examined.

4 See M. Alexiou and P. Dronke (1971), 'The Lament of Jephta's daughter: themes, traditions, originality', in *Studie Medievali* 3rd series No. 12, pp. 819–63.

5 Some commentators derive Delilah's name from a root which suggests she was a hierodule. See C. F. Burney (1918), *The Book of Judges with Introduction and Notes*, London, p. 407; and J. Gray (1967), *Joshua, Judges and Ruth* (New Century Bible), London, pp. 356–7.

6 See C. Hill (1977), *Milton and the English Revolution*, London, p. 442.

7 See *Genesis Rabbah* (the post-biblical *Great Midrash*) 66. 3.

8 Rowley and Jewby wrote a tragedy, *Sam(p)son*, in 1602.

9 C. Hill (1977), *op. cit.*

10 C. Zuckmayer (1970): *Part of My Life*, London.

11 See A. Solzhenitsyn (1972), *August 1914*, London.

12 G. Orwell (1954), *Nineteen Eighty-Four*, Harmondsworth, p. 192.

13 Virginia Woolf (1938), *To the Lighthouse*, London, p. 224.

14 For example, H. Lee (1974), *To Kill a Mocking Bird*, London, p. 45.

PART V

PARABLE AND ALLEGORY

The Rabbinic parables are clear clues to the disposition of the Rabbinic mind toward concreteness, rather than to the abstractions such as marked Greek thought.
S. Sandmel, in *Judaism and Christian Beginnings*, Oxford 1978, p. 106)

> The sower went forth sowing,
> The seed in secret slept. . . .

(W. St. Hill Bourne, from No. 486 in *Hymns Ancient and Modern Revised* London 1950)

10 ORIGINS OF MARK'S PARABLES

John Drury

The Anti-Allegorical Approach and its Faults

MODERN exegesis of the gospel parables show that a scholarly way of reading a set of texts can dominate in spite of being subjected to continuous scholarly objection. Students are referred to C. H. Dodd's *The Parables of the Kingdom*[1] and J. Jeremias's *The Parables of Jesus*.[2] There they learn that Jesus's parables were realistic, simple and, above all, free of allegory. It is no great difficulty that they are often not like that in the only texts of them we have. The techniques of restoration are confidently called in to peel off anything that does not fit the bill and attribute it to the theological over-painting of the early Church. That was where the allegorizing was done. This view goes back to A. Jülicher's *Die Gleichnisreden Jesu* of 1899–1910 with its insistence that a parable has only one point of comparison and no more. It has had the rare triumph of calling the tune, not only in the faculties but in the pulpit too.

But it has been doubted from the start and continuously, particularly by learned men trying to understand Mark's gospel. Wellhausen's *Das Evangelium Marci* of 1903 took up the cudgels promptly. This prince of Old Testament scholars observed that *mashal*, the Hebrew parable, makes no distinction between simile, proverb, parable and allegory. So the kind of sharp distinction drawn by Jülicher is wrong:

> Admittedly it is correct that the semitic parable very often hits off and illuminates only one point, while everything else is left *hors de comparaison* and in the dark. But it can make a comparison of several points and correspond to allegory or come near to it. One should not treat all alike, but rather adjust oneself to the individual instance. Only the protest against Philo and his followers is justified, finding allegory everywhere; and so the possibility of a double sense, natural and 'higher'. But we have got well beyond that.[3]

Paul Fiebig transcribed that bit of Wellhausen at the beginning of his *Altjüdische Gleichnisse und die Gleichnisse Jesu* of 1904, the first of his counterblasts to Jülicher from the stand-point of early rabbinic parables which likewise refuse to submit to Jülicher's procrustean method. He rejoices that the great orientalist confirmed what he had found in the Mekilta[4] and was only sorry that he had read it when his book was already at the printer's. Since then similar objections have been raised by Sanday,[5] Michaelis,[6] Benoit,[7] Hermaniuk,[8] Black,[9] Nineham,[10] Moule,[11] Goulder,[12] R. E. Brown,[13] the present author and Derrett[15]—by no means a roll-call of a party or national tradition or a comprehensive list. Time and again the Jülicher tradition, inherited and refined by Dodd and Jeremias, has been found too blunt and heavy for the delicate tasks of practical criticism, especially for the parables in Mark. Yet still it holds the fort. Why? The following reasons suggest themselves and have a general interest beyond this particular study:

1   The allegorical approach to Jesus's parables, like the British Empire, paid the penalty for dominating too successfully and too long. From the earliest Christian beginnings through the fathers to its last flowering in Archbishop Trench's *Notes on the Parables of Our Lord* it held sway, developing its complications inevitably and virtually unchallenged. Boredom with established ways of working is a strong and positive motive in all kinds of inquiry, including the literary and theological. Exasperation with truths not plain or literal is another. The two combined to unseat the age-old tradition that the parables of Jesus were allegories to be allegorically explored. They can be seen at work together in the first pages of Dodd's book. He quotes St Augustine's interpretation of the Good Samaritan in which the traveller is Adam, the thieves are devils, the priest and Levite are the Old Testament, the Samaritan is Christ, the inn is the Church and so on—and on. This sort of stuff, Dodd observes, prevailed until Trench and 'is still to be heard in sermons' (times have changed—to his advantage) but 'to the ordinary person of intelligence who approaches the Gospels with some sense for literature this mystification must appear quite perverse'. Help is at hand. Jülicher is invoked and his thesis approved 'that the parables in general do not admit of this method at all, and that the attempts of the evangelists themselves to apply it rest on a misunderstanding'.
2   Dodd's almost overwhelming success in the New Testament studies of his day was founded on the marriage of two qualities. He was a great scholar who wrote with clear elegance. He was a saintly and beloved churchman who did not lose sight of contemporary congregations and their preachers. Both came into play with his concept of 'realised eschatology'. Schweitzer had troubled scholarly and ecclesiastical waters with his picture of Jesus as a disappointed, passionate, apocalyptic preacher—the exponent of a 'thorough-going eschatology'[16] which staked all on an immediate end of the world. In comforting reaction Dodd portrayed one who preached the Kingdom of God present here and now in the continuing life of every day. John's subsuming of the End under the Eternal Now was imposed on Matthew, Mark and Luke. And the relief for preachers struggling to interpret the gospels was immense. Realised eschatology has since been qualified out of recognition, but it is organically connected to Dodd's exegesis of the parables which has not. Its combination of scholarship and usefulness (who wants to preach to allegorical, even apocalyptic, parables nowadays?) serves to keep it going. The gap between the study and the pew is bridged, but at the cost of blurring the gap between the first century and the twentieth.

3   The opposition has made nearly all its protests in essays, reviews and commentaries. There have been books, but Fiebig's have not been reprinted or translated; and Hermaniuk's fails, after a long and learned run-up, to get convincingly and thoroughly down to business in the gospels themselves. Written in 1947, it also failed to take account of Dodd's book (1935), which was culpable, and coincided with the first edition of Jeremias's, which was unfortunate. These practical facts of publishing matter a lot in the formation of ways of reading. One trouble with remarks made in essays, reviews and commentaries is that they have to be dug out of well-stocked libraries with a certain amount of persistence and footwork. Another is that they do not cope with the whole field and so oppose the grand strategy of Dodd and Jeremias with a more-or-less disjointed series of tactical raids.

But still, another such raid is worth making. There could be a cumulative effect and, more important, the protests have truth which could be more readily recognized by people who work in literature at large than within the specialised shop of New Testament Studies. If they have fallen for procrustean critical methods energized by reforming pastoral zeal in their own subjects (for example, for F. D. Leavis and his canon), they are likely to view them more coolly elsewhere. Nor are they likely to share the embarrassment and intolerance about allegory, though as recently as 1969 Northrop Frye had to remind them of the difference between 'debased' and 'genuine' allegory.[17] The way forward is historical—a point on which New Testament scholars and literary critics can agree. Negatively, it corrects the infection of one age with the standards and preferences of another. One century's obfuscation can be another's revelation: 'A Jesus who spoke exclusively in what moderns define as parable is a nineteenth century critical creation'.[18] Positively it reconstructs a moment in time past so that, however strange or apparently useless to present needs, it can be appreciated for its own sake and 'let be' in both senses of the phrase. St Mark's gospel, which is likely to be the earliest of the four, shows Jesus speaking in parables which are not 'what moderns define as parable'. So the usual procedure has been to chip away at them until they are—and become the sort of realistic, one-point illustrations or stories that are preferred. It does not work.[19] The parables in Mark are, briefly and clumsily put, historical allegories mixing concealment and revelation in the sort of riddling symbolism which is an ingredient of apocalyptic. The aim of this essay is to show that as such they fell plumb in the centre of what was called 'parable' at the time. The method is to trace the living tradition of such a literary (not excluding oral) form from the Old Testament, through inter-testamental literature, to Mark's Jesus. It will fall short of demonstrating that Jesus himself spoke these parables *verbatim*. But it will show that he formally could have done and that, in any case and above all, there is no call to cram them into a modern category of parable.

They have their own function and existence, and it is historically understandable.

The Old Testament Mashal—A Survey

The word *parable* translates *mashal* in the Hebrew Old Testament and *parabolē* in its Greek translation of the second century BC, the Septuagint. The Septuagint translators were consistent and careful in translating *mashal* as *parabolē* in all but fifteen instances which individually and together make no real difference.[20] That is to say that the Greek translators assented to the range and nuances of *mashal* in their Hebrews texts. Subsequent English translators usually have not. In the following categorization of the range I have adapted the Revised Version by always putting 'parable' for *mashal* (or, for Ecclesiasticus which is in Greek, for *parabolē*).

1   *A popular saying or commonplace* as at Ezekiel 12. 22f. 'What is this parable that ye have in the land of Israel, saying, The days are prolonged and every vision faileth'. At I Samuel 24. 13 David refers to a parable 'of the ancients, Out of the wicked cometh forth wickedness' and there are many such old sayings in the Book of Proverbs.

2   *A popular saying in figurative or comparative form* as at I Samuel 10. 12 'it became a parable, is Saul also among the prophets?' and at Ezekiel 18. 2ff. 'ye use this parable concerning the land of Israel, saying "the fathers have eaten sour grapes and the children's teeth are set on edge"'. Again, the Book of Proverbs has many examples.

3   *A wise saying*, not popular but belonging to the intellectual elite, which Eissfeldt calls *Kunstspruch*.[21] It has a riddling character which makes it hard to understand. At Proverbs 1. 6 the aim of the wise man is 'to understand a parable and a figure; the words of the wise and their dark sayings' and at Ecclesiasticus 39. 2 it is to 'enter in amidst the subtleties of parables. He will seek out the hidden meanings of proverbs, and be conversant in the riddles of parables'. The most majestic example is the perplexingly intricate allegorical parable of current history in Ezekiel 17. Israel is a cedar tree, its princes a seed which becomes a vine and the two eagles are the kings of Babylon and Egypt. Its impassioned absurdity is best called surrealism, which at least rings a warning bell for those set on realistic parables. Because it is a key passage which will be referred to again it is set out here:

And the word of the Lord came unto me, saying, Son of man, put forth a riddle, and speak a parable unto the house of Israel; and say, Thus saith the Lord God: a great eagle with great wings and long pinions, full of feathers, which had divers colours, came unto Lebanon, and took the top of the cedar: he cropped off the topmost of the young twigs thereof, and carried it into a land of traffic; he set it in a city of merchants. He took also of the seed of the land and planted it in a fruitful soil; he placed it beside many waters; he set it as a willow tree. And it grew, and became a spreading vine of low stature, whose branches turned toward him, and the roots thereof were under him: so it became a vine, and brought forth branches, and shot forth sprigs. There was also another great eagle with great wings and many feathers: and, behold, this vine did bend its roots toward him, and shot forth its branches toward him, from the beds of its plantation, that he might water it. It was planted in a good soil by many waters, that it might bring forth branches, and that it might bear fruit, that it might be a goodly vine. Say thou, Thus saith the Lord God: Shall it prosper? shall he not pull up the roots thereof, and cut off the fruit thereof, that it may wither; that all its fresh springing leaves may wither; even without great power or much people to pluck it up by the roots thereof? Yea, behold, being planted, shall it prosper? shall it not utterly wither, when the east wind touches it? it shall wither in the beds where it grew.

Moreover the word of the Lord came unto me, saying, Say now to the rebellious house, Know ye not what these things mean? tell them, Behold, the king of Babylon came to Jerusalem, and took the king thereof, and the princes thereof, and brought them to him to Babylon; and he took of the seed royal, and made a covenant with him; he also brought him under an oath, and took away the mighty of the land: that the kingdom might be base, that it might not lift itself up, but that by keeping of his covenant it might stand. But he rebelled against him in sending his ambassadors into Egypt, that they might give him horses and much people. Shall he prosper? shall he escape that doeth such things? shall he break the covenant, and yet escape? As I live, saith the Lord God, surely in the place where the king dwelleth that made him king, whose oath he despised, and whose covenant he brake, even with him in the midst of Babylon he shall die. Neither shall Pharaoh with his mighty army and great company make for him in the war, when they cast up mounts and build forts, to cut off many persons. For he hath despised the oath, breaking the covenant; and behold, he had given his hand, and yet hath done all these things; he shall not escape. Therefore thus saith the Lord God: as I live, surely mine oath that he hath despised, and my covenant that he hath broke, I will even bring it upon his own head. And I will spread my net upon him, and he shall be taken in my snare, and I will bring him to Babylon, and will plead with him there for his trespass that he hath trespassed against me. And all his fugitives in all his bands shall fall by the sword, and they that remain shall be scattered toward every wind: and ye shall know that I the Lord have spoken it.

Thus saith the Lord God: I will also take of the lofty top of the cedar, and will set it; I will crop off from the topmost of his young twigs a tender one, and I will plant it upon an high mountain and eminent: in the mountain of the height of Israel will I plant it: and it shall bring forth boughs, and bear fruit, and be a goodly cedar: and under it shall dwell all fowl of every wing; in the shadow of the branches thereof shall they dwell. And all the trees of the field shall know that I the Lord have brought down the high tree, have exalted the low tree, have dried up the green tree, and have made the dry tree to flourish: I the Lord have spoken and have done it.

This and other examples from the same book (for example, Jerusalem as a rusty cooking pot at 24. 1–14 and God's wrath as a forest fire at 20. 45–8) give force to the complaint of the prophet's hearers at 20. 49 'Ah Lord God! They say of me, is he not a speaker of parables?' meaning that which is barely, if at all, intelligible.

4 *A song of derision or taunting*, as at Isaiah 14. 4–23 when it is against Babylon, at Habakkuk 2. 6–8 against 'the Chaldeans', and at Micah 2. 4 against internal oppressors. Each is aimed into the historical future and the first is the most elaborately picturesque.

5 *A byword*, where the parable is not applied to the intermediate literary form but directly to the people or person in trouble, or about to be—and so 'become a parable'. Examples are at Deuteronomy 28. 37, I Kings 9. 7, Jeremiah 24. 9, Psalms 44. 14, Psalms 69. 11, II Chronicles 7.

20, Wisdom 5. 3 and Tobit 3. 4. Some are in the past, one (Psalm 44) in the present, and the rest in the future.

6   *An instructive discourse*, two examples of which are in the Book of Job, at 27. 1 and 29. 1. The second is an apologia.

7   *A prophetic oracle*, as at Numbers 23. 7 and 18, 24. 3, 15, 20, 21 and 23 where Balaam's oracles of Israel's future destiny are introduced with the formula 'he took up his parable, and said. . . .'

Fortunately it is not necessary for present purposes to arrange these categories in historical sequence. Eissfeldt offers such an arrangement[22] but it is very questionable: popular sayings, for instance, do not necessarily precede the harder 'wise' sayings of the elite which, vice versa, often subsequently find their way into common currency. These categories even impose an inappropriate clarity on the usage of the word because they conceal connections. The popular saying is obviously a brother of a figurative popular saying which in turn is related to the more elaborate figurative complexities of the *Kunstspruch* or wise saying described above. And this, because it is prophetic, has affinity with the prophetic songs of derision (see 4 above) and the prophetic oracles in 7 above. The byword (see 5) links with the taunt because of its connotation of jeering, and with the figurative popular saying (as in 2) because in both the people concerned are a *locus classicus* or ordinary point of comparison, whether of extraordinary behaviour (Saul among the prophets) or of God-forsakenness (the examples in 5).

To complicate things further before we select and clarify, it must be said that confining attention to instances which happen to be consciously labelled 'parable' gives firm ground for starting out but leaves out too much. There are, for instance, many more instructive discourses and prophetic oracles in the Old Testament than those noted above (in 6 and 7). Much more important to the point of this essay are some Old Testament forms which connect to Ezekiel 17 and 15.[23] These are:

1   *Prophetic utterances done figuratively and allegorically like Ezekiel's.* Nathan the prophet in II Samuel 12. 1–15 set a famous mousetrap for King David. He presented him with his own adultery and murder under the disguise of a story about a rich man who robbed a poor man of his pet lamb to feed an unexpected guest. The trap shut with 'thou art the man'. Isaiah, at 5. 1–7, lulled his audience with a love song about a vineyard gone wild, then let out that the well-beloved owner was God and the vineyard Israel. The same stock-figure of the vine is used in Ezekiel 15 and 17. The Book of Hosea begins with the prophet's own marriage to a whore being teased out in three chapters into an allegory of God's alliance with Israel. It is interesting as an allegory fastened to actuality, what the Germans call a *Symbolhandlung* or symbolic happening, and because Ezekiel picks it up again in his chapters 16 (Israel's

career as a whore's progress) and 23 (Jerusalem and Samaria as international whores).

2 *Riddles*. These are put with parables, virtually as synonyms, by Ecclesiasticus at 39.3 and at 47.15 where Solomon is said to have filled the earth with 'parables of riddles'. Samson's riddle about honey in a dead lion at Judges 14.14 is the classic example. Konrad von Rabenau[24] has argued cogently for the influence of this popular form on Ezekiel 17 and 15. There is the posing of it: 'a great eagle . . . came unto Lebanon', 'what is the vine tree more than any tree?' There are the paradoxical absurdities and pointed questions begging an answer. 'shall it prosper? shall he not pull up the roots thereof?', 'Is it profitable for any work?' There are, finally, the ominously negative answers to these questions: 'it shall wither', 'the fire shall devour them'.

3 *Fables*. David Daube[25] has claimed a place for fables 'within the wider category of parable, an account of one thing or event throwing light on another'. There are two undoubted fables in the Old Testament. At Judges 9. 7-15 Jotham satirizes the coronation of Abimelech with a fable about the trees choosing a king. None of the fruit trees wants to forsake its happily productive existence, so the crown goes to the bramble. At II Kings 14. 9 Jehoash king of Israel brushes off overtures from Amaziah king of Judah although the latter has just had a successful campaign against Edom. He uses a fable. The thistle asked the cedar for his daughter's hand in marriage for his son, but a wild beast came by and trod down the thistle. Amaziah should know his station, go home and stay there. Daube excludes the parable at Ezekiel 17 from the fold of fable because it distorts nature too violently—a surprising judgement after all these talking trees. Some affinity is certain in any case. Like the two classic fables, Ezekiel 17 is firmly set in a particular historical crisis and presents it enigmatically by beasts and plants. Again we have to notice that our labelling is artificial. Fables riddle, and prophetic utterances tease fabulously. But it is time to stop labouring that, though the incongruence of the chaotic richness of popular forms with nice critical discrimination is a worthwhile lesson. It is time to select and get some order.

The Major Features of the Parabolic Form

The range of the Old Testament parable is so ramifyingly extensive that to put it briefly only something as vague as 'striking saying' will do. Two major features can, however, be extracted from it. They do not define parable. But they do justice to major features of its major expressions. They are important in themselves and for the development to Mark's parables.

The first is the *use of 'tertia comparationis' or figures*, resulting in comparative rather than direct utterance. It is not present in the popular saying and is accidental rather than necessary to the taunt, the instructive discourse and the prophetic oracle (see pp. 175–6). In the

Old Testament comparison is not a sine qua non of the parable, and in view of much New Testament criticism this needs emphasis. But it is very common. It occurs in the figurative popular saying and the *Kunstspruch*, where it is integral. In the *Kunstspruch* it attains its fullest and most luxuriant development as allegory. The byword is interesting because it is intermediate. Insofar as it belongs with the taunt, it is not comparative. But of itself it shows a stock figure in the historical making as does Saul among the prophets at I Samuel 10. 12. Afflicted Israel or the afflicted individual becomes, or shall become, a *locus classicus* in common usage for affliction: becomes as 'proverbial', as much *the* figure, for affliction as pre-war Chicago for gangsterism or Mr Micawber for the belief that something will turn up.[26]

This note of history is very important and leads into the second major feature to be extracted from the confusion for future development. In all the categories, with the possible exception of the instructive discourse, *particular historical contexts* often inform the parables which are sometimes unintelligible without them. Again, these are not always present and so fail to define overall. They are absent from the great collection in the Book of Proverbs. But they dominate the taunt and the byword. And following Daube's suggestion that the two Old Testament fables should be included 'within the wider category of parable', it is striking that particular crises in history are as important to Jotham and Jehoash as they are insignificant to the great fabulist of antiquity, Aesop. The parables of Ezekiel, above all, are so complex in their inextricable binding into current international affairs that they are quite incomprehensible and useless without informed reference to them.

Ezekiel as Godfather of the Historical Allegory

Ezekiel is arguably the most important figure in the history of the Old Testament parable. He is a gathering-point and a creative initiator for its future.

He uses nearly all its range. Labelled as such he has the popular saying at Ezekiel 12. 21-2, 'the days are prolonged and every vision faileth'; the figurative popular saying at 16. 44, 'as is the mother, so is the daughter'; and at 18. 2-3, 'the fathers have eaten sour grapes and the children's teeth are set on edge'; the elaborate *Kunstspruch* at chapters 15, 17 and 20. 49. So the first three categories of parable are covered. At 24. 3 the *Kunstspruch* is extended into symbolic action with the cauldron, thus bringing into the fold of parable the sort of parabolic deed of Jeremiah with *his* cauldron (Jeremiah 1. 13), his loincloth (Jeremiah 13. 1-7) and his yoke (Jeremiah 27 and 28). It is a form which Ezekiel takes to bizarre and unprecedented lengths. The taunt and the oracle are in his book too. His lamentations over Tyre and Egypt in chapters 27 and 28, 31 and 32 are virtually taunting, and there is no shortage of prophetic oracles. Ezekiel thus contains a wider

illustrated use of the weltering range of parable than any other Old
Testament writer.

But his great achievement in the field is his passionate and sustained
combination of the two major features which have been isolated from
it: the use of comparative figures in the advanced form of sustained
allegory, and the determinative historical context. His parables of the
eagles and vine in chapter 17, of the cauldron at 24. 1–14, and the
forest fire at 20. 45–9 are labelled parables and have this combination
as their essence. They are far from being the whole story of his
prophetic historical allegorizing. It dominates the three great laments,
a form taken from popular custom. Each is double, with a switch of
comparison in the middle. In the first (Ezekiel 19. 1–9), Israel is a young
lion twice taken captive (Egypt, Babylon), and in 19. 10–14 the allegory
changes into a vine, once strong with branches which made sceptres(!),
but then transplanted to a desert and burnt. In the second (27–28. 19),
Tyre is mourned, first as the wreck of a superb trading ship and then as
a fallen angel. In the third (31–32. 16), Egypt is the tallest cedar tree in
the world, felled by 'the mighty ones of the nations' and abandoned,
then a stranded sea-monster become carrion. The whores in 16. 1–43
and 23 have been noticed already. So has the charred vine-wood in
chapter 15. His own role is allegorized by the watchman (3. 17–21 and
33. 2–9), his anguished repression of mourning for his beloved wife
made an example for Israel in its loss of its sanctuary. The allegories of
the shepherds and sheep in chapter 34, and of the resurrection of dry
bones at chapter 37, the numerous *Symbolhandlungen*—they testify with
all the rest to a man who virtually lived historical allegory, lived
parabolically. His utterances are the product of a personality stretched
to extremes: of tragedy and hope, of bold explicitness and riddling
obscurity, of tenderness and moral rigour, of a vision of divine
transcendence and a concrete physicality emerging in sensuousness
and disgust. The mediating powers of allegory served to hold these
together in the continuous prophetic concern with history—current
events, their past origins and future resolution. The violence of the
conjunctions is suited by the violence, to the point of fabulously
absurd distortion, which the moral and theological force behind
allegory inflicts on the materials it takes from nature, popular culture
and history. It results in a billowing obscurity from which rays of
dazzling revelation break out—as in the great vision of the chariot
throne in his first chapter, where concrete images are burned and
wrenched into indicating transcendant God. Ezekiel was a mystery-
monger, a fabulist and allegorist, a visionary and parabolic riddler—
and all these as an interpreter of history. 'Riddler' is, in the end, too
homespun and folksy a term for him. He was the father of apocalyptic,
that ultimate biblical answer to enigmatic history which lives on
allegory. He became William Blake's history tutor.[27] For our purpose
he is *the* great father of the allegorical historical parable and the
hammer of the anti-allegorical school of parable exegesis.

Parable and Apocalyptic

Ezekiel's visions were born in the humiliation of the Babylonian exile, those in the book of Daniel in the sharper test of the hellenizing persecutions Antiochus Epiphanes unleashed on orthodox Jewry in its homeland from 167 to 163 BC. Bad times forced a theology which took history seriously into a sustained symbolism:

The Jewish people, sorely tried, fighting desperately for their sanctuary, their law and the faith of their fathers, now needed *a new interpretation of history* which went beyond the glorification of the past in the 'praise of the fathers' [Ecclesiasticus 44–50] or in the work of the Chronicler and was displayed in God's hidden plan with his people and the powers of the world, to encourage and comfort the oppressed so that they would continue to persevere in an apparently hopeless world.[26]

The resolution of the appalling mess must lie elsewhere: in a secret design which could only be grasped by special revelation in symbolic or parabolic form. The prophet became a prophetic wise man, a dreamer and interpreter of symbols like Joseph in *his* affliction, who is given the clue in the symbols: *'J'ai seul la clef de cette parade sauvage'*.[29] The literary form to explore this interaction of hiddenness and revelation, darkness and triumphant illumination, was the historical *Kunstspruch* so majestically developed by Ezekiel. The past was not glorified but from it came figures such as Daniel, Enoch and Ezra to whom the apocryphal literature was attributed so that the readers could be comforted by the knowledge that all this had been foreseen, as it was foreordained, long ago—and as it would be resolved in a not-too-distant future, which these worthies had seen in vision too. It gave comfort to set the negative present between a positive point in the past and a positive future. But historiography done between the two had to be riddling and visionary rather than plain and earthy. It had to be parabolic.

Daniel's visions are not called parables as some of Ezekiel's are. Like Joseph's they come in dreams and waking dreams. But their sustained historical allegory, their content whatever their label, fix them in the same category with the same alliances with oracle, fable and riddle. The dream of the great tree in Daniel 4. 10–37 has Ezekiel's tree visions as its conscious source and shares his violent confusion when the tree stump becomes a man and the man is given the heart and grazing habits of a beast. 'Daniel' is every bit as allegorically surrealistic as Ezekiel. In his division of international history into periods with the statue-dream of chapter 2 and the beasts of chapters 7 and 8 he comes out as an historian—or 'philosopher' of history—of greater scope and sophistication. The obscurity which bothered Ezekiel: 'Ah Lord God! they say of me, Is he not a speaker in parables?' (20. 49), he rejoices in as something deliberate and integral to God's plan which gives him a privileged place in it (2. 20–23) and screws up the eschatological tension: 'Shut up the words and seal the book, even to the time of the end' (12. 4).

Enoch, like Daniel, is a great human spirit summoned up from the legendary past. He is the father of Methuselah who walked with God and was translated to heaven (Genesis 5. 21–4). The visions in his pseudepigraphical book[30] are called parables. The negligible influence they have had on parable exegesis can be excused by the treacherously composite nature of the work. The concomitant lack of a definitive historical crisis is a factor too. 'Enoch's' times were bad and muddled but not dreadful. So the general moral question of the fate of good men and bad takes over from sharp historical crisis—with consequent slackening of narrative tension. Enoch tours the secrets of heaven, particularly the culmination of God's historical plan and the solving of the moral enigma at doomsday, in a pedestrian way, interrupted by his questions and the cross rebukes of his angelic guide. But the indissolubility of parables from the mystery of theological/moral history is insisted on from the first and throughout. 'Not for this [that is *Enoch's own long-past*] generation but for a remote one which is to come. Concerning the elect I said, and took up my parable concerning them' (1. 3). The angel is a sort of celestial super-scribe and prophetic wise man, Enoch his not very apt pupil.

II Esdras[31] brings back Ezra, the fifth-century reformer and rebuilder after the Babylonian exile, as the pseudepigraphical writer of a book of tormented broodings over the destruction of Jerusalem in AD 70. Actual historical disaster and a sharper sense of history brought forth a book much more profound and searching than 'Enoch's' parabolic ramblings. It shapes his moral concern with humanity at large, but with a deeper and more sensitive heart which 'reminds us of Job'.[32] In the eschatological age to come he has a visionary solution to his problem, though in a tension of hope far more highly strung than 'Enoch's'. It informs the parables and visions of the book and is not abolished by the inconclusive interpretations of them given by the angel Uriel. We are back, not only with a mind as passionate as Ezekiel's, but also with his more pointed parabolic method. The parables given by Uriel (4. 4ff.) are in his tradition. The first is a riddle. 'Weigh me a pound of fire, measure me a bushel of wind; or call back a day that is passed' (4. 5). There is no solution. The riddle is meant to show up human incapacity for divine mystery: 'If you cannot understand things you have grown up with, how can your small capacity comprehend the ways of the Most High? A man corrupted by the ways of the world can never know the ways of the incorruptible' (4. 10–11). The second is a fable with echoes of Jotham's—

I went out into a wood, and the trees of the forest were making a plan. They said 'Come, let us make war on the sea, force it to retreat, and win ground for more woods'. The waves of the sea made a similar plan: they said, 'Come, let us attack the trees of the forest, conquer them and annex their territory'. The plan made by the trees came to nothing, for fire came and burnt them down. The plan made by the waves failed just as badly, for the sand stood its ground and blocked their way. If you had to judge between the two, which would you pronounce right, and which wrong? (4. 13–18).

Again Ezra cannot answer and Uriel agrees that 'only those who live above the skies can understand the things above the skies'. Here is apocalyptic with a vengeance in its refusal to reveal. But Ezra persists: 'Why have I been given the faculty of understanding? My question is not about the distant heavens, but about the things which happen every day before our eyes. Why has Israel been made a byword among the Gentiles; why has the people you loved been put to the mercy of godless nations?' (4. 22–3). And what is God going to do about it? At last Ezra gets a parable with some moral and historical meaning and a strong eschatological bent:

This present age is quickly passing away; it is full of sorrows and frailties, too full to enjoy what is promised in due time for the godly. The evil about which you ask has been sown, but its reaping is not yet come. Until the crop of evil has been reaped as well as sown, until the ground where it was sown has vanished, there will be no room for that which has been sown with the good. A grain of the evil seed was sown in the heart of Adam from the first; how much godlessness has it produced already! How much more will it produce before the harvest! Reckon this up: if one grain of evil seed has produced a crop of godlessness, how vast a harvest will there be when good seeds beyond number have been sown.

It is not just the symbols there which remind us of Mark's sower (Mark 4. 3–20) and Matthew's wheat and tares (Matthew 13. 24–30). There is the over-riding eschatological thrust too. Ezra's 'When will the harvest begin?' is answered with 'As soon as the number of those like yourselves is complete' (see Mark 13. 20). It will be soon, for 'the past far exceeds the future in length; what remains is but raindrops and smoke' (4. 50). Mark's other great allegorical parable of the vineyard (Mark 12. 1–12) is also paralleled in II Esdras. At 5. 23ff. Israel is the one chosen vine and chosen plot.

With II Esdras the parabolic tradition we have traced is contemporary with Mark, contemporary at the point of the aftermath of the destruction of Jerusalem in AD 70:[33]

1   It is *historical.* That is to say that its realm is not, as with Aesop and the Book of Proverbs, the repetitive everyday but the particular grand crisis. It is there that the questions which provoke it are raised and there that its 'answer' is directed.
2   It is *allegorical.* Sometimes there may be only one *tertium comparationis* but usually there are more, as in fables. As in historical crises more than one force is at work, so in their parabolic symbolizing more than one figure is needed. The enigma of the crises is congruent with the enigma, the riddling, of the allegory, so—
3   It is deliberately and properly *obscure.* Baffling at first glance, interpretation springs its revelation and makes it in its small way *apocalyptic* and a little apocalypse (literally 'disclosure'). The allegorical representation of God's secret historical plan first parades its secrecy then cracks it—often by an indispensable interpretation.

4   But not completely. The resolution is for later, for some future denouement in history or for the denouement of history itself at doomsday. So it is *eschatological*. Which is to say again that its concern is not so much with the everyday, even in the light of the eternal, but with history's goal.

If this long road has had no other surprises, it has certainly shown that the allegorical parable, informed by a moral and theological wrestling with history, is not some sort of aberration but a vehicle exactly tuned to a serious (to say the least) purpose. It was not the encrusting obfuscation by petty minds of something basically simple, but the art of energetically visionary minds caught in riddling complexities, which they refused to evade and through which they *hoped* for the simplicity of a resolution.

Mark and the Parabolic Tradition

Mark 4. 10–12—'And when he was alone'

And when he was alone, they that were about him with the twelve asked of him the parables. He said unto them, Unto you is given the mystery of the Kingdom of God, but unto them that are without, all things are done in parables: that seeing they may see and not perceive, and hearing they may hear and not understand; lest haply they should turn again, and it should be forgiven them.
(Mark 4. 10ff. quoting Isaish 6. 9–10)

This is the crux of interpreting Mark's parables. The long and tortured history of such interpretation will at least make clear that two major disadvantages hamper it, not least in modern times; that Mark is at cross purposes with nearly all his readers in two ways.
    The first is that for them the Christian Gospel is usually a plain revelation for all plain people, universally and fairly easily accessible. But for him it was a revelation of a subtly different kind: an enigma balancing disclosure with obscurity; a mystey for initiates who have been given the key by their divine master, which yet discloses itself in public history. The preceding pages of this essay should have prepared us for it by opening up a way into the parabolic tradition in which Mark stands, and in which he is intelligible by an exercize of historical imagination which takes leave of modern hopes and fears.
    The second obstacle is more obstinate. It is Mark himself, only rivalled by Paul in his passionately extreme and often self-contradictory presentation of Christianity. Even when we have soaked ourselves in the obscurities of the historical-allegorical tradition of parables he is awkward, to say the least. For example, how can we reconcile 4. 11ff. above with 4. 33 'And with many such parables spake he the word unto them as they were able to hear it'? In one parables seem to be used to hide things, in the other to explain them. It is like

the equally intractable Markan problem of Jesus's wish to hide himself and his provocatively public deeds and words. Internally and from his own mouth Mark is not entirely intelligible historically, and so not historically entirely probable. *Could* Jesus have behaved like this? 'If he had not wished them to hear and be saved, he would have kept quiet, not spoken in parables': John Chrysostom,[34] wrestling in the pulpit in the fourth century with 4. 11ff., does not only speak for subsequent interpreters. The same thought seems to have crossed the minds of Mark's earliest exegetes and editors, Matthew and Luke. Matthew makes the more determined effort (Matthew 13. 13-5). The crux is explained historically as a deliberate fulfilment of Isaiah's oracle: the fulfilment of prophecy is Matthew's conscious historiographical method. It is also explained morally by a fuller quotation of Isaiah than Mark's which includes 'for this people's heart is waxed gross' etc., implying that it is their fault: moralizing is Matthew's strong point. Luke whittles it down and waters it down (Luke 8. 9-15), his usual way with Mark's ferocities. But this obstacle is not going to be overcome in any interpretation which, unlike their's, takes Mark as he is instead of altering him. What we do have in Mark, though, is the parabolic tradition traced so far stretched to extremes and virtually *ad absurdum* —continuity with tension to breaking point. Such a climax has its own literary and historical interest.

Mark 7. 14-9—Declaring all foods clean

The parable about digestion at Mark 7. 14-9 falls fairly and squarely into the category of *Kunstspruch*. Physical digestion stands for intellectual-cum-spiritual digestion in an artificially made 'wise saying' *ad rem*. It foxes the disciples' pedestrian realism by its figuratively enigmatic form. They do not understand it, so it has—with rebukes— to be explained by the master. It is set in the argument about internal against external purity in Mark 7. 1-23. So it apparently belongs in the realm of general and abiding, rather than particular and historical, truth. But it comes in an historical book and with emphasis that Jesus made it so: 'this he said, making all meats clean'. It marks an historical difference. There are historical and allegorical elements here. But they are slighter than in the other three labelled parables. Here the *Kunstspruch* is of Ecclesiasticus's sort, there it is of Ezekiel's.

Mark 4. 1-9, 13-32—The Sower parable and its adjuncts

The Sower has big features in common with Ezekiel's vine/eagle allegory. It is surrealistic—the realism imposed by Dodd and Jeremias simply does not stick.[33] The sower is no hard-headed and hard-fisted peasant but a wild, vague figure flinging his seed all over the place: a vision heralded by the solemn beginning 'Hearken: Behold the [not 'a'] sower went forth to sow'. Like Ezekiel's, this parable is followed by its interpretation. According to Mark it was unintelligible without it. That is surprising to us who find it perfectly intelligible as a general illustration of general truths about perception. But was it that for Mark? Partly perhaps, if only because the general and the particular are never quite independent of one another. But again we must remember that Mark is writing a history, a 'gospel' rather than an 'epistle'. The parable is not set in a frame of moralizing and dogmatizing at large so much as in the *narrative* of the cataclysmic difference made by a divine invasion of history. In particular it is about the waste and success, tragedy and triumph, loss and resurrection, involved in that terrific action. It has, too, an eschatological drive stronger than in Matthew's and Luke's subsequent versions, more like that in Ezra's parable of sowing and reaping. So it is decidedly historical. It is an allegory of what happened when the times were changed by the ministry, death and resurrection of Jesus. According to the interpretation in verses 14–20 its *termini* are the sowing of the word and the final harvest, with all the disappointments which happened between—disappointments which will be historically instanced and realised in Mark's narrative. They spring from attitudes of mind (the bad ground), but attitudes brought out historically by the proclamation of the gospel, the events of the sowing of the word. The notion of Satan taking away the word sown on the path (4. 15) is instanced by, for example, Peter at 8. 33 ('Get thee behind me Satan, for thou mindest not the things of God but of man'); those who stumble in tribulation and persecution by, for example, the disciples at 14. 50 ('They all forsook him and fled'); those choked by riches by, for example, the rich man of 10. 17–25 ('how hard it is for them that trust in riches to enter into the kingdom of God').

The parables which follow in Mark 4 are explanatory pendants to the sower. The lamp has surrealism in the absurd suggestion of putting it under a bushel or bed. That brings in the motif of hiddenness—but this time only to be dismissed or used as a foil for the dominant motif of revelation. Verses 24 and 25 hark back to the interpretation of the Sower. So do verses 26–9, the seed growing secretly. They too use mystery and revelation, but this time with added emphasis on mystery: 'he knoweth not how'. Mark switches back and forth between these poles of allegory. The realism is rooted in the unknown. The mustard seed is surrealistic again, growing into a veritable tree with 'great branches'—Daniel's tree of Daniel 4. 10–37 and its forebears in Ezekiel, the apocalyptic kingdom-tree.

Mark 12. 1–12—The parable of the vineyard
With the parable of the Vineyard (12. 1–12) we do not have to make the sort of adjustment of view we needed for the sower. The historical substance of this allegorical parable, a sort of strip-cartoon of salvation history, stares us in the face as boldly as it did Mark's 'chief priests and scribes'. So it needs no explanation—and is even the point at which anti-allegorical exegetes lay down their arms, at least for a moment.[36] It is not clear because it is realistic. Dodd's and Jeremias's efforts do not

stick here either.[37] It is clear because it uses the familiar outlines of biblical history and the well-known and traditional figure of the vine and vineyard for Israel: Isaiah 5. 1–7 is quoted at the outset (and see the vine figures in Ezekiel discussed above). So the key is in the reader's hand already, if like Mark and his readers he has his Scriptures. God is the landlord, Israel his vineyard, the Jewish nation the tenants, the prophets the servant-messengers, Jesus the son, the crucifixion his death, the fall of Jerusalem to the Roman army the destruction of the tenants, the gentile expansion of the Church the giving of the vineyard to others. If there remains any doubt that it is all an allegory of God's up-ending action in history the stone text at verses 10 and 11 (Psalm 118. 22ff.) dispels it: 'They perceived that he spake the parable against them'. Only the hedge, pit, winepress and tower of verses 1 can possibly be unallegorical—and they come with Isaiah 5. 1–7. Otherwise the cap fits ominously well. Its obviousness is the most exceptional thing about it, and needs some explanation. The allegorical parable of history, in fact, stands between obscurity and revelation: less plain than straight narrative from the realistic viewpoint, it is plainer in its thrust of meaning. Mark pulls it both ways. Usually people are puzzled by it, this time it hits them between the eyes. The energetic contradiction is typical of him.

Mark 13. 28–9—The parable of the fig tree

There remains the fig tree of 13. 28–9. It is realistic enough, but 'from the fig tree learn her parable' is a command not to look at it with ordinary eyes but allegorically. As its leaves are a sign that summer is coming, so the catastrophes, which have been predicted in the previous verses of the chapter, are a sign of the impending end of history in apocalyptic harvest. It will be soon, as in II Esdras 4. 50. The fig tree does not tell of ordinary, but of pan-historical, doomsday weather.

Conclusions

> Discuss unto me; art thou officer?
> Or art thou base, common and popular?
>
> (Pistol, *Henry V* IV.1)

Like so many (? all) literary forms, the remote origins of the parable are in the life of the people. The common saying is the oldest kind of Hebrew *mashal* according to Eissfeldt.[38] It presses a wealth of ordinary experience into tough little maxims, popular gems, which are sometimes figurative and always unambiguous. To set Jesus's parables in this milieu has been the aim of three generations of New Testament scholarship, undeterred by more-or-less continuous sniping. They ought to belong in the everyday life of Palestinian country folk. But this fails to do justice to a major and determinative episode in the history of the form. It got into the hands of the intelligentsia, the literary, scribal officer class. Ecclesiasticus congratulated himself on a parabolic skill which was quite beyond the capacity of artisans: 'where parables are they shall not be found' (38. 31–4). Ezekiel knew the parable as common saying but spent his own dazzling energies on the development of it into something which ordinary people complained was too difficult, the elaborate historical allegory. It was, literally, a heaven-sent vehicle for the writer of Daniel in his dark historical crisis. It thrived with the writers of Enoch and II Esdras, becoming an apocalyptic stock-in-trade.

The combination of two major features of primitive Christianity disposed it towards this first, rather than the common and static, form of parable. It was apocalyptic. And it arose at a time when the Scriptures, the literary revelation, were coming into their authoritative kingdom. In the Scriptures of the Christian Churches were these historical allegories labelled 'parable'. And they, more than the homely proverbs, were needed by the new sect with its acute historical consciousness and sense of impending, liberating doomsday. Mark had much in common with Daniel, in particular. They were both in their different times confronted with the sight of Jerusalem, the holy place, desecrated by triumphant paganism. To both it was appalling—if less drastic for Mark who could fall back on his gospel of Jesus's death at its hands and his resurrection, and on allegiance to a sect already thriving more in gentile territory than there. To both it brought the conviction that the end was near, with concomitant meditation on that secret divine plan for history which was about to be made plain in its resolution. Both expressed themselves, and comforted their public, by putting this in a story of a man from the past who had suffered for his faith, seen the secret plan and set it out in historical allegory. Present and future trouble had been parabolically foretold by a holy man, a divinely privileged prophet-seer, in the past. But Mark's Jesus is something much more than Daniel. Daniel stood for the law. Mark's Jesus, as son of God and the realisation of Daniel's visionary Son of Man, stood for God and himself. The salvation he brought made the law an anachronism; for Mark as for his theological mentor, Paul. God's historical plan had been allegorically proclaimed and historically accomplished through one who would soon return.

So Mark stands within the tradition of the parable as historical allegory—and at its point of *non plus ultra*. Later the apocalyptic fires of Christianity died down, except for the writers of Revelation and II Peter. Mark's successors in gospel writing assented to apocalyptic but had other things to do. This shows in their parables. Matthew takes up Mark's vision of the end, but uses it in his (M) parables[39] to enforce morality as much as for its own historical sake. Luke was an historian but of a very different and earthier sort, taught by the Deuteronomic school of the books of Samuel and Kings rather than by Ezekiel and Daniel. His (L) parables are like that too: plain tales of everyday and always, cunningly told. So they are not strictly parables and not labelled as such, but rather stories. It is these that the anti-allegorical critics have rejoiced in as authentic parables of Jesus. They have striven to make Mark (and Matthew) deliver similar goods. Perhaps Mark prepared the way for the parables of Matthew and Luke by stretching the poles of allegory until it snapped and there was nothing to do but get down to morals and more ordinary history, leaving allegory for the less time-bound historical concerns of John and his Alexandrian successors. Perhaps the tight fit in his parables and their succinctness led that way. But a backward reading is always something of an imposition, something to be corrected as far as possible in historical literary criticism. Mark had his own way and an august pedigree for it.

Notes

1 C. H. Dodd (1935), *The Parables of the Kingdom*, London, revised ed. 1961.
2 J. Jeremias (1954), *The Parables of Jesus*, (trans. S. H. Hooke) London, third revised ed. 1972.
3 J.. Wellhausen (1903), *Das Evangelium Marci*, pp. 30ff., my translation.
4 An exposition of Exodus 12–23, one of the oldest *midrashim* originating with the Tanraim, the first rabbinic 'school'. In English parallels to the Hebrew: edition of 1944 by J. Z. Lauterbach. But see B. Z. Wacholder (1968), in *Hebrew Union College Annual XXXIX*, pp. 117–44 for a later dating, though it is not accepted by J. Neusner (1970), *Development of a Legend*, Brill, Leiden, pp. xiii ff.n.
5 A. Sanday (1899), *Journal of Theological Studies*, p. 174.
6 W. Michaelis (1956), *Die Gleichnisse Jesu* (third ed.), Hamburg, especially p. 15.
7 M. Benoit (1948), *Revue Biblique*, iv, pp. 594–9.
8 M. Hermaniuk (1947), *La Parabole Evangélique*, Paris/Bruges.
9 M. Black (1959–60), 'The parables as allegory', *Bulletin of the John Rylands Library*, XLII, pp. 284 ff.
10 D. E. Nineham (1963), *St. Mark*, London, pp. 131–4 and 311.
11 C. F. D. Moule (1969), 'Mark 4: 1.20 yet once more' in *Neotestamentica et Semitica: Studies in Honour of Principal Matthew Black*, Edinburgh; C. F. D. Moule (1954–5), *Expository Times*, pp. 46–8.
12 M. D. Goulder (1968), 'Characteristics of the parables in the several gospels', *Journal of Theological Studies*, April 1968, pp. 50–69.
13 R. E. Brown (1962), 'Parable and allegory reconsidered', *Novum Testamentum*, V, pp. 35–45.
14 J. H. Drury (1973), 'The sower, the vineyard and the place of allegory in the interpretation of Mark's parables', Journal of Theological Studies, October 1973, pp. 367–80.
15 J. D. M. Derrett (1974), 'Allegory and the wicked vineꞇ ꞇ sers', *Journal of Theological Studies*, October 1974, p. 246.
16 A. Schweitzer (1911), *The Quest of the Historical Jesus*, London.
17 N. Frye (1969), *Fearful Symmetry*, Princeton, pp. 10ff.
18 R. E. Brown (1966), *The Gospel According to John, Vol. I*, London, p. 390.
19 In the present author's article in the *Journal of Theological Studies* in October 1973 he showed why, and the part of it spent doing so has not been challenged (but his speculative remarks at the end of it have, cogently, by J. Bowker in the *Journal of Theological Studies* in October 1974 and the present essay is indebted to his strictures).
20 Listed in O. Eissfeldt (1913), 'Der Maschal im Alten Testament', *Beihefte zur Zeitschrift*

für die Alttestamentliche Wissenschaft, XXIV, p. 22, and explained mainly by the greater freedom and hellenism of the translators of Proverbs and Ecclesiasticus. B.T.D. Smith (1937), *The Parables of the Synoptic Gospels*, Cambridge, p. 11 n. 2 also gives a list, but with less thorough explanation.

21 O. Eissfeldt (1913), *op. cit., passim.*

22 O. Eissfeldt (1913), *ibid.*, p. 43.

23 In his chapter 15 Ezekiel exploits Isaiah's figure of the vine for Israel. If it is not useful viticulturally it has no use in carpentry—still less if it has been charred in the fire of divine wrath, as Israel will be.

24 K. von Rabenau (1957), 'Die Form des Rätsels im Buche Hesekiel' in *Gottes ist der Orient: Festschrift für O. Eissfeldt*, Berlin, pp. 129–31.

25 D. Daube (1973), *Ancient Hebrew Fables: Inaugural Lecture of the Oxford Centre for Postgraduate Hebrew Studies*, Oxford, especially pp. 8 and 21ff.

26 For the limitations of this see O. Eissfeldt (1913), *op. cit.*, pp. 39–41.

27 See H. Bloom (1976), *Poetry and Misprision*, New Haven and London.

28 M. Hengel (1974), *Judaism and Hellenism Vol. I* (trans J. Bowden), London, p. 194. The chapter on 'The Hasidim and the first climax of Jewish apocalyptic' here is an excellent combination of literary and political history. Margaret Barker in *Expository Times*, August 1978, pp. 324–9 unravels much of the tangle surrounding the concept of apocalyptic.

29 A. Rimbaud *Les Illuminations IV* ('I alone hold the key of this wild parade').

30 A composite work of circa 165–64 BC according to R. H. Charles whose translation is available in R. H. Charles (1913), *Apocrypha and Pseudepigrapha of the Old Testament*, Oxford. According to Milik its chapters 37–71, the so-called 'Book of Parables', does not belong to the original 'Enochian Pentateuch'. But parables are scattered throughout the Enochian collection. See J. T. Milik (1976), *The Books of Enoch, Aramaic Fragments of Qumran Cave 4*, Oxford.

31 Available in the Apocrypha of the New English Bible (used here) etc.

32 O. Eissfeldt (1966) *The Old Testament, an Introduction*, (trans P. R. Ackroyd), Oxford, p. 626.

33 I accept the dating of Mark in S. G. F. Brandon (1956), *The Fall of Jerusalem and the Christian Church*, London pp. 185–205.

34 In Matt. Hom. 45 n. 2.

35 J. Drury (1973), *op. cit.*, pp. 368–71.

36 For example, Jülicher II, pp. 385–406 and J. Jeremias (1954), *op. cit.*, p. 70 overtly, C. H. Dodd (1935), *op. cit.*, p. 94 tacitly after a bold refusal on the previous page.

37 J. Drury (1973), *op. cit.*, pp. 371–4.

38 O. Eissfeldt (1913), *op. cit.*, pp. 34ff.

39 'M' in the shorthand of New Testament criticism, is material found only in Matthew, 'L' that only in Luke.

11 PARABLE AND TRANSCENDENCE

Bernard Harrison

Nous vénérons tous secrètement cet idéal d'un langage qui, en dernière analyse, nous délivrerait de lui-même en nous livrant aux choses.

(Maurice Merleau-Ponty, in *La Prose du Monde*)

Part I

Parable is a thorn in the side of theology. Parables defy precise doctrinal or moral interpretation; or, more infuriatingly still, admit it only on the level of moral commonplace, escaping all our attempts to articulate the more profound and numinous meanings which we feel to be obscurely present in them. Even the word 'parable' is a shifting sand:

The word 'Mashal' and its synonyms, which underlie the 'parabolé' of the gospels, cover a wide range of utterance, varying from, at the one end, the brief and self-explanatory proverb, through manifold forms of extended metaphor to, at the other end—and this is most surprising—the riddle or enigma.[1]

You cannot found a state religion, or a practical homilectic, upon a collection of riddles. Hence, perhaps, the long tradition, from Augustine and Origen onwards, of treating parable as allegory. To allegorize a parable is to turn it at one stroke into something altogether easier for our minds to grasp: a cipher; a piece of 'Aesopian' discourse with an esoteric, but nonetheless perfectly fixed and definite meaning. Thus Augustine, following Origen, interprets the parable of the Good Samaritan (Luke 10. 30–35) as darkly adumbrating the central events of divine history. The Samaritan is Christ, the man going down from Jerusalem to Jericho is fallen Adam: 'the inn is the church, the innkeeper St. Paul . . ., and the two pence are the sacraments'.[2] Every element of the parable is associated with a definite designation, with the result that the whole becomes a brief statement of orthodox theological doctrine in code.

It is not easy to see, as Professor C. F. Evans remarks, 'Why there should have been this curious arrangement in which fundamental theological truths had to be secured by being uttered twice and in two such different modes, once explicitly in the doctrinal language fitted to them, and then over again in the language of cipher. . . .'[3]

Nor, of course, is this the only reason for dissatisfaction with the allegorical method. To view a parable as allegory generally involves wrenching it from its narrative context. If Augustine's interpretation of the Good Samaritan were correct, for instance, it would make it hard to see how the parable could be read as any sort of reply to the question 'And who is my friend?'[4] to which, according to Luke's narrative, Jesus offers it as an answer.

Again, the grammatical form of its introduction is sufficient in many cases to show that the parable was intended as a *parallel*, or complex simile; and a parallel is not at all the same thing as an allegory. Each of the elements of an allegory has an independent significance: to grasp the significance of the allegory just is to see what each separate *motif* represents, or stands for. A parallel, or simile, does not work like that: it is only when taken as a whole that it has significance. One common form of parable introduction, it seems, begins with an abbreviation of a lengthy rabbinic formula which runs thus: 'I will relate a parable to you. With what shall the matter be compared? It is the case with it as with. . . .'[5] What is proposed, in short, is a comparison, between the whole matter of debate and the whole content of the parable, not the delivery of a statement of doctrine concealed within an allegorical cipher.

Such considerations gain added force when we learn that a number of scholars, following Adolf Jülicher, have argued, using the methods of form-criticism, that the interpretation of the parable of the Sower offered by Jesus at Mark 4. 11–20, an explicit scriptural example of allegorical interpretation, does not in fact represent the original tradition of the words of Jesus, but a fragment of later apostolic teaching.[6]

The present critical orthodoxy concerning the parables, which rests mainly upon two books, C. H. Dodd's *The Parables of the Kingdom* and Joachim Jeremias' *The Parables of Jesus*, avoids the pitfalls of the allegorizing tradition. Its central methodological conviction is that the parables must be taken in their context as arguments or responses given by Jesus in particular circumstances in his ministry, and taken, moreover, as responses which take on their fullest sense only against the background of contemporary life and the contemporary religious situation. We must not wrench parables from their context, as allegorical interpretation requires us to do: we must look instead at the concrete circumstances which situate them in the fabric of the recorded life and ministry of Jesus: at their *Sitz im Leben*. Moreover we must treat parables as complex similes or parallels, not as doctrinal statements in an allegorical code consisting of essentially discrete elements each of which is capable of being allegorically decoded quite separately from the other elements.

Dodd and Jeremias both see the parables as *arguments*, or rather as moves in a polemic. They point out that parables are often replies to a questioner, who may be openly hostile, like the Pharisees of Luke 14. 1–3, who question Jesus' association with tax-gatherers and other disreputable elements and receive in reply the parables of the Lost

Sheep, the Lost Coin and the Prodigal Son, or smoothly enquiring like the lawyer of Luke 10. 29, who asks 'And who is my friend?' and is answered by the parable of the Good Samaritan. But parables are of course not 'arguments' in the sense of sets of propositional premises entailing conclusions which confute opposing *propositions*. What they confute is a certain religious outlook, and they confute it by announcing and adumbrating an eschatology which that outlook in no way prepares its adherents to receive. The eschatological message of the parables is that the Kingdom of God has arrived, either wholly realised in the actions and words of Jesus, according to Dodd, or partly realised in the presence of Jesus and in process of further realisation according to Jeremias. On either view the parables speak primarily to Jesus' immediate hearers in the hour of eschatological crisis produced by his presence. The parables announce different aspects of the eschatological crisis, revealing the nature of the Kingdom of God now realised or in process of realising itself; and they accuse the 'scribes and Pharisees', the religious leaders who are blind to the nature of the crisis, and unwilling to accept the Kingdom now that it is here.

Thus Jeremias, in a passage dealing with a group of parables which he takes to contain the central message of the Gospels, which is not merely that 'the Redeemer has appeared, but also that salvation is sent to the poor, and that Jesus has come as a saviour for sinners', says:

The parables which have as their subject the gospel message in its narrower sense are, apparently without exception, addressed, not to the poor, but to opponents. That is their distinctive note, their *Sitz im Leben*: their main object is not the presentation of the gospel, but defence and vindication of the gospel; they are controversial weapons against the critics and foes of the gospel who are indignant that Jesus should declare that God cares about sinners, and whose special attack is directed against Jesus' practice of eating with the despised. At the same time, the parables are intended to win over the opponents.[7]

According to Jeremias, the vindication of the gospel in these parables proceeds on three levels. First, the critics' attention is directed to the poor to whom the message of the Gospel is being proclaimed. Second, the critics are themselves rebuked:

In the parables of this group the vindication of the gospel is accompanied by the sternest rebuke. 'You,' he says, 'are like the son who promised to obey his father's command, but afterwards neglected to fulfil his promise (Matthew 21. 28-31). You are like the husbandmen who refused year after year to render to their Lord his due share of the produce of his land, heaping outrage upon outrage upon him (Mark 12. 1-9, par.; Gospel of Thomas 65). You are like the respectable guests who rudely declined the invitation to the banquet—what right have you to pour scorn and derision upon the wretched crowd that sit at my table?'[8]

And, third, the parables in the central group expound the mercy of God for sinners, most clearly in the Prodigal Son (Luke 15. 11-32):

The parable was addressed to men who were like the elder brother, men who were offended at the gospel. An appeal must be made to their conscience. To them Jesus says: 'Behold the greatness of God's love for his lost children, and contrast it with your own joyless, loveless, thankless and self-righteous lives. Cease then from your loveless ways and be merciful.'[9]

In Dodd's and Jeremias' analyses, in short, the crucial questions are the questions to whom, to what sort of people, that is, and in what circumstances, the parables were originally addressed. The later use of the parables, for homiletic and hortatory purposes, within communities which were already Christian, is secondary to their original use in defending and justifying Christ's teaching against those who could not understand it or were opposed to it; and the meanings acquired by parables in later, Christian, contexts are likewise to be regarded as secondary and to some extent, though of course not entirely, for there are clearly degrees of distortion involved, unjustified.

One merit of this way of looking at parables is that it steers clear of the main alternative to treating them as allegories: the alternative of regarding them as containing moral lessons, or instructions embodied, as if for the edification of children, in simple, naturalistic stories. Jülicher, wishing to cut off at the root the radiating alternative possibilities of allegorical interpretation, opted for 'the broadest possible application'[10] of each parable to common life. The result is to make the interpretation of each parable end in a moral generality such as the one ascribed by Jülicher to the Parable of the Talents (Matthew 25. 14–30/Luke 19. 12–27): 'fidelity in all that God has entrusted to us'.[11] Dodd's comment upon such methods is pointed:

Was all this wealth of loving observation used merely to adorn moral generalities? Was the Jesus of the gospels just an eminently sound and practical teacher, who patiently led simple minds to appreciate the great enduring commonplaces of morals and religion? This is not the impression conveyed by the gospels as a whole. There is one of His parabolic sayings which runs: 'I have come to set fire to the earth, and how I wish it were already kindled!' . . . It is exactly the phrase we need to describe the volcanic energy of the meteoric career depicted in the gospels. The teaching of Jesus is not the leisurely and patient exposition of a system by the founder of a school. It is related to a brief and tremendous crisis in which He is the principal figure and which indeed His appearance brought about.[12]

One might add to Dodd's criticism that unless one has critical and theoretical reasons for taking 'the broadest possible application' of a parable to life as identifying the specific moral generalization it was intended to convey, it is not at all obvious what moral generalization is to be drawn from most parables. The moral point of the Great Feast (Matthew 22. 1–10/Luke 14. 16–24), for example, might be, and this is particularly plausible if we accept the Matthaean identification of the feast-giver as 'a king', that it is unwise to refuse the invitations of the great, because they have it in their power to make people who do that look foolish.[13] The 'moral' of the Prodigal Son might be taken to be that one should receive errant children with joy no matter what they have done and no matter how much it involves damaging the interests of one's other children, and so on. Of course, this is a problem with all religious narrative. Kierkegaard, in *Fear and Trembling*,[14] has ghoulish fun at the expense of the plain, commonsensical pastor who, having preached one Sunday in glowing terms about the faith of Abraham, is confronted by a parishioner who, in response to voices, has 'sacrificed' his own son. No doubt that was not what was intended: that is not how we are to read such a narrative: but how, then *are* we to read it?

Dodd, in attacking the allegorical tradition, makes a great deal of the fidelity of the parables to the concrete circumstances of everyday life,[15] his point being that allegory need not be true to nature, because its significance lies not in the terms of the story but in what each element of the story 'stands for', whereas the point of parable, in Dodd's view, is precisely to present the eschatological crisis in terms having all the vivid immediacy of everyday life. But the accuracy of the commonplace setting of the behaviour described in the parables can be contrasted with the fact that the behaviour itself is frequently odd to the point of craziness: a man gives a feast for beggars and any chance travellers his servants can pick up on the highway; an employer pays his servants the same wage for quite different hours of labour; an absentee landlord sends one slave after another to collect his rents, despite the fact that they all get beaten up, and finally sends his son, who predictably enough gets killed. The most natural conclusion to be drawn from these stories is merely, perhaps, the deflating one that their protagonists are mad, with the consequence that no moral conclusions whatsoever, let alone general moral maxims, can be extracted from their peculiar doings.[16]

Here, then, is a second set of reasons why the polemical-eschatological account of parables may come as a relief: it frees us not merely from the need to extract an allegorical significance from the text, but from the need to extract any set of general moral injunctions from it either. Moreover it heals the gap between parable and dogma, considered as two distinct scriptural *genres*, or modes of scriptural discourse. If Dodd and Jeremias are correct, the parables are polemical comments upon an eschatology and a moral outlook which can be reconstructed from non-parabolic material in the gospels. Like the allegorical interpretation, Dodd's and Jeremias' account connects parable with the formal, non-parabolically expressed body of Christian doctrine, but it does so without doing violence to the essential nature of parable.

Nevertheless, I find myself dissatisfied with the Dodd-Jeremias reading of the parables. I speak not as a biblical scholar, but as a literary critic writing in some respects from a philosophical standpoint. Moreover, it is not exactly that I think Dodd and Jeremias have *misread* the parables: indeed, what I am about to say, even if it carries conviction, will leave their position virtually intact as a reading of the parables adequate enough within its limits. My dissatisfaction concerns a series of questions upon which the Dodd–Jeremias interpretation is comparatively silent, but which do seem to demand an answer.

The first, oddly enough, concerns the problem of what general moral interpretation, if any, is to be attached to the parables, about which I have just been so scathing. No doubt we misread the parables if we try to reduce them to narrative illustrations of general moral principles. But is there, then, *nothing* 'general' about the parables; nothing which enables them to speak to all ages, and not merely to Jesus' immediate hearers? In tying them so closely to their historical context the Dodd-Jeremias orthodoxy gives us no explanation of why the parables, for all their brevity, should seem to us to have such resonance, such universality. Parable, after all, is a literary form, and one exemplified in writings, by Kafka or Kierkegaard, for example, which do not belong to the scriptural canon of any religion. And if we took the parables of Jesus out of any scriptural setting which might illuminate their eschatological significance, they would still resonate, would still tease the mind and heart, in the way that, say, Kafka's parables[17] do.

Dodd feels the force of this objection, and tries to answer it:

What then are the parables, if they are not allegories? They are the natural expression of a mind that sees truth in concrete pictures rather than conceives it in abstractions.[18]

. . . The Gospels do not offer us in the first place tales to point a moral. They interpret life to us, by initiating us into a situation in which, as Christians believe, the eternal was uniquely manifested in time, a situation which is both historical and contemporary in the deepest possible sense.[19]

But such talk butters few literary-critical, or for that matter epistemological parsnips. How can a 'picture' express a 'truth', or to put it another way, how can we say, without benefit of an immense amount of more-or-less *ad hoc* interpretative scene-setting, what truth a picture expresses? Is not the very diversity of theories concerning the interpretation of parables itself evidence of their fragility and uncertainty as a means of conveying 'truths'? What is the difference, exactly, between a 'tale to point a moral' and a tale which 'interprets life to us'? We cannot, as Dodd does, answer this question by gesturing, half-apologetically, towards the eschatological content of Christian belief; because one of the main grounds of Christian belief, once we cast aside the rotten staff of rational or 'natural' theology, must be the inherent force or impressiveness of Christ's teaching in the gospels; and a great deal of that teaching takes the form of parable; so that we are thrown back once again on the question of what it is that gives the parables of Jesus the profundity and numinousnes which we obscurely feel them to possess, irrespective of all questions of polemical context or eschatological significance, just as parables.

The problem, indeed, arises at the heart of Jeremias' or Dodd's interpretation, as the question of what it is exactly that gives the parables, so far as they can be understood as contributions to a polemical controversy between Jesus and his opponents, their force *as polemic*. Jeremias and Dodd have no difficulty in showing how the religious leaders rather vaguely characterized as 'scribes and Pharisees' might detect oblique references to themselves in such figures as the son who agrees to do his father's bidding (Matthew 21. 28–32), or the servant who buries his talent wrapped in a napkin (Matthew 25. 14–30/Luke 19. 12–27), or the guests who refuse the invitation to the Great Feast (Matthew 22. 1–10/Luke 14. 16–24). But this, taken just in itself, is polemic at a fairly low level: no more than a kind of figurative jeering. Both Jeremias and Dodd want to say more than this: that the parables in some way justify Christ's message against its detractors. What Dodd, for example, *wants* to say, as I think is clear from the passage I quoted a page ago, is that the parables confute the detractors and draw in the uncommitted mind because they communicate a vision—a general way of looking at life—against which the offered objections appear thin and insubstantial. But how can a vision sufficiently powerful to bear the historical weight of the Christian tradition be communicated by narrative, especially narrative of the brief and rudimentary kind employed in the parables?

Faced with this question we can reformulate it in a still sharper form. Why does any of Christ's teaching take the form of *narrative* in the first place? If, as the current orthodoxy maintains, the function of the parables is to announce and to describe the broad outlines of an eschatological crisis, and to accuse those who remain blind to the significance of the events in which that crisis is manifesting itself, why does Jesus not express himself directly and explicitly in the languages of accusation and eschatological annunciation which, as many passages in the gospel show, he was perfectly capable of doing when the occasion demanded it? Narrative and metaphor, indeed, seem devices peculiarly weak and ill-suited to the purposes which the conventional orthodoxy supposes the parables to have been designed to serve.[20] Why, then did Jesus use narrative at all? This is the fundamental question to which I shall address myself in what follows.

Part II

My suggestion is that parabolic narrative has as one of its functions the subversion of the conceptual scheme in terms of which its hearers construe the world and their lives in it.

Put as baldly as this, the suggestion may seem too drily abstract, and too fashionably semiological, to carry much weight. For that reason it will be best, I think, to start by explaining what I have in mind through the medium of some textual exegesis. I am not sure that the story I am going to tell will work for everything called 'parable' in the gospels—as we noticed earlier, the word *'mashal'* is ambiguous, and covers a number of different literary forms—but I think it will work at least for a number of those central parables which fall into the second of Jeremias' eschatological categories, which he labels 'God's Mercy for Sinners.' These are the parables, Jeremias says (p. 124), 'which contain the Good News itself'. I shall concentrate on three of them: the Great Feast (Matthew 22. 1–10/Luke 14. 16–24), the Good Employer (Matthew 20. 1–16) and the Prodigal Son (Luke 15. 11–32).

A narrative is not merely a description that recounts a sequence of events. Scientists often describe very precisely the sequences of events which take place when, say, a cell divides, or a ball-bearing travelling with a certain velocity strikes a tray of moon dust; but such descriptions are not *narratives*: they are simply descriptions with tenses in them. A narrative contains exposition, developments, and denouements, moments of crisis and relaxations of tension, which give it a structure which is more than mere sequence; and this structure is relative to the point of the narrative, in that grasping which parts of the narrative are expository and which constitute a denouement or a relaxation of tension involves grasping the point of the story as a whole, and vice versa. So much is obvious. What is perhaps less obvious is that a narrative cannot determine its own structure, by a purely internal fiat, as it were. The writer of narrative cannot arbitrarily choose that certain events in the narrative shall constitute background to a denouement, that certain other events shall constitute the denouement, and so on, merely in virtue of his so designating them. Such a fiat would be meaningless, like stipulating that the point in cell-division at which the nuclear membrane re-forms around the genetic material in each daughter-cell is to be regarded as the denouement of the narrative of cell-division. What would be the point of such a stipulation?—It would not, after all, have the effect of turning the biological description of cell division into a narrative: despite the stipulation, it would remain just a description with tenses in it. In short, a narrative is dependent for its point, and hence for the kind of structure which makes it a narrative rather than a tensed description, upon something outside it. The freedom which narrative writers enjoy is the freedom to invent any fictional events they please, but this freedom, if it is to produce *narrative*, rather than tensed description, must be exercized under the constraint of those extra-fictional considerations (a very diverse lot) which give point to narratives. And of course the art of narrative fiction consists precisely, from one point of view, in living successfully with the tensions which spring from that freedom and those constraints.

Jeremias, in discussing the Great Feast, relates it to a story which occurs in Aramaic in the Palestinian Talmud, and which, as other evidence seems to confirm, was evidently known to Jesus. It concerns a rich tax-gatherer, Bar Ma'jan, and a poor scholar. The Palestinian

Talmud tells us that Bar Ma'jan died and was given a splendid funeral. At the same time a poor scholar died, but nobody followed his body to the grave, since the whole city was escorting Bar Ma'jan's body. How could the justice of God permit this? The answer given is that Bar Ma'jan, though not a pious man, had done one splendid good deed. He had invited the city councillors to a banquet, and they, to insult him, refused to come. So in a rage he gave orders that the poor should come and eat the food, in order that it not be wasted.

Jeremias comments that the parallel between the Great Feast and the story of Ma'jan gives us a clear explanation of the otherwise inexplicable behaviour of the guests who refuse the invitation to the Feast. Then he says:

Just as Jesus does not hesitate to illustrate from the behaviour of the deceitful steward the need for decisive action, or from the conduct of the unscrupulous judge, the despised shepherd, and the poor woman, the boundless mercy of God, so he has not the slightest hesitation . . . in choosing the behaviour of a tax-gatherer to illustrate both the wrath and the mercy of God. That the man's motive was . . . selfish and ignoble . . . has not in any way disturbed Jesus, but has rather induced him to choose just these persons as examples.[21]

Jesus' reasons for making the tax-gatherer's ambiguous revenge on his guests emblematic of the wrath and mercy of God are, according to Jeremias, dramatic ones. Jesus' hearers would be likely to smile at the familiar story of the parvenu's revenge upon snobbish insolence, so that the shock of realising that what is being described is not, after all, a parvenu's mock banquet but the Kingdom of God, and that the hallful of beggars and cripples upon whom the doors finally close are the final inheritors of that Kingdom would be all the greater.

But I think more is at stake here than dramatic emphasis. What gives point to the narrative of Bar Ma'jan is the social gulf between Bar Ma'jan and his guests, taken together with the function of the institution of feast-giving as a device for conferring and confirming honour or social standing. The honour conferred by giving or attending a banquet is reciprocal. The host, if he is a man of sufficient social standing, confers honour on the guests whom he invites to a banquet. But they, of course, if they are persons of social standing, increase his standing by accepting his invitations. Social standing is the aim of both host and guests, but social standing is defined merely by whose parties one attends and who can be got to attend one's parties. The concept of this kind of honour, defined as it is solely by reciprocal social relationships, seems, in a sense, gratuitous and without real foundation, despite the emotional capital invested in it. Proust speaks of the social talents of Madame Verdurin, the dreadful society hostess in *À la Recherche du Temps Perdu* as an expertise in 'sculpturing the void'.

Nonetheless this is the conceptual structure which gives a point to the narrative of Bar Ma'jan, which makes no sense unless we see that this is the kind of honour which Bar Ma'jan and his invited guests are interested in: the goal of the race in which host and guests are jockeying for position. Bar Ma'jan wishes to use his 'guests' to enhance his social standing; those invited choose not to be so used. Bar Ma'jan then publicly insults them by inviting beggars, the implication being that beggars are better guests than the invited ones; or that one might as well invite beggars as such beggarly noblemen. But the insult is an impotent one: Bar Ma'jan, the one shot in his locker fired, remains socially excluded: one does not win the social game, after all, by dining with beggars.

The Talmudic story and the synoptic parable use this basic narrative material in different ways, each of which involves changing the context of the narrative in ways which throw its point into doubt. The Talmudic narrative encloses the story in another narrative: the narrative of the funerals of Bar Ma'jan and the poor scholar. The effect is to shift the point of central interest in the narrative from the question whether Bar Ma'jan's revenge was a good way of replying to the insolence of the nobles, to the question of whether it constituted, incidentally, a good deed. At once we encounter the receding ambiguities, the deep water, characteristic of parable in general and religious parable in particular. Bar Ma'jan fed the poor. But that was only to insult the absent guests. But still, the poor *were* fed, and God saw to it that he got a grand funeral as a reward. Ah, but the reward was a *funeral*. . . . Still, it was a *grand* funeral. . . . So you might say Bar Ma'jan's pride was satisfied in the end. . . . , (But was God just, to let the poor scholar go without mourners to the grave? Well, the justice of God was certainly manifest in the nature of Bar Ma'jan's reward.)

The synoptic parable does something of the same sort (that is, it effects a change of context for the narrative) but something rather simpler, and I think rather more radical. Jesus tells the Bar Ma'jan narrative more or less straight, but prefaces it (explicitly in Matthew, by implication, given the context, in Luke) with the words 'The Kingdom of Heaven is like this'.

This at once puts the whole point of the story under strain. The point depends upon Bar Ma'jan's being, despite his wealth, the social inferior of his guests. But if the story of the revenge is a description of the Kingdom of Heaven, the giver of the feast is presumably God. What then, can be the point in inviting the beggars, the crippled, the blind and the lame? In the Bar Ma'jan story the point is to jeer at the nobility by giving the food meant for them to the scourings of the gutter. But such a display of social pique cannot, surely, with any meaning be ascribed to the maker of the universe. Why then does the master of the feast invite the poor? The only answer left is that he wants to give a feast, and that the poor will do as well as guests as the nobility. But this cuts at the whole conception of honour implicit in the Bar Ma'jan story. That story depends for its point, and its structure as a narrative, on the conception of honour as sculptured from the void; a bauble dependent solely upon questions of who knows whom and who dines with whom. But for the narrative to have a point *as a parabolic description of the Kingdom of Heaven*, the honour conferred upon the poor guests at 'the feast in the Kingdom of God' must be an *absolute* honour. That is, their title to be guests at that feast depends not at all upon their social standing, upon any place which they occupy in human society. God, the master of the heavenly feast, is thus seen as a kind of absolute fountain of honour. He has no need to consider the social standing of his guests: they are *made* fit guests for his table by the bare fact that He has invited them, and that they have accepted the invitation.[22]

In short, to read the description of a sequence of events *as a narrative*, with a point and a structure, involves reading it against a background consisting of a set of presuppositions, together with the conceptual scheme in terms of which those presuppositions are formulated. The presuppositions and the underlying conceptual scheme direct the narrative. But the relationship is reciprocal, and hence narrative can be used to influence, to change, the underlying conceptual scheme. The technique is to tell the narrative in such a way that the mind, in order to discover a point and a structure in it, has to shift and rearrange the underlying conceptual structure. The story of Bar Ma'jan is a story about honour, or dignity, in the ordinary sense of social standing. The parable of the *Great Feast* is about the difference between worthiness for the feast as it is understood among men and as it is understood in Heaven. It succeeds in introducing the idea that the value, the worth, the standing of a man in the eyes of God is not dependent upon his standing in the eyes of other men, but is absolute; that *anyone* is a fitting guest at the great feast (provided he will accept the invitation, whereby hangs a longer but equally parabolic tale), because the mind has to grasp towards such a conception in order to construe the parable as something having the point and structure proper to a narrative. The parable thus compels its hearers to transcend the limits of their ordinary conceptual vocabulary; to grasp a new concept: a new sense in which a man may be said to have dignity or honour.

Something of the same sort happens in the Good Employer (Matthew 20. 1–16). The narrative is about an employer who hires labourers for his vine harvest. 'Employer' and 'labour' are terms in the common language, and like 'host' and 'guest' they are defined, as linguists say, 'structurally',[23] that is, in terms of one another, so that it is not possible to explain the meaning of either without at some point explaining the meaning of the other. Of course, you cannot 'define' two words in terms of one another, if the notion of *definition* you have in mind is verbal, or dictionary, definition. But you can do so if your conception of what is involved in giving the meaning of a word has a more Wittgensteinian tinge; if 'giving the meaning of a word' is showing how it fits into a structure of relationships or 'ways of proceeding': for two or more terms can certainly occupy relationships to one another within such a structure of relationships, and it can certainly therefore be the case that we cannot explain the meaning of either word without explaining how it fits into that structure, and thus how it is related to the other word, and thus how *that* word fits into the structure.

This is pretty obviously the case with 'employer' and 'labourer': what defines them is that they label certain points, certain rôles, in a single structure of economic relationships. That structure is set up like this. Men trade goods with one another, with the general aim of diversifying, and at the same time maximizing, the advantages that each individually possesses. In the trading game, labour is one kind of commodity that is sold, the point of buying it being that its possession can enable one to utilize potential goods in the shape, for example, of unharvested grapes; while the point of selling it is that one divests oneself of a commodity for which one has no use (because one possesses no potential goods, such as unharvested crops, capable of being realised by labour) in exchange for a commodity, money, which can be converted into commodities for which one does have a use. An 'employer' is, now, simply someone who buys labour; a 'labourer' is simply someone who sells his labour ('selling' and 'buying', of course, being defined, also, merely as marking correlative relationships within the general structure—the 'language-game', or 'form of life' in Wittgenstein's terms—known as 'trading', or 'commodity exchange').

All the parable tells us about the Good Employer is that he is an employer; a landowner. However, he behaves in a way which makes no economic sense, hiring batches of labourers at different times during the day, but paying all of them, at the end of the day, the wages for a full day's work, even though some of them only started work an hour before sunset. When the men who have worked longest complain, he says 'Am I not allowed to do what I choose with what belongs to me? Or do you begrudge my generosity?' (Matthew 20. 5). Again the whole narrative is enclosed by the introductory rubric, 'The kingdom of heaven is like this'.

What, then is the point of the story? It is a story about an employer who hires labour, so we are driven to search for a point in the system of economic relationships which define the correlative relationships of labourer and employer. But the narrative immediately frustrates that search, since it describes the employer as behaving in a way which precisely removes the point, economically speaking, of hiring extra labour. The economic point of hiring extra labour late in the day is presumably to get the last few grapes harvested; but any profit gained in that way will be wiped out with interest if one pays these marginal labourers a full day's wage for an hour's labour. Such behaviour only has a point if the primary interest of the landowner is not in maximizing his profit, and perhaps not even in getting the grapes harvested, but in *the labourers*. His behaviour does make sense if his primary object is to make sure that every out-of-work man gets a full wage in his pocket. If that is his aim, we can see why he goes out scouring the town for fresh groups of unemployed men at different times of day: it is not that he wants to increase the marginal profit on his grape harvest, it is that he wants as many unemployed men as possible in his employ at the end of the day. The point is sharpened if one takes Jeremias' point,[24] that the day's wage is a *subsistence* wage: all the labourers are paid alike what is necessary in order *that they may live*.

The parable is thus, like the Great Feast, about the difference between the value men find in one another and the value God finds in men. The value of labourers for an employer is, given the whole structure of economic relationships and practices in terms of which the terms 'employer' and 'labourer' find their meaning, relative to the profit which their labour can produce: labourers are ranked in relative value according to their relative profitability to the employer. The value of men for the employer of the parable is absolute: he feels the same concern for one as for another, irrespective of the economic advantage he has derived from the labour of each, and his concern in each case is the same: that the man should receive the wage that guarantees subsistence: that he should receive life, in other words.

The Prodigal Son (Luke 15. 11–32) has a similar structure. The younger son asks for and gets his share of the estate, converts it into cash and spends it all on drink and women, until he is reduced to working as a common labourer minding the pigs of a local landlord who starves him. He decides that if he has to spend his life as a common labourer he will at least spend it working for his father, who pays a good wage, so he goes home. The father welcomes him as a lost son, and kills the calf for a feast. The elder son is furious and complains that not even a kid has been killed for him and his friends, though he has always done as his father wished. The father replies, 'Son, you are always with me, and all that is mine is yours . . . this your brother was dead, and is alive; he was lost, and is found' (Luke 15. 31–32).

Just as the Good Employer's behaviour makes nonsense of economic commonsense, so the father's behaviour makes nonsense of common considerations of fairness and justice in the management of family affairs. The younger son has made all the claims on the estate he has a right to make. Indeed, the elder brother could perfectly reasonably claim that the fatted calf killed for the prodigal is really a part of his portion. In terms of the ordinary reciprocal rights and duties of parents and children, and ordinary considerations of justice in the disposition of an estate between different members of a family, the parable is a story of a besotted old fool. But we cannot take this as its point, because the father's reply to his son is clearly supposed to be in some way a telling one; and in any case the parable is offered as illuminating the nature of the Kingdom of Heaven. So we must look again for a point. The first clue is perhaps that the returned prodigal does not want to be treated as a son, or think he has any right to his father's best robe and a feast of welcome: he simply wants employ-ment as a paid servant. The father does not, then, weakly accede to a request to let bygones be bygones. He goes, in his response, instantly beyond anything the prodigal hoped or could have hoped for. He orders up a feast, and orders the prodigal to be dressed in his best robe, because he thinks that that is the appropriate response to the situation. What, then, does he think it an appropriate response *to*? Certainly not to the prodigal's *deserts*: if the feast were a feast to reward *desert* it would be a feast given for the elder son (one can, indeed, imagine a parable in which the prodigal returns, asks to be taken on as a paid servant and is indeed taken on in that capacity, at which point a feast is given for the elder son: that would not, indeed, be a parable, but a moral fable). But if the feast is not to reward desert, what on earth is it for? The explanation given by the father to the elder son is that it is simply a celebration for 'a happy day'; the sort of feast that one gives when some great good descends upon the family. What is the good? Again, it cannot be anything which the prodigal has done or that he brings with him. Therefore it can only be the prodigal himself. *He* is the thing of great value which the father has regained, and whose recovery he is therefore celebrating. This is why the elder son's objection is peculiarly out of place. And, of course, it is also what he finds so hard to stomach. In the gulf between the father's joy and the reaction of the elder son at being seriously asked to treat his wastrel younger brother as some sort of Pearl of Great Price, an object of immense intrinsic value, for whose restoration to the family a celebratory feast is in order, we see the abyss which separates the everyday morality which we all know well enough how to handle, from the extraordinary outlook which Christ is not only recommending to us but asserting as a condition of our salvation.

Part III

These three parables each presuppose some system of practices in terms of which a field of moral concepts (using 'moral' in the old, broad sense) are defined relative to one another: the system of formal social contacts in terms of which social standing, snobbery, social ambition and the corresponding kinds of mortification and chagrin are defined; the systems of economic relations which define the corresponding roles and interests of labourer and employer; the structure of a family around a property or *oikos* which defines the roles and rights of brothers and sons and determines where, for example, it is and is not proper to feel moral outrage at the flouting of those rights.

But the parabolic narrative is in each case set askew to these underlying structures of social practices and their corresponding systems of concepts, so that the mind can find no resting-place in the story: cannot find, in terms of the underlying scheme of practices and associated concepts, a clear point and structure in the story, as it can, for example, in the simple, pre-parabolic story of Bar Ma'jan's revenge.

In order to find a point, to see why the vineyard-owner's behaviour might not be just economic muddle-headedness, or the father's simply parental affection turned soft and besotted, or the feast-giver's summons to the cripples and beggars not social mortification expressing itself in savage mockery of the reluctant guests, the mind must reach beyond the conceptual resources offered by the commonplace underlying conceptual structures to something which transcends those structures and constitutes a kind of judgement upon them.

In each case the behaviour of the central protagonist (father, landowner, feast-giver) is explicable only if the value he places upon other protagonists (beggar-guests, labourers, son) is not a value which those protagonists acquire through their position in an underlying system of practices, which defines a set of morally significant social roles (the good, obedient son, the man of social standing, the worthy, profitable labourer who has worked long hours to increase his master's harvest), but an absolute value; a value which inheres in the person concerned merely *qua* person. Or, to put it another way, it is the *guests*, and not their social standing, who justify the feast; it is for *labourers*, or *in order that labourers should not be unemployed*, that the landowner scours the town, and not for *labour* to increase the profits of the vine-harvest; it is for *the son* that the father gives the feast of thanksgiving, and not to reward the son's deserts, or for any ulterior benefit that his return may or may not bring to the household.

So there *is*, after all, something general which these parables give us. They give us what, if we want to put a familiar and therefore reassuring name to it, we can call the concept of the dignity of the person; and correlatively with that they give us the concept of God's grace as absolute; as something which transcends all human moral categories, and thus perhaps as something (there is a chain of suppressed steps here, but not a very long one) which does not depend upon works. The role of both these concepts in the subsequent development of Christendom has been sufficiently momentous and ambiguous to make it I think obvious that (and why), these sayings of Christ have had a resonance and an influence beyond the immediate circumstances of their original utterance. John Stuart Mill, in the essay on *Utilitarianism*, tried to represent Christ's central message as a form of that doctrine; as a universal benevolence, a concern for the felicity of mankind in general. One's feeling that this is an altogether bizarre reading both of the Gospels and of the general content of the Christian tradition is brought to a head by these three parables. The outlook which these parables adumbrate is one which involves infinite concern for single individuals, and which therefore precisely does not proportion its concern for individuals to the demands of any arithmetical computation of the common good. One might say that according to these parables the justice of God, like logic, 'contains no numbers'; or that the God who is seen through them, if he is a mathematician, is one who does not take into account, morally speaking, any numbers between unity and infinity. Whereas, of course, the calculation of a guest's value to his host, or a son's to his family, or a labourer's to his employer, is as much a computation as any other estimation of utilities.

So, I want to say, these parables do offer us something general. They originate a moral outlook. And that is what gives them polemical force as replies to the question 'How can a respectable religious teacher spend his time consorting with tax-gatherers and riff-raff?' They have polemical force because the moral outlook which they communicate goes beyond and undercuts the moral outlook out of which that question springs.

And yet all this is in one way altogether too pat. In putting a name, 'the Concept of the Dignity of the Person', to what is communicated by these parables, have I not fallen victim to the most ancient and profound of linguistic illusions, the illusion that once we can put a name to something we know what it is?

For, suppose I am impressed by this new idea of 'the dignity of the person', and I want to make it the basis of all my relationships with other people. What, exactly, in practical terms, will constitute doing that? What, when it comes down to it, *am I to do*? Am I, for example, with my strength of character, my moral vision and my remarkable powers of love transcending all commonplace moral relationships, to take charge of my weaker fellow-men in the manner of Dostoevsky's Grand Inquisitor? Or more prosaically should I, if I have servants, treat them 'as one of the family', taking an interest in their lives, helping them in trouble and so on? The parables do not say: notoriously, they do not offer specific moral principles or injunctions, and the moment we try to reduce them to illustrated moral copybook maxims we trivialize them. And yet it is obvious that in each of these cases, not to mention many others, the attempt to follow 'the teaching' of the parables is fraught with ambiguity. Spiritual guidance becomes spiritual tyranny; help to those in inferior social positions becomes an odious and hypocritical paternalism, unless we are very careful. And how can we know? What can enable us to tell, can make us sensitive to the difference?

Well, what *can* I do, if I want to articulate, to become sensitive to such a difference, to make it concrete enough to apprehend, but tell a story? For example I must tell a story about just such a Grand Inquisitor, or about a servant who was treated in a certain way as one of the family, so as to show how that in the end made him only more of a servant, bound him more helplessly to the service of the family interests, than a more openly economic way of treating him would have done. Of course that story will be as little amenable as the synoptic parables to being reduced to a general moral injunction; of being reduced, that is, to a safe guide in all future moral difficulties. But then, *that* story was not supposed to deal with *future* moral difficulties, let alone with *all* future moral difficulties, but only to make clear the nature of a *present* moral difficulty.

In telling such a story, what we should do is to rely on our readers grasping the point and rationale of some scheme of values, in this case the values of Christian love, concern for others, and so forth, and we should make the narrative demonstrate a new way in which you can take those values, a way in which you can secure yourself against taking them wrongly. The narrative would say, in effect, 'You think it is simple to love your neighbours as yourself, that it is clear what that involves. But, look. . . .' But is that not, in turn, exactly what the synoptic parables do? They say, in effect, 'You think you know what a guest, or a friend is, or what it is to be a just employer, or to exercize well paternal rule over a family. But, look. . . .' And in the space after the invitation to look comes the parable. In each case the concept of fatherhood, of being a good employer, of being a friend or a host, is not dispensed with. It is precisely what it is to be a friend, a host, a father, and so on, that we are talking about (one cannot, that is, construct parables, or narrative in general, at random). But something is added to the concept, or drawn out of it, or revealed in it, by the parable.

The parables are not, therefore, it seems to me, merely illustrations of a Christian moral outlook capable of being fully expressed in non-parabolic terms, and thus they cannot be *merely* eschatological in content, for Christian eschatology is itself defined partly in moral terms (it concerns not just the arrival of a Kingdom of Heaven, but of a Kingdom of Heaven of a certain kind). Jeremias is closer to the mark, it seems to me, when in refusing to translate 'friend' as 'neighbour' he remarks that the parable of the Good Samaritan *constructs*, and does not merely *employ*, the Christian concept of a neighbour. The parables, in short, do—or better, commence—the work of conceptual construction upon which the eschatology of Christianity partly depends. That is why they are connected with eschatology but are not *simply* eschatological in purport.

Let me try, even at the risk of repetition, to be a little less parabolic myself. What is it to grasp a moral concept? It is, presumably to grasp the form, the structure, which is common to a number of cases. That is why you can introduce a new moral concept by telling stories: the content of the stories presents your hearers with a number of cases to consider, and the moral structure, the concept, is shown by (or 'shows itself in', to use a Wittgensteinian tag) the point and narrative structure of the story. This is, in effect what our three parables do. Each one sets up a different tension between the structure of a narrative and a body of underlying conceptual material in terms of which, if at all, the narrative has to be construed *as a narrative*, and the tension reveals a way of structuring the narrative which is the same in each case. But what does the *same* mean here? Well, in each narrative we are driven to postulate a concern for persons as ultimate objects of value as the predominating interest of the central character in each narrative. But what does this new phrase, this piece of jargon, 'to have a concern for persons as ultimate objects of value', *mean*? How, if we were asked to, could we explain its meaning? We might, of course, try to replace it with some other verbal formula, such as the Kantian 'treat others as ends and not as means' (a verbal formula which also, incidentally, depends upon narrative illustrations, which have also, like the parables, been felt to be notoriously ambiguous, and to fall lamentably short of the respectable clarities of doctrine).[25] But ultimately, I think we should be reduced to pointing at the parables, or rather at a complex structural similarity which recurs in all of them, but which cannot in the end be disentangled or abstracted from their narrative content.

But if 'what the parables have to tell us' cannot be disentangled from their narrative content, how can we be sure that we have understood it correctly? Let us rephrase the question. How can we *show* that we have understood correctly? Wittgenstein says that we show that we have understood the principle of a series by continuing the series. What we have in the parables, or some of the parables, as I have tried to show, is precisely a series of narratives bound to one another by a single principle: a single complex pattern of structural similarity. How could we show our understanding but by continuing, in other narratives or in our own lives, the series of which we have been given, as it were, the first few integers? Of course, as I have already suggested, in the process of doing this we shall at times stop short because we see that what looked from one point of view like a continuation of the series is not so from another: that what can be seen from one point of view as bearing to the other members of the series the same complex structural similarity that they bear to one another can be seen from another point of view as either lacking or incompletely manifesting that similarity. (Thus, if the father in the *Prodigal Son* took on his younger son as a paid labourer and treated him kindly and correctly as one in that position, that would in a sense be *justice* all right, but not the fullness, the rather baffling perfection of justice that we find in the parable, where the father does indeed do what is 'due' to the son, or 'due' to the occasion of the son's return, but where *that* turns out to be something infinitely more than the son could have considered to be 'in justice' due to him). And, of course, one can then describe what happens when we are brought up in this way either by saying that we have, by an act of self-transcendence, changed or transformed the moral concept which forms the principle of the series; or by saying that we have seen more clearly what was already implicitly given in the set of relationships between cases which set the series in motion.

This duality is, I think, the reason for the *riddling* character of parables. For if it is true that parables are given in answer to questions, it is also true that they answer those questions only by asking a further question, and a question, moreover, which can only honestly be answered 'Yes and no'. Was the landowner just to the servants who had worked so long in paying the ones who had worked so short a time the same wage? Yes and no. Was the father unjust to his eldest son? Yes and no. Does the feast-giver, by using the beggar-guests to rebuke the guests who refused, use the beggar-guests as a mere instrument of his wrath? Yes and no. The doubleness here is not the indeterminacy of bafflement or wilful mystification: it is the necessary duality of self-transcendence: the slow climb to successively more adequate levels of vision.

A few paragraphs ago, I said that grasping a moral concept involves grasping a form—a complex structural similarity between cases—and that that is why telling stories is one way of introducing a new moral concept. It now looks as if we can say something stronger than this: that parabolic narrative is not just one way, but the only way of introducing a new moral concept. For on the one hand, whatever verbal label I attach to the moral concepts in question can only ultimately be explicated by appeal to a series of cases, and on the other hand the full significance of the moral outlook demonstrated by associating or dissociating specific cases to form such a series can only be grasped when one sees what further cases, seen from what points of view, turn out to associate themselves to, or to dissociate themselves from, the series of cases as so far formed. Terms of moral categorization: 'honour', 'justice', 'respect for the person' and the rest, are at best only signposts or markers in this process; markers which, admittedly are not to be dug up and moved about casually at will, but which life, or moral experience, inevitably eventually digs up and moves in spite of us, unless we are very stubborn indeed.

If I am right, then, we have an explanation of why so much of the teaching of Jesus consists of narrative. It is because narrative offers, in the end, the only way of talking seriously about the moral life. It is serious because it is content to *show* what all other kinds of moral talk attempt, in the face of our condition as beings in a state of becoming, to *say*.

Our age dislikes riddles, and stories, because it is still in love with a notion promulgated in the seventeenth century by the founders of modern science, and still believed by many to be central to the practice of science despite the rise of relativistic physics: the conception of the Ideal Observer. The Ideal Observer neither affects nor is affected by what he observes. Hence he can speak a language of detached objective description. The description of the world which he is able to give in this language may increase in richness, and indeed will increase in richness, as a result of the steady advance of science. But the *language* does not change: it remains a neutral medium for recording fact. And hence the observer does not change. Indeed the notion of a change in the observer is, on this view of the nature of knowledge, both something conceptually absurd and something obstructing and theoretically scandalous to the view of knowledge in question. The observer *cannot* change, because the observing mind, *qua* observing mind, is not supposed to possess any content, or structure, of its own. It is simply a camera recording reality. What is observable from the viewpoint of the Ideal Observer (this is why he *is* an *Ideal* Observer) is what would be observed by any other observer. There is nothing, in short, to distinguish one observer from another, if the scientific study of nature is properly conducted; for change in the observer would imply differing observation-states, and the possibility of passing from one of these states to another. But on the Ideal Observer view of knowledge there is only one possible viewpoint from which anything deserving the name of knowledge can be apprehended: the viewpoint from which the properly trained observer observes what any other properly trained observer observes: the viewpoint of the Ideal Observer, in short.

We like to think that everything that is true and worth saying can be put into such a language, and one consequence of this hankering is that we want to know, once and for all, what parables, or for that matter poems or novels, *have to say*: what they 'come down to' (the very phrase suggests that we think of the language of poetry and narrative fiction as a sort of pink cloud or afflatus, upon which perfectly solid, down-to-earth objects are floated about, tantalizingly and infuriatingly in mid-air, just out of reach) in the language of an Ideal (or commonsense) Observer. But the hankering itself is an illegitimate one, not because the notion of an Ideal Observer is an absurd or dispensable one, but because it is a notion which we have allowed to get out of its proper place in our conceptual scheme.

The notion of an Ideal Observer is, I think, essentially that of a *properly trained* observer: the man who knows what he is looking for and knows also what sorts of thing could prevent him from noticing it if it is there, or make him think that it is there if it is not. In this sense a competent chemist looking for barium in a sample is an Ideal, because a trained, Observer. Because he knows chemical theory, and has acquired a certain skill in manipulating the techniques of qualitative analysis, he will get, quite independently of other trained observers, the results which they get, thus providing one step in that endless chain of independent corroboration which both confirms the general adequacy of chemical theory, and entitles us to say that his training *is* a training in the accurate observation of reality, and not just in some conventional ritual mumbo-jumbo.

But at the same time, the concept of a trained observer in chemical analysis is defined against the background of chemical theory. And chemical theory is not something which could be 'observed' in nature at all. The notion of training somebody to observe, say 'the constitution of matter' is, indeed, senseless, except against the background of some specified theory of the constitution of matter, which we must already possess. Theory, in short, is not read off from experience by a process of *observation* at all, and there is no ideal posture of observation in which a scientist can place himself which will guarantee that he will succeed in making an advance in theory. Nor is there any neutral descriptive language, given antecedently to a theoretical advance, into which the specific content of that advance can simply be transcribed. Any language adequate to express the content of a theoretical advance in science must be formulated in the process of making that advance, and this effort of conceptual formulation is commonly the most difficult part of the process of discovery. Whatever else one accepts of the relativist or 'anarchist' philosophies of science put forward by Kuhn or Feyerabend,[26] for example, this much is certainly true.

In erecting a theory of knowledge founded upon the concept of an Ideal Observer, what seventeenth- and eighteenth-century empiricism and its modern philosophical descendents have done is to take an essential but secondary part of the practice of scientific enquiry, and treat it as if it were primary and ultimate in that practice. In reality, in science, as elsewhere, there is a level at which an advance in our comprehension of reality can only come by way of a change in us: in our stand-point as observers: a change in the conceptual schemata in terms of which we ultimately order the world and which direct all our observations, and our responses to what we observe.

We are, in short, beings in a continual process of becoming and self-transcendence. And just as the theoretical languages of science both express and engineer this transcendence in our understanding of nature, so narrative and the language of poetry and parable both express and engineer our self-transcendence as moral beings (taking 'moral' once again in the broad sense which it formerly had). There is no other language in which one can express the life that is in parable, because, for reasons which I hope I may have made a little less opaque in this paper, the life is in the language (that is, what the parable makes us see is already 'put into words' in the only way it can be—by the parable). I do not think that in saying that I have said anything very original; which is not, of course, to say that I do not think that what I have said needs saying. What I want to say was said quite clearly, though parabolically, by Kafka, and his words will serve very well as summary and conclusion:

Many complain that the words of the wise are always merely parables, and of no use in daily life, which is the only life we have. When the sage says: 'go over', he does not mean that we should cross to some actual place, which we would do anyhow if the labour were worth it; he means some fabulous yonder, something unknown to us, something too that he cannot designate more precisely, and therefore cannot help us here in the very least. All these parables really set out to say merely that the incomprehensible is incomprehensible, and we know that already. But the cares we have to struggle with every day: that is a different matter.

Concerning this a man once said: Why such reluctance? If you only followed the parables you yourself would become parables and with that rid of all your daily cares.

Another said: I bet that is also a parable.
The first said: You have won.
The second said: But unfortunately only in parable.
The first said: No, in reality: in parable you have lost.[27]

Notes

1 C. F. Evans (1977), *Parable and Dogma*, London, p. 5.
2 C. F. Evans (1977), *ibid.*, p. 4. Augustine's interpretation is in *Quaestiones Evangeliorum*, II, 19.
3 C. F. Evans (1977), *ibid.*
4 'The import of the story is obscured if *plesion* (= *rea'*) in Luke 10. 29 is translated 'neighbour'. The Christian concept of the 'neighbour' is not the starting point of the story, but that which the story was intended to create'. J. Jeremias (1954), *The Parables of Jesus*, (trans S. H. Hooke) London, third revised ed. 1972, p. 202, n. 53. The last clause of Jeremias' remark cuts close, I believe, to the heart of the matter.
5 J. Jeremias (1954), *op. cit.*, pp. 100–102.
6 C. H. Dodd (1935), *The Parables of the Kingdom*, London, revised ed. 1961, p. 3.
7 J. Jeremias (1954), *op. cit.*, p. 124.
8 J. Jeremias (1954), *ibid.*, pp. 127–8.
9 J. Jeremias (1954), *ibid.*, p. 131.
10 A. Jülicher, *Gleichnisreden Jesu*, II, p. 481, quoted in C. H. Dodd (1935), *op. cit.*
11 A. Jülicher, *ibid.*
12 C. H. Dodd (1935), *op. cit.*, p. 13.
13 The moral codes of primitive peoples, as reflected in, for example, the Norse Eddas, contain many injunctions of this kind, and it is only obvious to us that they are not 'moral' injunctions.
14 S. Kierkegaard (1939), *Fear and Trembling* (trans R. Payne), Oxford, pp. 31–4.
15 'I have shown elsewhere what a singularly complete and convincing picture the parables give of life in a small provincial town—probably a more complete picture of *petit-bourgeois* and peasant life than we possess for any other province of the Roman Empire except Egypt, where papyri come to our aid'. C. H. Dodd (1935), *op. cit.*, p. 10.
16 For a view attacking the notion of realism in the parables, and arguing for an allegorical interpretation, see J. Drury (1973), 'The sower, the vineyard and the place of allegory in the interpretation of Mark's parables' *Journal of Theological Studies* October 1973, pp. 367–379.
17 F. Kafka (1946), *Parables and Paradoxes*, New York.
18 C. H. Dodd (1935), *op. cit.*, p. 5.
19 C. H. Dodd (1935), *ibid.*, p. ix.
20 C. F. Evans (1977), *op. cit.*, p. 13, puts essentially the same point in the form of a doubt about the propriety of the term *Sitz im Leben* as used by Dodd and Jeremias:
    A more general, and possibly far-reaching criticism could be made that in this reconstruction the term *Sitz im Leben* is being used in a significantly different sense from that which it originally has in form criticism, where it refers to the situation which best accounts not for the content of a passage but for the particular form of utterance the passage takes, whether that form be regarded from an aesthetic or a sociological point of view. For, whatever the subsequent use made of parable in the tradition, it is not obvious, nor perhaps likely, that it elects itself as a form of utterance for proclaiming an eschatological message, or for defending it.
21 J. Jeremias (1954), *op.cit.*, p. 179.
22 This interpretation is inconsistent with the episode of the guest without a wedding garment in the Matthaean version of the parable (Matthew 22. 11–3). But there is good ground for regarding the episode as belonging to a quite independent parable; see J. Jeremias (1954), *op. cit.*, p. 65.

23 The most pithy and informative definition known to me of the terms 'structural' and 'structuralism' is given by J. Lyons *(1977) Semantics* Vol. 1, Cambridge pp. 231–2.

24 J. Jeremias (1954), *op. cit.*, p. 37.

25 See B. Harrison (1979), 'Kant and the sincere fanatic', in S. Brown (ed.) *Philosophers of the Eighteenth Century; Royal Institute of Philosophy Lectures 1977–78*, Brighton.

26 See T. Kuhn (1962), *The Structure of Scientific Revolutions*, Chicago; P. Feyerabend (1975), *Against Method*, London.

27 F. Kafka (1946), *op. cit.*, p. 11.

ACKNOWLEDGEMENTS

The editor and publishers are indebted to the following for permission to use material which originally appeared under their auspices:

Messrs. Faber and Faber Ltd.,
for the quotations from 'Burnt
Norton' and 'Ash Wednesday' by
T. S. Eliot.

Messrs. Macmillan and Co. Ltd.,
and Macmillan Inc. for the
quotation from 'Among School
Children' by W. B. Yeats.

I. INDEX OF REFERENCES TO BIBLICAL AND ANCIENT POST-BIBLICAL WRITINGS

1. BIBLICAL (Old Testament)

Genesis

1.3–4	136	11.10–32	11
2.21	138	11.32	135
3.8	136	12.1–3	11
5	134	15.7	11, 12
5.21–24	181	22	141–2, 139, 156
8.7–8	134	27.22	137
10–12	11	27.26–30	140
10.11–11a	12	27.33–35	140
11	134		

Exodus

3.4–5	138	12–23	188n.
3.11–12	138	12.25	8
4.10	145	20.2	12
4.12	145		

Deuteronomy

4.12	142	5.6	12
4.15–16	143	26	8
4.20	143	28.37	175

Joshua

24.2	12

Judges

9.7–15	177	16.4–22	157
11.30–31	140	16.5	14
11.35	141	16.22	158
11.38	155	16.26	158
13	156	16.28	158
14.5–9	156	16.31	157
14.10	159	17	14–16
14.14	177	17.2	14
14.15–18	156	17.3	15
15.1–7	157	18	14–16
15.18–19	157	19	16
16	16	20	16
16.1–3	157		

2. BIBLICAL (New Testament)

218 Ways of Reading the Bible

II. GENERAL INDEX